Post-Development from the Global South

Post-development advocates and decolonial thinkers are calling for radical alternatives to development, but how do these ideals sit with the day-to-day reality of marginalised communities struggling with poverty, precarity, and the deprivation of human rights?

This book investigates how post-development alternatives are being understood and negotiated on the ground in the Global South. Indigenous concepts and practices attributed to people in the Global South are seen by post-development thinkers as offering transformative alternatives to dominant development models of progress and economic growth. For example, *buen vivir* from particular regions of South America points to a 'culture of life' and *ubuntu* in Southern Africa emphasises human connectedness and mutuality. Such terms are associated with social and environmental sustainability, and a greater connection to Southern epistemologies. Drawing on extensive fieldwork, this book takes us directly to Global South communities from around the world, to consider the complex ways in which they negotiate the ideas and practices associated with (post)development, and their views on the supposed Indigenous alternatives. The book encourages a contextual approach that embraces the tensions and contradictions that exist within different communities.

Taking the reader from abstract post-development theory right into the heart of communities directly impacted by development, this book will be an important guide for students, researchers and practitioners looking for better ways to address the desires and aspirations of marginalised communities in the Global South.

Sally Matthews is an Associate Professor in the Department of Political and International Studies at Rhodes University, South Africa. She is interested in a rather eclectic range of topics – post-development theory, the politics of knowledge production on Africa, the role of NGOs in Africa, higher education transformation and decolonisation – which are all loosely related to the question of whether and how those who occupy positions of privilege can act in the interests of the marginalised and oppressed.

Alba Castellsagué is an Assistant Professor (Lecturer) in the Pedagogy Department at the University of Girona (UdG). She has teaching and research experience in the fields of education and international development, gender equality and migration studies.

Rethinking Development Series

Rethinking Development offers accessible and thought-provoking overviews of contemporary topics in international development and aid. Providing original empirical and analytical insights, the books in this series push thinking in new directions by challenging current conceptualizations and developing new ones.

This is a dynamic and inspiring series for all those engaged with today's debates surrounding development issues, whether they be students, scholars, policy makers and practitioners internationally. These interdisciplinary books provide an invaluable resource for discussion in advanced undergraduate and postgraduate courses in development studies as well as in anthropology, economics, politics, geography, media studies and sociology.

Dear Development Practitioner: Advice for the Next Generation
Edited by Simon Milligan and Lee Wilson

Foreign Aid and its Unintended Consequences
Dirk-Jan Koch

Reformers in International Development
Five Remarkable Lives
David M. de Ferranti

Young People in the Global South
Voice, Agency and Citizenship
Edited by Kate Pincock, Nicola Jones, Lorraine Van Blerk and Nyaradzayi Gumbonzvanda

Community-Led Development in Practice
We Power our Own Change
Edited by Elene Cloete and Gunjan Veda

Post-Development from the Global South
Radical Alternatives or Ambivalent Engagements?
Edited by Sally Matthews and Alba Castellsagué

For more information about this series, please visit: http://www.routledge.com/Rethinking-Development/book-series/RDVPT

Post-Development from the Global South

Radical Alternatives or Ambivalent Engagements?

Edited by
Sally Matthews and Alba Castellsagué

Routledge
Taylor & Francis Group
LONDON AND NEW YORK

First published 2025
by Routledge
4 Park Square, Milton Park, Abingdon, Oxon OX14 4RN

and by Routledge
605 Third Avenue, New York, NY 10158

Routledge is an imprint of the Taylor & Francis Group, an informa business

Designed cover image: Neil Maheve

British Library Cataloguing in Publication Data
A catalogue record for this book is available from the British Library

ISBN: 9781032762982 (hbk)
ISBN: 9781032762968 (pbk)
ISBN: 9781003477921 (ebk)

DOI: 10.4324/9781003477921

Typeset in Galliard
by Taylor & Francis Books

Contents

Illustrations

Figures

Table

Contributors

Joseph Edward B. Alegado is a PhD candidate at the Crawford School of Public Policy at the Australian National University in Canberra, Australia. His research sits at the intersection of degrowth, zero waste, and forms of alternatives to development in the Global South. Prior to starting his doctoral research, he worked with non-profit organizations and environmental movements in the Asia Pacific region in the areas of advocacy, campaigns, and communications. He also teaches undergraduate and postgraduate courses at Ateneo de Manila University and De La Salle University in the Philippines.

Vanessa Azañedo Gamarra has a BA in Anthropology from the Pontifical Catholic University of Peru (PUCP) and is pursuing a Diploma in Data Science for Social Science at the same university. She currently works as a research analyst. Her research deals with informality and gig economy, rural health and agrarian development, and youth leadership.

Maria Fernanda Córdova Suxo is a PhD candidate in Sociology at the University of Kassel. She holds an MA in Peace and Conflict Studies and an MSc in Critical Approaches to Development. A scholar of the Global Partnership Network, she also lectures in the Faculty of Human Sciences at the University of Kassel.

Hadi Darvishi holds a PhD in Sociology from Mazandaran University, Iran, and has previously lectured at Mazandaran University and Tehran Azad University. Considering religion as a central element of Iranian society and a significant political factor, his fields of interest include the sociology of religion and development, with a focus on gender studies.

Simphiwe Gongqa holds a Bachelor of Social Science with Honours in Political and International Studies from Rhodes University. He is currently pursuing a Master of Social Science degree in Political and International Studies at Rhodes University. His research interests are on alternative 'bottom-up' approaches to development. His Master's study investigates the experiences of recipients and practitioners of the Asset-Based Community Development (ABCD) intervention, a bottom-up participatory approach to development, in a South African semi-urban context.

Emile Kwa is a cultural anthropologist with a Master's degree in International Development Studies from the University of Amsterdam. He has teaching experience within the Anthropology and Cultural studies programmes of this university. His research interests lie at the intersection of political ecology and Indigenous social movements, focusing on the interplay of environmental politics, activist practices, cosmology and spirituality of Indigenous communities, with theoretical interests in ontology and globalising knowledges.

Neil Maheve is a Global Partnership Network (GPN) Thomas Sankara scholarship recipient and PhD candidate in the Department of Political and International Studies at Rhodes University. His research interests include development discourses, development in marginal communities, environmental history, human-wildlife conflict, and the extractive mining industries in Zimbabwe. His research is mainly ethnographical and tells mundane everyday stories that portray people's attitudes. He has a history background, with his first and second degrees attained in African history. Neil recently submitted his PhD dissertation titled 'Rethinking Development in Post-Colonial Zimbabwe, the Case of the CAMPFIRE Programme in Kanyemba'.

Nhlanhla Mkhutle holds a Master's degree in Political and International Studies from Rhodes University, South Africa. His research interests include Democratic Theory, African Political Philosophy and Grassroots Mobilizations. He is currently a part-time politics lecturer at Rosebank College, South Africa.

Greg Molecke is a Lecturer in Social Entrepreneurship, Greg Molecke researches how organizations secure resources and support based on the social value they generate and how they navigate tensions between social, environmental, and financial goals. Greg is Co-Director for Postgraduate Research and the Master of Research in Management and Global Political Economy programs. He teaches Qualitative Methods and Entrepreneurship courses. Greg also has over 15 years of management experience in the technology, energy, and health sectors.

Somaye Momeni is a PhD candidate in Sociology of Economic and Development at the University of Tehran, Iran, and a former lecturer at Elmi Karbordi University. She is currently working on women and alternative development. Holding an MA and BA in Sociology, she has years of research experience in the fields of gender, urban and development studies.

Justin Dodd Mullikin grew up on one of the last tobacco farms in central Kentucky, USA, sparking a life-long interest in agrarian change. Before completing a PhD in geography at Rutgers University, Justin worked in Rwanda for six years with an agrarian development NGO. His dissertation research on ambivalence and agrarian change was motivated by the many questions, expectations, and hopes expressed by farmers in Eastern Rwanda that seemed to be ignored by mainstream development discourse and practice. Justin currently lives in Philadelphia where he is a Lecturer in the Critical Writing Program at the University of Pennsylvania.

Injina Panthi is a development professional based in Lumbini Province, Nepal. She works closely with civil society and media organizations to uplift and empower women, youth, and marginalized communities by connecting them with resources and opportunities. Previously, she has worked with Panos South Asia and Tribhuvan University (TU). She holds a Master's degree in International Relations and Diplomacy from TU.

Léna Prouchet recently obtained her PhD from the University of Exeter and is currently a postdoctoral researcher at Copenhagen Business School. Her doctoral project focused on initiatives implemented by development organisations to promote entrepreneurship among Indigenous communities in the Peruvian Amazon. Léna is particularly dedicated to contributing to evidence-based policymaking in international development and nature conservation, collaborating with practitioners to ensure the societal impact of her work. Her current research interests centre on the emergence of discourses promoting entrepreneurship as a development tool in the Global South and the impact of these discourses, especially on marginalised communities.

Stefano Pascucci is a Professor in Sustainability and Circular Economy at the University of Exeter Business School (UK) and visiting professor in Sustainable Business at the University of Auckland Business School (NZ). He holds a position as Visiting Researcher at the Business Management and Organization Group, Wageningen University (NL). He is a social scientist interested in sustainability and circular economy, focused on understanding the role of businesses, communities, and other forms of organizing to ensure transitions into a more fair and sustainable society. His research includes food community organising, agribusiness management, and regenerative agriculture.

Eija Ranta is an Academy of Finland Research Fellow and University Lecturer in Global Development Studies at the University of Helsinki, Finland. Her work focuses on development, politics, and democracy from ethnographic and decolonising perspectives. She is the author of *Vivir Bien as an Alternative to Neoliberal Globalization* (Routledge, 2018) and has recently published in such journals as *AlterNative: An International Journal of Indigenous Peoples*, *Journal of Latin American Studies*, and *Third World Quarterly*.

Reihaneh Saremi is a PhD candidate in Social Policy at the University of Tehran, Iran, and a GPN (Global Partnership Network) scholar at the University of Kassel, Germany. Her research interests include poverty studies and policies toward marginalized groups, where she also brings years of social activism experience. In her research, she seeks to uncover the discourses behind policies alongside the everyday experiences of the targeted groups

Yves Van Leynseele is a social and political anthropologist and works as a senior lecturer at the University of Amsterdam where he teaches critical development theory and is involved in initiatives to diversify the Master's programme in International Development Studies, including decolonising of the curriculum and research methodology. His research focuses on the dynamics and emerging properties of rural and urban transformation processes in sub-Saharan Africa, with a particular interest in unravelling knowledge regimes and related contestations by local actors and social movements, the role of privileged brokers in land reform and nature conservation initiatives and the rationale and contestations in community-public-private-partnerships.

Jane Wills is Professor of Geography at the University of Exeter, Cornwall. She has worked on labour and community organising, living wage coalitions and localism. Her current research focuses on place-based nature recovery and its integration into regional development paths in the rural-periphery.

Cecilia Zenteno Lawrence is an Afro-Bolivian activist and lecturer at the Faculty of Rural and Territorial Development at the Universidad Mayor de San Simón, Bolivia. She holds a doctoral degree in Rural Development. Her research interests and work experiences relate to the management of development processes in territorial planning, water management, food sovereignty, and feminisms in Latin America, Asia, and Europe. She is passionate about discovering, designing, and facilitating educational and organisational processes that highlight the connections between society and nature through just, diverse, and sustainable local practices and dynamics.

Aram Ziai has studied sociology, history and English literature in Aachen and Dublin, got a PhD in political science in Hamburg, and is Professor of Development and Postcolonial Studies at the University of Kassel. He has also taught in Vienna, Amsterdam, Accra, and Tehran. More than two decades ago he wrote his PhD on Post-Development, although sympathetic professors had strongly advised him not to – because scholars in development studies would detest this and other scholars would hardly care and he would never get a job with this topic. He was lucky and got one nevertheless.

Acknowledgements

This edited collection has its origins in a panel presented at the 2023 conference of the European Association of Development Research and Training Institutes (EADI). We are grateful for EADI's support of the panel and their subsequent support for several blogs related to the book, which have been published on their Debating Development Research blog.

We would also like to thank our editors at Routledge, Helena Hurd and Katerina Lade, for their enthusiasm and support for this project. They were warm, understanding and helpful throughout the process.

Several of the contributors to this book are part of the Global Partnership Network, an international research network based at the University of Kassel. The GPN brought together many of the book's contributors and also provided financial support towards the completion of the book. We thank the GPN for this support.

Bringing a book together requires all kinds of work behind the scenes. We are very grateful to Lesego Monyai, a postgraduate student at Rhodes University in South Africa, for her research assistance and to Jean Schafer for preliminary language and copy editing.

Of course, a book cannot come together without contributors! Our contributors were very responsive to suggestions and – mostly – good with deadlines. For that, we are very grateful. The book process was a lovely opportunity to connect with researchers in a variety of contexts.

Our sincere thanks go to all the anonymous participants in the studies compiled in this book. Their generosity in sharing their views, opinions, and insights – often during challenging times – has been invaluable to the success of this project.

Finally, acknowledgement and gratitude are also due to the families of the editors. Alba would like to thank Aldy for taking such good care of the family. Special thanks to Mai for becoming my little officemate, and to Lola for coming into our lives just as this book was taking shape. Sally would like to thank Pedro, Noah and Lithalelanga for providing meaning and love which ground everything else.

1 Introduction

Sally Matthews and Alba Castellsagué

The idea of development is one of the most influential ways of explaining differences and inequalities between parts of the world. Some parts of the world, we have come to believe, are 'developed' while others might be described as 'developing' or 'underdeveloped' or 'least developed'. The development narrative tells us that this difference in 'development' explains why people in some parts of the world live wealthier, healthier lives while others struggle to meet their needs. This narrative also suggests that those who supposedly lack 'development' need to emulate those who are ahead of them on a universal path to development.

This familiar narrative has by now been subjected to varied and robust critique. One of the most vigorous strains of critique has come from so-called post-development[1] theory which rose to prominence during the 1990s and which remains influential today. The recent increased influence of so-called decolonial thinking includes critiques of development which are similar to those first raised by the post-development thinkers. One common theme in both post-development and decolonial theory has been the idea that people in the so-called developing world are rejecting the development narrative and embracing alternatives to it, with these alternatives emerging from ideas and practices that are typically presented as being 'Indigenous'[2] or as coming from the 'grassroots'.

Our book is situated in this context. The long-standing debates about development and its alternatives have made contributors to this book ask questions about exactly how people living in what has been called the developing world engage with development and with the alternatives to development advocated by post-development and decolonial scholars. We would like to move beyond theoretical and conceptual debates about alternatives, to explore exactly how people are engaging with development and its supposed alternatives. We want to know whether and how people are embracing (or rejecting) development and whether and how they are promoting alternative ways to improve their lives. This book responds to questions like: Do people seem to want development? Are people rejecting development and proposing alternatives to it? If so, what do those alternatives look like?

The book originated in an email conversation between the editors after one of us, Sally Matthews, presented a seminar on the concept *ubuntu* and whether it can be understood as a viable alternative to development. This seminar was

DOI: 10.4324/9781003477921-1

motivated by a sense of frustration that *ubuntu* was regularly being listed (often alongside *buen vivir*) as a supposed alternative to development without reference to any meaningful research about whether or not the term is understood that way by those who use it most often. The conversation between the two of us led to a panel at the European Association of Development Research and Training Institutes (EADI) 2023 conference in which we invited participants to reflect on how development and proposed alternatives to development are being understood and negotiated on the ground. Our sense is that there are many ambivalences and complexities in how people engage with development projects and in whether and how they reject hegemonic forms of development in favour of the kinds of alternatives which are *en vogue* in post-development and decolonial circles. The scholars brought together by the conference panel share our commitment to finding out how particular communities negotiate the idea of development and whether and how they propose alternatives to it. Subsequent to the conference, we invited the conference panellists and some other scholars to join us in putting together a book that takes seriously the complicated and often conflicted ways in which people try to improve their lives in spaces where the concept of development looms large. All the chapters are based on research conducted in and with communities in the Global South and refer to specific groups of people and their specific ways of interacting with projects purporting to bring about development or supposed alternatives to development. We set out to avoid making grand claims about development (or alternatives to it) in favour of exploring the ambiguities and nuances that we believe are typically to be found when we look at how particular groups of people engage with development.

Before continuing, it is necessary to briefly explain what we mean by the term 'Global South'. Our book looks at post-development from the perspective of the Global South, so it is important to explain what we mean by this term. While this term has greatly increased in prominence in recent years, it is used in slightly different ways – hence the need for clarification. Mahler (2018) identifies three usages for the term. Firstly, it is used as an alternative to the term 'Third World' which has become irrelevant in the post-Cold War era. Secondly, it can be used to refer to those who are negatively affected by capitalist globalisation. In this second sense, it does not refer to geographical location and it can be said that there are 'Souths in the geographic North and Norths in the geographic South' (Mahler 2018: 6). A related third use of the term points to a shared political subjectivity on the part of those who experience subjugation in the contemporary global order. In this book, it is principally to the third sense of the term 'Global South' that we refer. As Grovogui (2011: 176) explains, the term is not a 'directional designation', but rather refers to a 'symbolic designation' that points to 'the semblance of cohesion that emerged when former colonial entities engaged in political projects of decolonization and moved toward the realization of a postcolonial international order'. We understand the Global South to refer to those who share an experience of colonialism and who are today working to undo their oppression or marginalisation within the global capitalist order. In particular, as our book focuses on the question of development, we use the term to refer to those people who are seen, within standard development discourse, as in need of development but who are presented, in post-development and decolonial thinking, as potential agents who can help shape post-development alternatives. All the chapters in the book draw on research conducted in the Global South, so defined. Furthermore, while we acknowledge Mahler's (2018: 6) point that there may be 'Souths in the geographic North', we have decided to focus particularly on those situated in the countries of the world that have, over the last century, been labelled as 'underdeveloped', 'developing' or 'less-developed', in an attempt to understand exactly how those so-labelled engage with and contest development.

Another term that might need some clarification is the term 'marginalised community'. We use this term, for want of a better one, to describe the kinds of people who have typically been regarded as in need of development. But, as becomes clear in this book, not all people who are the 'targets' of development intervention are positioned the same way. Some, such as those organising to promote *mupo* in Venda, South Africa, are able to connect with international allies and engage with and appropriate international environmentalist discourses to advance their interests (see the chapter by Kwa and Van Leynseele). Others, such as the Tembo Mvura in Kanyemba, Zimbabwe, are marginalised even in relation to others living in the same region and have hardly any contact with national and international allies (see the chapter by Maheve). Nevertheless, all the communities we describe in this way are communities with two key features: they are communities that the development industry would regard as being in need of development, and they are communities post-development thinkers regard as being potentially a source of alternatives. Rather than seeing these communities in either of these ways, we try to draw out the varieties of experiences that such communities have.

In this introduction, we will begin by introducing the post-development debate and its embrace of alternatives to development. We will also briefly introduce the chapters in this book. In so doing, we will briefly highlight some common themes, but we will leave a longer discussion of such themes to the concluding chapter in which we summarise the insights presented in this book and raise some proposals for further research and reflection.

Post-development as a critique of mainstream development

Since the early 1990s, post-development theorists have offered a strident critique of development and, especially in recent years, have put forward a range of alternative approaches which they propose would be preferable to mainstream development. Books like *The Development Dictionary* (Sachs 1992), *Encountering Development* (Escobar 1995), *The History of Development* (Rist 1997), *The Post-Development Reader* (Rahnema 2008) and *Grassroots Postmodernism* (Esteva and Prakash 1998) first helped to popularise a new and varied critique of development that became known as 'post-development theory'. Since then, the critiques offered by post-development thinkers have moved in a range of different directions, sharing in common a sceptical and critical stance towards mainstream development and a commitment to attending to and valorising perspectives that come from the Global South or from marginal communities in the Global North.

While post-development theory is varied, core to post-development thinking is a sceptical and critical approach to development. Post-development thinkers highlight the colonial origins of the idea of development (Esteva 2010; Ziai 2016) and point out that development tends to be associated with the promotion of unlimited and unsustainable economic growth which pays insufficient attention to the ecological limits of the planet (Bassey 2019; Tortosa 2019). Furthermore, they argue that the idea of development presents those in the Global South in a negative and reductionist way while presenting the Global North as a model to be emulated by the Global South (Esteva 2010; Bassey 2019). Mainstream development advocates assume that the features that characterise the so-called 'developed' world will gradually spread to other parts of the world as these parts of the world 'catch up' through processes of economic growth, industrialisation and modernisation. In contrast, post-development thinkers argue that the idea of development is Eurocentric and has been used to defend and advance Western hegemony (Ziai 2016: 54–69). They argue that the idea of development implies that Global South communities are deviant and in need of intervention and assistance from the Global North (Escobar 1995; Esteva and Prakash 1998). In contrast to mainstream development perspectives, post-development writing suggests that when thinking about how to improve people's lives, it is important to look to societies in the Global South for inspiration rather than to treat such societies as needing to emulate the Global North.

In recent times, the increased prominence of decolonial theory has given new impetus to some of the critiques of development offered by post-development theory. As with post-development theorists, decolonial theorists reject the idea that the poorer parts of the world ought to follow along behind the richer on a universal path to development. Escobar, author of the prominent post-development text *Encountering Development* (1995), is now an important contributor to decolonial critiques of development (Mignolo and Escobar 2010; Escobar 2020). In his recent writing, he continues to insist upon the failure of conventional approaches to development, the importance of rejecting the West as a model for the rest of the world, and the value of recovering and revitalising ways of thinking and being from the Global South. Other decolonial thinkers, such as Mignolo (2011; 2019) and Ndlovu-Gatsheni (2020) take up similar themes. Recent post-development and decolonial critiques of development highlight the ways in which development continues to be rooted in coloniality and how it entrenches Western domination. Both approaches turn to the Global South to find the conceptual and practical resources to address the devastation they believe is caused by mainstream development.

What distinguishes post-development and decolonial critiques of development from other critical discussions of development, is the more extreme position they tend to take up. Since the rise of the idea of development, there have been many attempts to respond to criticisms of development by reforming it in some way, hence the rise of various qualifiers used to describe development: sustainable development, human development and the like. While advocates for the reform of development have much in common with post-development thinkers, the latter thinkers push more for something more radical than reform. For example, early on in the post-development debate Latouche (1993: 149) declared that talk of 'alternative development' was simply a 'siren song' which might entice people to continue to accept development, whereas in his view, the idea of development needs to be rejected entirely. More recent post-development thinking continues to insist on going beyond reform as can be seen in the introduction to *Pluriverse: A Post-Development Dictionary* in which the editors reject the idea of 'sustainable development' (Kothari et al. 2019: xxvi-xxvii). While sustainable development is supposed to be a form of development that takes on and addresses critiques of mainstream development, the editors argue that it maintains faith in the idea of endless economic growth and 'depoliticize[s] genuine political antagonisms between alternative visions for the future' (Kothari et al. 2019: xxvii). Instead of reformist solutions, post-development thinkers of the past and present have in common a commitment to a search for more fundamental transformative alternatives.

Criticisms of post-development

Post-development theory has been subject to a wide range of criticisms on a number of fronts. First, the post-development literature has tended to present mainstream development in a static and homogeneous way (Corbridge 1998; Kiely 1999; Nederveen Pieterse 2000). Development approaches have evolved and diversified in recent decades as a result of critical debates in academia and among development practitioners. However, such heterogeneity is not taken into account by some post-development writers who adopt an 'over-generalised' conception of development (Storey 2000: 42), and present it as a 'monolithic structure' (Ziai 2004: 1047). Moreover, the ways in which mainstream and alternative approaches have had an impact and influence on one another have not been sufficiently taken into account (Nederveen Pieterse 2000).

Secondly, while post-development has done much to highlight the consequences of development practices in the Global South, in doing so, it has focused exclusively on the negative impacts (Storey 2000). While such criticism has certainly been necessary to reassess the *modus operandi* of the development industry, post-development may have overlooked some of the improvements that development has made possible (Ziai 2004; McGregor 2009).

A third recurrent critique has accused post-development theorists of romanticising the lives of those in the Global South (Corbridge 1998; Kiely 1999; Nanda 1999; Asher and Wainwright 2019). Local communities have been portrayed as equal and in balance with each other and with nature (Nederveen Pieterse 2000). Post-development theorists have constructed a nativist and essentialist narrative of the 'Noble South' (Kiely 1999: 38), by repeatedly omitting conflicts and hierarchies within local communities, as well as ignoring reactionary elements such as racism, sexism and other practices of exploitation (Kiely 1999; Sylvester 1999; Pailey 2020). Not only is this problematic for its cultural relativism, but it is a remarkable inconsistency in post-development thinking in which 'one romantic parochialism (Eurocentrism) is replaced by another (Third Worldism)' (Kiely 1999: 39). More recent decolonial approaches to development, which share many features with post-development theory, have also been accused of a rather simplistic, essentialising defence of non-Western epistemologies. Naicker (2023: 222) accuses decolonial approaches to development of engaging in a 'simple inversion of colonial stereotypes' which sets up a 'binary distinction between indigenous subaltern epistemology as morally good and all secular Western epistemology as morally evil'. This, he argues, is an unacceptable simplification (Naicker 2023: 222).

A further critique relates to post-development theory's focus on discourse. Post-development is part of the discursive turn in development studies that has challenged the hegemonic ways of thinking about the world and their impact on international power relations (Escobar 1995). With its focus on discourse and ideology, post-development has been accused of being reduced to these and of neglecting material realities, real cases and field experiences (Nederveen Pieterse 1998; Kiely 1999; Ramírez-Cendrero 2018). Similarly, recent decolonial approaches to development have also been accused of focusing on discourse to the neglect of attention to material realities (Smith and Lester 2023).

Other scholars have warned about the potential anti-democratic implications of post-development by problematising the question of people's agency and voice through suggesting that those who support development have 'colonised minds' (Matthews 2017). Paradoxically, the 'alternative' future envisioned by post-development could be said to be based on universalist notions of progress (Thornton et al. 2015) and has been criticised for being prescriptive and authoritarian (Ziai 2004).

Finally, issues of positionality have been raised by critics, as post-development thinking has largely been generated by scholars situated in the comfortable and settled Global North. They have been exposed as paternalistic and hypocritical, enjoying the benefits of 'modern', 'developed' lifestyles while denying the same privileges to the Global South in the name of 'preserving traditions' (Sylvester 1999; McGregor 2009; Matthews 2017). A related problem is that while post-development and decolonial thinkers are ostensibly committed to decentring the Global North, their most prominent spokespersons are based in the Global North. Puwar (2020: 542) notes with discomfort the way in which the current increased interest in knowledge from the Global South is often advanced through 'the centring of ambassadors from the North, whose project is to decentre the centre by centring the margins' while Chetty (2023: 388) scathingly accuses decolonial thinkers of behaving like 'self-ordained oracle[s] of the Other' (see also Altschul 2022).

Post-development scholarship has certainly engaged with such critiques (Storey 2000). This has resulted in multiple variations and positions within post-development theory. Not to present it as such would be to fall into the over-simplification of which post-development has been accused.

Ziai (2004) identifies two conflicting discourses in the post-development literature. On the one hand, a 'neo-populist' variant 'which romanticises traditional culture, portraying it as static and rigid, is based on a complete rejection of modernity and promotes the return to subsistence agriculture' (Ziai 2004: 1054). On the other, a different orientation 'which is more sceptical in evaluating local communities and cultural tradition, more cautious in criticising modernity, employs a constructivist perspective on culture and avoids sketching models of future transformations of society' (Ziai 2004: 1054). Some of the criticisms of post-development theory apply only to its neo-populist variant rather than the more careful, sceptical variant.

In recent years, post-development theory has shifted somewhat from making radical calls for the writing of development's obituary (Sachs 1992: 1) to a focus on building a diverse range of alternatives to mainstream development (Klein and Morreo 2019). Gibson-Graham (2005: 6) modifies and tones down the post-development argument by stating that 'The postdevelopment agenda is not, as we see it, anti-development. [...] The challenge is to imagine and practice development differently'. McGregor (2009) argues that post-development thinking has undergone a metamorphosis, from the 'negativity of anti-development' to a more constructive approach that seeks new and alternative pathways. Recent post-development scholars have responded to their critics by presenting post-development perspectives generated by in-depth fieldwork (see McGregor 2009).

Looking at past and current contributions, there seems to be a broad acceptance of post-development theory's critique of development hegemony (Nederveen Pieterse 1998), while its attempts to formulate a model for social change remain questionable (Storey 2000). Therefore, there are different strands regarding the question of 'alternatives' in post-development theory, some of which place more emphasis on the pursuit of alternatives from the Global South while others are more compatible with traditions endorsing radical democracy (Ziai 2004).

As shown above, post-development thinking continues to be the subject of much debate, as many questions remain unanswered. How are the more nuanced positions adopted by some thinkers compatible with the 'complete break' with development and the 'radical rupture' that post-development stands for? How do they differ from the many attempts to redefine 'alternative' development that post-development seeks to distinguish itself from? In sum, there is a rich internal ongoing debate within post-development theory to which we hope this book will contribute.

Alternatives to development

As discussed above, one of the key shortcomings of post-development theory has been that its focus has been on critiquing the discourse of development, while playing insufficient attention to the material realities and aspirations of the people in the so-called 'developing' world. Moreover, post-development has been accused of not being able to move beyond the development critique and of not offering viable alternatives in practice (Ziai 2004: 1050; McKinnon 2008: 286; McGregor 2009: 1695). These shortcomings have at least partly been addressed in some recent post-development writing which fleshes out the idea of 'alternatives to development' by providing detailed accounts of real-world attempts to move beyond the framework of development. A good example here is the book *Postdevelopment in Practice* edited by Klein and Morreo (2019), which brings together detailed discussions of various attempts to build alternatives to development. Kothari's (2020; 2023) discussion of the 'global tapestry of alternatives' is another example of an attempt to provide detail about how alternatives to development might work.

There is also a burgeoning interest in degrowth as a possible alternative to the idea of development (see for example Bendix 2017; Bendix et al. 2019; D'Alisa et al. 2015; Escobar 2015; Latouche 2018; Schmelzer et al. 2022). Like post-development theorists, advocates of degrowth reject the idea of continuous economic growth and believe that we need to build alternative forms of livelihood which are less damaging to the environment. Thus far, degrowth has mostly been discussed in relation to the Global North with advocates arguing that the industrialised countries of Europe and North America should aim to reduce their economic growth rather than to continue to grow their economies. The relevance of the degrowth movement for the people of the Global South is not quite so clear, although some degrowth advocates do discuss its applicability beyond the industrialised countries (see for example Dengler and Seebacher 2019; Gräbner-Radkowitsch and Strunk 2023).

Another avenue taken by those interested in alternatives to development is to discuss and validate concepts from the Global South which are considered potential alternatives to replace the idea of development. Most prominent here is the concept of *buen vivir* which is often put forward as a possible alternative to development (see for example Acosta 2012; 2017; Escobar 2015; Gudynas 2011; Villalba 2013). Loosely translated as 'living well', discussion of *buen vivir* draws on Indigenous Latin American concepts and practices to think through possible alternatives to mainstream development. There have also been some attempts to think about alternative approaches to development in relation to the African concept of *ubuntu* (see Molefe 2019; Shumba 2011; Zondi 2016). Furthermore, several prominent post-development and decolonial thinkers make reference to such concepts in their calls for the rejection of development, even though they do not necessarily elaborate much on whether and how these terms are being used as alternatives to development. For example, Mignolo (2021: 54) claims that 'the philosophies of *ubuntu* (a Nguni Bantu term, living for the extended communal) or *sumak kawsay* (a Quichua term, living in harmony and plenitude with the living Earth) would allow us to divest ourselves from *democracy and development*'. Similarly, Acosta (2019: 282) says: 'It is crucial to recuperate alternative epistemes like *buen vivir*, *eco-swaraj*, *ubuntu*, or communitarianism – to understand and re-organise the world without falling into mandates such as *development*' (italics in the original for both quotes).

Thus it can be said that a prominent and enduring feature of post-development thought is this interest in and advocacy for alternative concepts and practices emerging from the Global South. It is this interest in alternatives that is at the heart of this book. But while the contributors to this volume are all open to and interested in the idea of alternatives, we are also committed to exploring those alternatives in relation to the experiences of particular communities within the Global South. Rather than thinking about alternatives in a fairly abstract and discursive way, we would like to pay attention to whether and how these alternatives are being articulated in particular places and how entangled they might be with more mainstream development projects. It is in this regard that the idea of ambivalence comes to the fore.

The notion of ambivalence

This book argues for the relevance of the notion of ambivalence in post-development debates, even though it has received considerably less attention than other issues. First, at the discursive level, both development and post-development have tended to be represented in a rather homogeneous and simplified way. The notion of ambivalence is therefore useful in terms of considering the diverse and conflicting discourses and meanings that post-development thinking might represent. Following Ziai (2004: 1058), who calls for caution in celebrating post-development critique, we think it is important to take account of its ambivalence.

The simplistic and dichotomous way in which classical development discourses have created categories (e.g. developed/underdeveloped; rural/urban; modern/traditional) has been at the centre of post-development critiques (Escobar 1995). However, such critiques have often fallen short of overcoming this limitation by working with opposing constructs (e.g. First/Third World; traditional/modern). In particular, such critiques have presented the possibilities for 'alternatives' in a rather polarised way, by distinguishing between 'transformative initiatives' and 'reformist solutions' (Kothari et al. 2019). Kiely (1999: 35) has argued against such binary opposition, by stating that such distinction is 'rhetorical' and 'meaningless'. While post-development and decolonial thinkers reject the way in which these kinds of oppositions have tended to devalue those who are labelled as 'underdeveloped', they have often failed to sufficiently interrogate the distinction itself. As Naicker (2023: 222) observes, by engaging in a 'simple inversion' of these kinds of binaries through rejecting the 'Western' and valuing the 'traditional' and 'Indigenous', such an approach 'unwittingly continues to adopt the moral and epistemological norms of colonial discourse'.

This book seeks to move beyond such binaries, both of development and of post-development, by bringing together empirical accounts of how development is experienced in practice. Each chapter draws on a rich ethnographic knowledge of the different ways in which people from around the world interact and engage with the complexities of development. The everyday experiences that the authors reflect on are far from fitting into the clear-cut post-development categories of 'rejection of' or 'alternatives to' development, or into easily identifiable discourses that can be aligned with a theoretical position within the abovementioned academic debates. Therefore, it seems that while such binaries may make sense at a rhetorical level, empirical realities are much more complex and nuanced. As Ramírez-Cendrero (2018: 2) puts it, 'much controversy becomes diluted when concrete experiences of action and transformation are analysed'. The notion of ambivalence reappears as relevant, this time in relation to the empirical, as Sylvester (1999: 719) notes that

> there are plenty of critiques and dreams of development circulating ambivalently in the villages and urban areas of specific Third World locales. The challenge is to reach into those spaces, pull out and analyse the stuff of everyday postcolonial deprivation and desire.

This book tries to do this by exploring the notion of ambivalence in relation to both its theoretical and empirical domains.

The structure of the book

This book is divided into three distinct sections. The book begins with four chapters which all explore the ambivalence that many feel in relation to development. Mainstream development discourse presents development as unambiguously desirable while post-development writing suggests that communities in the Global South are rejecting development. The first four chapters in the book complicate these two positions by reporting on how the desire for development, rejection of aspects of development, nostalgia for past ways of being, and profound disappointment with the failure of development initiatives may all be present at the same time within many marginalised communities.

The first chapter – by Matthews, Mkhutle and Gongqa – explores the ways in which some marginalised South African communities talk about development, as well as their views on *ubuntu,* which some post-development theorists are suggesting could be seen as an alternative to development. The chapter shows that such communities express a desire for development, although community members do not always define development in line with hegemonic discourses of development. Contrary to what is suggested in some post-development writing, the respondents discussed in the chapter do not view *ubuntu* as an alternative to development, but rather see it as compatible with development arguing that if government officials had more *ubuntu* – understood as an ethics of care, compassion and cooperation – such officials would help marginalised communities achieve their dreams of development.

This chapter is followed by a chapter by Castellsagué and Panthi which explores how *bikas*, a Nepali term used to refer to development, is understood in two regions of Nepal. The chapter explores the way in which many Nepalis associate *bikas* with what they refer to as 'hardware' development. 'Hardware' development is focused on infrastructure, the economy and the provision of financial resources. It is contrasted with 'software' development which places less emphasis on material resources and more on empowerment and education. Castellsagué and Panthi argue that while development organisations in Nepal are shifting their discourse towards 'software' development, the people interviewed for this study tend to insist upon the implementation of 'hardware' development, calling into question the idea that people in the Global South are rejecting development.

Mullikin's chapter, which focuses on the experiences of farming communities in Eastern Rwanda, makes up the third contribution to this section. These communities have been greatly impacted by state-sponsored agrarian development programmes which have substantially changed farming practices as well as shifted the ways in which people imagine their futures. Mullikin discusses how these farmers experience development as a precarious and ambivalent state between nostalgia and reverie. They feel nostalgia for the rituals and rhythms that used to characterise agrarian life but which are being eroded by agrarian modernisation schemes. At the same time, however, they dream of achieving the opportunities that development is supposed to open up for them and their children. Their nostalgia for past practices can thus not be understood as a rejection of development, but more as a recognition of what they have given up to pursue what they hope will be a more prosperous future. Mullikin emphasises that rather than proposing alternatives to development, what his respondents most want, is to be fully and meaningfully included in it.

The final chapter in the first section, by Maheve, takes us to Kanyemba, a remote area in northern Zimbabwe. He relates the experiences of Kanyemba residents with CAMPFIRE, a conservation-based Zimbabwean development programme. Maheve's chapter brings out the complexities and ambivalences that emerge when we look carefully at the everyday experiences of those affected by development programmes. The CAMPFIRE programme did not affect all Kanyemba residents in the same way, with the more marginal Tembo Mvura community receiving fewer benefits from the programme than their Chikunda neighbours. Maheve shows that these differences also lead to different ways in which the two communities speak about development, with the Tembo Mvura community generally showing more explicitly negative feelings towards CAMPFIRE and development. Like the Rwandan farmers discussed by Mullikin, some Kanyemba residents express nostalgia for past ways of life, but at the same time they also long for inclusion in the benefits they expect development to bring to them, such as the provision of formal housing.

The second section of the book focuses on the concept of *vivir bien/buen vivir* which, as discussed earlier, has received much attention among those advocating for alternatives to development. As such, *vivir bien* could be considered to be the most promising alternative put forward by post-development and decolonial advocates for radical alternatives. It is typically presented as a concept that arises from the beliefs of Indigenous South Americans and which emphasises solidarity with others and harmony with the environment, thereby serving as a contrast to the individualistic and economistic approaches associated with Western narratives on development. However, as the three chapters in this section show, the *vivir bien* rhetoric adopted by political leaders and scholars does not adequately capture the much more ambivalent ways in which many people living in South America engage with this concept.

The first chapter in this section, by Ranta and Zenteno Lawrence, focuses on the experiences of Afro-Bolivian women. They show that while Afro-Bolivians initially had high hopes in relation to the concept of *vivir bien* and felt that this concept resonated well with their experiences, they have come to be disappointed with the ways in which the Bolivian government has implemented its *vivir bien* vision. By focusing on their experiences, Ranta and Zenteno Lawrence highlight the gap between a romanticised *vivir bien* rhetoric advanced by the Bolivian state, and the concrete experiences of Afro-Bolivian women who continue to experience marginalisation and discrimination. Ranta and Zenteno Lawrence describe the ways in which *saya*, an Afro-Bolivian dance and music genre, has provided Afro-Bolivian women with spaces for resistance and enabled them to advance their own alternative approaches to counter their disillusionment with the *vivir bien* approach officially adopted by the Bolivian state.

The next chapter, by Córdova Suxo, also focuses on Bolivia, but looks at the ways in which social movements representing Indigenous communities in Bolivia contest the concept and relate it to narratives about indigeneity. While much writing on *vivir bien* presents such communities as the originators of this concept, Córdova Suxo paints a much more complicated and ambiguous picture. The incorporation of *vivir bien* into official state policy has resulted in the concept sometimes being aligned with projects which result in natural resource exploitation, modernisation, the displacement of Indigenous communities and standard neoliberal economic approaches, despite the concept supposedly serving as an alternative to hegemonic forms of development. The chapter explores the way in which discourses around indigeneity relate to narratives about alternatives to development, in a context where developmental modernisation and its related marginalisation of many people persist, despite the rhetoric that *vivir bien* provides a new and alternative approach.

The final chapter in this section, by Prouchet and her colleagues, focuses on the perspectives of the Awajún people in the Peruvian Amazon. Several entrepreneurship-for-development projects are present in this area and the chapter explores how people engage with such programmes. In contrast with the rather romanticised images of Indigenous life present in some post-development writing, this chapter shows that even within one community, people respond in diverse ways to development programmes, with most neither rejecting nor fully supporting such programmes. While the concept of *vivir bien* is presented as arising from Indigenous communities, people in this Awajún community seem to regard it as a concept brought from outside. Furthermore, many embrace aspects of mainstream development and seek inclusion in it. However, as the chapter makes clear, multiple conceptions of 'the good life' coexist in the community, leading the authors to conclude by emphasising the importance of context-based approaches that are not shaped by predetermined ideas about how Indigenous communities prefer to live.

The last section of the book brings together three chapters which set out to explore potential alternatives to development in three very different contexts: urban Iran, rural South Africa and an island in the Philippines. While the contexts are very different, all three chapters are concerned with whether and how communities try to advance approaches which could be considered to constitute alternatives to development. Like all the chapters in this book, the authors in this section bring out some of the complexities and ambiguities that emerge when we are attentive to the ways in which marginalised communities try to improve their lives in contexts saturated with the idea of development.

The first chapter, by Saremi and her colleagues, looks at the economic practices of four marginalised groups in Tehran, Iran, with the view to see whether or not such groups are building practices that challenge the logics of capitalist development. The authors set out to investigate whether the economic practices of such communities constitute economies of solidarity that could be considered examples of post-development practice. They conclude that while these communities do engage in alternative economic practices which do not conform to the standard capitalist model, it is less clear whether such practices demonstrate the values of reciprocity and solidarity advocated for by some post-development approaches. Furthermore, it is also not clear to what extent such alternative practices would be abandoned if inclusion in mainstream economic development was possible for these marginalised communities. The chapter shows that the marginalised communities in the study do engage in practices that call into question many of the assumptions of mainstream development discourse, but that it is less clear whether such practices can be considered to constitute positive and sustainable alternatives.

Kwa and Leynseele's chapter also explores an attempt to create an alternative to mainstream development by looking at the activities of a social movement, Dzomo la Mupo, in the Venda region of South Africa. They argue that this social movement's eco-centric defence of sacred spaces is based on Indigenous ways of understanding nature and demonstrates resistance to state-led extractivist development projects. In exploring the practices of this social movement, they show how the movement articulates community claims by connecting with local and global networks and narratives. This includes their adoption of eco-mapping practices which they learnt through connecting with South American Indigenous social movements, as well as their attempts to translate Indigenous concepts in ways that make them legible within legislative language and Western bio-conservation discourses. The chapter helps us see how marginalised communities might use alternative discourses, rooted in Indigenous epistemologies and ontologies, alongside more mainstream discourses to pursue their ends.

The final chapter in this section, by Alegado, explores the relevance of the idea of degrowth on the island of Siquijor province in the Philippines. Degrowth is one of the most popular new concepts emerging from post-development theory and other critiques of capitalist development, but it has mostly been discussed in a Global North context. Alegado sets out to relate the concept of degrowth to the concepts of ***kalamboan*** (development) and ***ginhawa*** (wellbeing) which are used in the Philippines. In so doing, he explores potential connections between debates on degrowth and the ways in which people in Siquijor think about development.

Why this book at this time?

There is a lot of interest at the moment in alternative epistemologies and alternative concepts such as ***vivir bien*** and ***ubuntu***. Widespread and ongoing disillusionment with development and increasing awareness of the negative environmental consequences of development is leading many people to look for alternatives to mainstream development. While disillusionment with mainstream development is certainly not new, the interest in finding alternatives rooted in supposedly Indigenous concepts is a feature of recent attempts to move beyond mainstream development. An interest in such alternatives has been a long-standing feature of post-development theory but has been given new impetus in recent decolonial critiques of development.

This book connects with the increased interest in these topics but does so in a way that is attentive to some of the critiques of post-development theory. One of the long-standing critiques of post-development theory's interest in alternatives to development is that it approaches such concepts theoretically without providing much empirical detail (Nederveen Pieterse 1998; Kiely 1999; Ramírez-Cendrero 2018). The enthusiasm for alternatives rooted in Indigenous epistemologies is often not accompanied by careful and detailed descriptions of these epistemologies and attentiveness to the communities from which such concepts supposedly originate. Critics – and indeed many of the contributors to this book – experience much frustration when appeals to the experiences of Indigenous or 'grassroots' communities are made in ways that seem to flatten and generalise these experiences. Expressing such frustration in relation to recent decolonial advocacy for Indigenous alternatives, Chetty (2023: 388) complains that such appeals are part of a Western 'existential crisis' which leads Western-based scholars to reach out to the Global South for alternatives like ***ubuntu*** and ***buen vivir***. He argues that the 'actual content of these ideas is entirely irrelevant' and asks what happens when individuals from such Global South communities behave like 'wrong natives' by refusing to endorse the visions of the future that supposedly align with the Indigenous epistemologies receiving so much attention in the West.

This book sets out to be different by showing how tensions and contradictions arise when these supposed alternatives to development are approached ethnographically and contextually rather than rhetorically. When we focus on particular marginalised communities in the Global South, we do not find communities full of people who all endorse the values attributed to them in some post-development and decolonial thinking. We find plenty of 'wrong natives' (Chetty 2023: 388) who seek inclusion in development rather than advancing alternatives.

However, we also find people who are resisting mainstream development projects and trying to build alternative livelihoods. When putting this book together, we did not seek out contributors who share the same view on whether alternatives to development are desirable. Rather, what we wanted was a shared commitment to taking seriously the beliefs and practices of marginalised communities, rather than making generalised claims about what such communities believe or want.

The book is a compilation of cases from different geographical regions and is based on fieldwork in each of these regions. Many similar books focus on one region, whereas this book brings together different Global South perspectives, including regions of the world that are rarely discussed in post-development theory, such as Africa. Indeed, if any region is somewhat over-represented in this book, it is Africa, which is featured in four chapters (those by Maheve; Mullikin; Kwa and Leynseele; and Matthews, Mkhutle and Gongqa). But the book also includes chapters focused on South America (Córdova Suxo, Prouchet et al., and Ranta and Zenteno Lawrence) and Asia (Alegado and Castellsagué and Panthi) and a chapter focusing on the Middle East (Saremi et al.'s chapter on Iran). In doing so, the book makes connections between different contexts and different concepts being advanced as alternatives to development (such as *buen vivir* or *ubuntu*), rather than studying them separately.

The contributors to this book have varied positionalities and it is important to briefly touch on how these might have influenced the book. As we discuss earlier, cultural relativism and romanticism are major concerns in development and post-development debates and these concerns are often related to the positionality of the scholars who advance post-development positions. While many post-development and decolonial critiques of development make rhetorical gestures towards centring the Global South, the most prominent advocates of alternatives to development are based in the Global North. In comparison, most of the chapters in this book include at least one Global South-based author. Of course, where scholars are based is only one aspect of their embeddedness within the global and unequal distribution of power and privilege. Indeed, most of the contributors to this book could be described as beneficiaries of this unequal distribution. However, we hope that by including so many contributors who are from or currently live in the Global South, we are making a small contribution to shifting the inequities in global knowledge production. Relatedly, we have also tried to strike a balance between young and more experienced scholars, giving those at the beginning of their careers a place to have a voice in an edited volume with a wide reach. That's something worth noting in an increasingly competitive and unequal academia. Similarly, in a world where knowledge production remains dominated by men, this book is edited by two women and around half of the chapter contributors are women.

The editors have tried to make this book as much about the process as the outcome. It began as a discussion at the EADI conference 'New Rhythms of Development' and continued through the editors' work and refinement of the book's scope. Several meetings were held with the contributors to engage with each other's perspectives and work. The review process was collaborative, with authors commenting on each other's chapters and identifying common issues and connections across the cases presented. As a result, the book has strong links between chapters and sections, which we believe contributes to a better and more meaningful overall discussion of current development and post-development debates.

This book is the culmination of the collective efforts of numerous individuals, including authors, editors, research assistants, linguistic editors and the participants of each study. We extend our gratitude to all of them for their willingness to collaborate and for their dedication and enthusiasm in pursuing this project. It is our intention that this book, and the ideas presented in each of its chapters, will prove valuable to students, researchers, practitioners and activists engaged in the field. It is our contention that this book represents a valuable contribution to the ongoing debates on development and post-development.

Notes

1 We have chosen to use the term post-development (with a hyphen) because it is the more accepted form among scholars who identify with this school of thought. More recently, however, other scholars have advocated the use of the term without a hyphen (postdevelopment) to point out that there is no complete break before and after development, and that the alternatives in practice exist alongside each other (See Klein and Morreo 2019).

2 In line with the advice given in most recent publishing guidelines, we will capitalise the word 'indigenous' when referring to people groups and concepts (as in 'Indigenous communities in Bolivia') while using lower-case when using the word in other ways (as in 'protecting indigenous forests in Venda'). Similarly, we will capitalise words referring to other people groups, using capital letters to refer to Black people, *Mestizo* people and so on. This is in recognition that when using the word in this way, we are referring to the name of a group of people and so, just as one would use capitals when speaking of Belgian people or Kenyan women, we should use capital letters when referring to other groups of people. However, we acknowledge that referring to people in respectful ways is more complicated than simply using capital letters and that there are instances where it can be unclear what the most appropriate usage is.

References

Acosta, A. (2012). *Buen vivir. Sumak kawsay: Una oportunidad para imaginar otros mundos.* Quito: AbyaYala.

Acosta, A. (2017). 'Living Well: ideas for reinventing the future', *Third World Quarterly*, 38 (12), pp. 2600–2616.

Acosta, A. (2019). 'Post-Economia'. In *Pluriverse: A Post-Development Dictionary*, edited by Kothari, A., Salleh, A., Escobar, A., Demaria, F. and Acosta, A.New Delhi: Tulika Books, pp. 280–282.

Altschul, N.R. (2022). 'The Decolonial Imperative: A Postcolonial Critique'. *Gragoatá*, 27 (59), pp. 1–19. Available at: https://doi.org/10.22409/gragoata.v27i59.53591.

Asher, K. and Wainwright, J. (2019). 'After post-development: on capitalism, difference, and representation', *Antipode*, 51 (1), pp. 25–44. Available at: https://doi.org/10.1111/anti.12430.

Bassey, N. (2019). 'Breaking the Chains of Development'. In *Pluriverse: a post-development dictionary*, edited by Kothari, A., Salleh, A., Escobar, A., Demaria, F. and Acosta, A.New Delhi: Tulika Books, pp. 3–5.

Bendix, D. (2017). 'Reflecting the Post-Development gaze: the degrowth debate in Germany'. *Third World Quarterly*, 38 (12), pp. 2617–633. https://doi.org/10.1080/01436597.2017.1314761.

Bendix, D., Müller, F. and Ziai, A. (2019). 'Postdevelopment alternatives in the North'. In *Postdevelopment in practice: alternatives, economies, ontologies*, edited by Klein, E. and Morreo, C. E.London: Routledge.

Chetty, K. (2023). 'The politics of decolonial investigations', *Social Dynamics*, 49 (2), pp. 386–388. Available at: DOI:doi:10.1080/02533952.2023.2239010.

Corbridge, S. (1998). '"Beneath the pavement only soil": The poverty of post-development', *Journal of Development Studies*, 34(6), pp. 138–148. Available at: https://doi.org/10.1080/00220389808422549.

D'Alisa, G., Demaria, F. and Kallis, G. (eds.). (2014). *Degrowth: A Vocabulary for a New Era*. London: Routledge.

Dengler, C. and Seebacher, L. M. (2019). 'What about the Global South? Towards a feminist decolonial degrowth approach', *Ecological Economics*, 157, pp. 246–252. Available at: https://Doi.org/10.1016/j.ecolecon.2018.11.019.

Escobar, A. (1995). *Encountering development: the making and unmaking of the Third World*. Princeton University Press.

Escobar, A. (2015). 'Degrowth, postdevelopment, and transitions: a preliminary conversation', *Sustainability Science*, 10, pp. 451–462. Available at: https://doi.org/10.1007/s11625-015-0297-5.

Escobar, A. (2020). *Pluriversal politics: the real and the possible*. Translated by D. Frye. Durham: Duke University press.

Esteva, G. (2010). 'Development'. In *The development dictionary: a guide to knowledge as power*, edited by Sachs, W.London: Zed Books, pp. 1–23.

Esteva, G. and Prakash, M. S. (1998). *Grassroots Post-Modernism: Remaking the Soil of Cultures*. Palgrave Macmillan.

Gibson-Graham, J. K. (2005). 'Surplus possibilities: Postdevelopment and community economies', *Singapore Journal of Tropical Geography*, 26 (1), pp. 4–26. Available at: https://doi.org/10.1111/j.01297619.2005.00198.x.

Gräbner-Radkowitsch, C. and Strunk, B. (2023). 'Degrowth and the Global South: The twin problem of global dependencies', *Ecological Economics*, 213, p. 107946. Available at https://doi.org/10.1016/j.ecolecon.2023.107946.

Grovogui, S. (2011). 'A revolution nonetheless: The Global South in International Relations', *The Global South*, 5 (1), p. 175. Available at: https://doi.org/10.2979/globalsouth.5.1.175.

Gudynas, E. (2011). 'Buen Vivir: Today's tomorrow', *Development*, 54 (4), pp. 441–447.

Kiely, R. (1999). 'The last refuge of the noble savage? A critical assessment of post-development theory', *European Journal of Development Research*, 11, pp. 30–55.

Klein, E. and Morreo, C. E. (eds.) (2019). *Postdevelopment in practice: alternatives, economies, ontologies*. London: Routledge.

Kothari, A. (2020). 'Earth Vikalp Sangam: proposal for a Global Tapestry of Alternatives', *Globalisations*, 17 (2), pp. 245–249.

Kothari, A, (2023). 'Towards Post-Development in India Lessons of Community Resilience in Times of Crises', *DPS Working Paper Series: Activist Special Issue*. Department for Development and Postcolonial Studies: University Kassel. Available at https://dx.doi.org/doi:10.17170/kobra-202311249091.

Kothari, A., Salleh, A., Escobar, A., Demaria, F. and Acosta, A. (eds.). (2019). *Pluriverse: A Post-Development Dictionary*. New Delhi: Tulika Books.

Latouche, S. (1993). *In the wake of the affluent society: an exploration of post-development.* Zed Books.

Latouche, S. (2018). 'The Path to Degrowth for a Sustainable Society'. In *Eco-efficiency in industry and science*, edited by Lehmann, H. Cham: Springer. Available at: https://doi.org/10.1007/978-3-319-50079-9_17.

Mahler, A. G. (2018). *From the Tricontinental to the global South: race, radicalism, and transnational solidarity*. Durham: Duke University Press.

Matthews, S. (2017). 'Colonised minds? Post-development theory and the desirability of development in Africa', *Third World Quarterly*, 38 (12), pp. 2650–2663. Available at: https://doi.org/10.1080/01436597.2017.1279540.

McGregor, A. (2009). 'New Possibilities? Shifts in post-development theory and practice', *Geography Compass*, 3 (5), pp. 1688–1702. Available at: https://doi.org/10.1111/j.1749-8198.2009.00260.x.

McKinnon, K. (2008). 'Taking post-development theory to the field: Issues in development research, Northern Thailand', *Asia Pacific Viewpoint*, 49 (3), pp. 281–293. Available at: https://doi.org/10.1111/j.1467-8373.2008.00377.x.

Mignolo, W. D. (2011). *The darker side of Western modernity: global futures, decolonial options*. Durham, NC: Duke University Press (Latin America Otherwise).

Mignolo, W. D. (2019). 'Sustainable development or sustainable economies? Ideas towards living in harmony and plenitude', *Socioscapes: International Journal of Societies, Politics and Cultures*:1, 1, 2019 [Preprint]. Available at: https://doi.org/10.48250/1004.

Mignolo, W. D. (2021). *The Politics of Decolonial Investigations*. Durham: Duke University Press.

Mignolo, W. and Escobar, A. (2010). *Globalisation and the decolonial option*. London New York: Routledge.

Molefe, M. (2019). 'Ubuntu and Development: An African Conception of Development', *Africa Today*, 66 (1), pp. 96–115.

Naicker, V. (2023). 'The problem of epistemological critique in contemporary decolonial theory', *Social Dynamics*, 49 (2), pp. 220–241. Available at: https://doi.org/10.1080/02533952.2023.2226497.

Nanda, M. (1999). 'Who Needs post-development? Discourses of difference, the green revolution and agrarian populism in India', *Journal of Developing Societies*, 15 (1), pp. 1–31.

Ndlovu-Gatsheni, S. J. (2020). *Decolonisation, development and knowledge in Africa: turning over a new leaf.* Abingdon, Oxon: Routledge (Worlding beyond the West).

Nederveen Pieterse, J. (1998). 'My paradigm or yours? Alternative Development, Post-Development, Reflexive Development'. *Development and Change*, 29, 343–373.

Nederveen Pieterse, J. (2000). 'After Post-Development', *Third World Quarterly*, 21 (2), pp. 175–191.

Pailey, R. N. (2020). 'De-centring the "white gaze" of development', *Development and Change*, 51 (3), pp. 729–745. Available at: https://doi.org/10.1111/dech.12550.

Puwar, N. (2020). 'Puzzlement of a déjà vu: illuminaries of the Global South', *The Sociological Review*, 68 (3), pp. 540–556. Available at: https://doi.org/10.1177/0038026119890254.

Rahnema, M. (ed.). (2008). *The post-development reader*. London: Zed Books.

Ramírez-Cendrero, J. M. (2018). 'Limits and contradictions of post-developmentalism as a heterodox approach to capitalist development', *Capitalism Nature Socialism*, 29 (4), pp. 68–87. Available at: https://doi.org/10.1080/10455752.2017.1334220.

Rist, G. (1997). *The history of development: from Western origins to global faith*. Zed Books.

Sachs, W. (ed.). (1992). *The Development Dictionary: A Guide to Knowledge as Power*. London: Zed Books.

Schmelzer, M., Vetter, A. and Vansintjan, A. (2022). *The Future Is Degrowth A Guide to a World beyond Capitalism*. London: Verso.

Shumba, O. (2011). 'Commons thinking, ecological intelligence and the ethical and moral framework of Ubuntu: An imperative for sustainable development', *Journal of Media and Communication Studies*, 3 (3), pp. 84–96.

Smith, M. N. and Lester, C. A. (2023). 'From "dependency" to "decoloniality"? The enduring relevance of materialist political economy and the problems of a "decolonial" alternative', *Social Dynamics*, 49 (2), pp. 196–219. Available at: https://doi.org/10.1080/02533952.2023.2220588.

Storey, A. (2000). 'Post-development theory: romanticism and Pontius Pilate politics', *Development*, 43 (4), pp. 40–46.

Sylvester, C. (1999). 'Development studies and postcolonial studies: disparate tales of the "Third World"', *Third World Quarterly*, 20 (4), pp. 703–721. Available at: https://doi.org/10.1080/01436599913514.

Thornton, A., Dorius, S. F. and Swindle, J. (2015). 'Developmental idealism', *Sociology of Development*, 1 (2), pp. 277–320. Available at: https://doi.org/10.1525/sod.2015.1.2.277.

Tortosa, J. M. (2019). 'Maldevelopment'. In *Pluriverse: a post-development dictionary*, edited by Kothari, A., Salleh, A., Escobar, A., Demaria, R. and Acosta, A.New Delhi, India: Tulika Books, pp. 9–11.

Villalba, U. (2013). 'Buen Vivir vs development: A paradigm shift in the Andes?', *Third World Quarterly*, 34 (8), pp. 1427–1442.

Ziai, A. (2004). 'The ambivalence of post-development: between reactionary populism and radical democracy', *Third World Quarterly*, 25 (6), pp. 1045–1060. Available at: https://doi.org/10.1080/0143659042000256887.

Ziai, A. (2016). *Development discourse and global history: from colonialism to the sustainable development goals*. New York, NY: Routledge.

Zondi, S. (2016). 'Ubuntu and sumak kawsay: The Inter-Parliamentary Union and the search for a Global South humanist paradigm of development', *South African Journal of International Affairs*, 23 (1), pp. 107–120.

Part I

Ambivalence, Nostalgia, Complexity

In this section, we bring together chapters that highlight the ways in which marginalised communities seem to want some aspects of development while rejecting or feeling more ambivalent about others.

DOI: 10.4324/9781003477921-2

2 In search of post-development alternatives

Ubuntu and development in South Africa

Sally Matthews, Nhlanhla Mkhutle and Simphiwe Gongqa

Introduction

For several decades now, post-development thinkers have put forward a detailed and varied critique of the idea and practice of development. While debate about post-development theory was most vigorous during the 1990s, post-development theory arguably remains 'the most popular critical approach to development' (Asher and Wainwright 2019: 25). One of the key features of post-development theory is its call for alternatives to development. Rather than joining the many voices calling for some kind of alternative way of achieving development (such as participatory, human or sustainable development), many post-development theorists call for the 'full abandonment of "development" as a discourse, as a vision and as a practice' (Garcia-Arias and Schöneberg 2021: 866) in order to 'open a way for cultural alternatives that nurture and respect life on Earth' (Kothari et al. 2019a: xvii).

In recent years, post-development thinkers have presented certain Indigenous concepts as potential alternatives to the idea of development (Acosta 2012; 2017; 2019; Escobar 2015; Gudynas 2011; Klein and Morreo 2019; Kothari et al. 2019a; 2019b; Villalba 2013). Most prominent among such concepts has been that of *buen vivir*. This Indigenous South American concept translates literally as 'good living' and suggests a way of living that is in harmony with others and the environment. While African concepts have been less commonly discussed as potential post-development alternative concepts (and Africa has, in general, been under-represented in post-development thinking), the southern African concept *ubuntu* has received some attention with some commentators suggesting that *ubuntu* could be a useful concept to guide alternative approaches to development (see Boogaard and Van Norren 2022; Metz 2017; Molefe 2011; 2019; Shumba 2011; Zondi 2016). While such commentators do not necessarily link *ubuntu* to post-development thinking (but rather see it as an alternative approach to development), it has also been linked directly to post-development thinking. For example, Ziai (2014: 148) describes *ubuntu* as a 'potential [post-development] concept', and the term is included as one of the entries in the recently published *Pluriverse: A Post-Development Dictionary* (2019). Concepts like *buen vivir* and *ubuntu* are increasingly being discussed in new contexts. Careful thought is required about the implications of the appropriation and translation of such

DOI: 10.4324/9781003477921-3

concepts for use in broader struggles against hegemonic forms of development. Furthermore, ***ubuntu*** has to some extent been picked up on and used within political and governance spaces in South Africa, although not nearly as much as ***buen vivir*** which has been institutionalised in some South American countries such as Bolivia (see chapters in this volume by Ranta, Zenteno Lawrence and Cordova Suxo) and Ecuador (Radcliffe 2012).

This chapter is intended as a preliminary exploration into whether and how ***ubuntu*** is related to development in the South African context. While there is some scholarly writing relating ***ubuntu*** to development (see Boogaard and Van Norren 2022; Metz 2017; Molefe 2019), such writing does not report on whether and how the terms are being related in 'grassroots' or everyday settings. This article responds to the question of whether, in everyday contexts, people connect development and ***ubuntu*** and, if so, how. As Ziai (2014: 148) points out, it is not clear that the term ***ubuntu*** is being used to advance anti-hegemonic approaches to development. If ***ubuntu*** is being proposed as a concept that can drive alternatives to development aligned with some of the key concerns centred by the post-development critique of development, it is important to tease out how the terms development and ***ubuntu*** are interpreted by 'ordinary' people in 'grassroots' contexts. This is what this chapter sets out to do. The chapter begins with a brief overview of post-development thinking and of the concept of ***ubuntu***, followed by a discussion of the findings of preliminary research conducted in four marginalised South African communities. We show that our respondents value both development and ***ubuntu*** and see the two concepts as related to each other, but not necessarily in the way that either development or post-development theorists imagine.

Post-development theory and alternatives to development

As noted in the introduction to the book, post-development theory remains a popular critical approach to development. As the book's introduction provides a lengthy introduction to post-development theory, it is not necessary to introduce it at length here. However, it is important here to point out that one key feature of post-development theory has been its interest in finding alternatives to mainstream development through drawing on the ideas and practices of people situated in the Global South. Early post-development theorists such as Alvares (1993), Mies and Shiva (1993) and Rahnema and Bawtree (1997) drew on non-Western thinkers, such as Gandhi or Confucius in attempts to create alternatives to development. More recently, post-development and decolonial thinkers have suggested that the ideas and practices of 'Indigenous' people can provide valuable alternatives to mainstream development. For example, in *Pluriverse: A Post-Development Dictionary*, the editors identify 'Indigenous worldviews' as an important source for the alternative vision the book seeks to present (Kothari et al. 2019: xxviii). As there is great variety among post-development thinkers, a common feature is an interest in the ideas and ways of life of those who are seen by mainstream development thinking as deficient and in need of development. It is this interest that has led to increased reference to terms like *buen vivir* (and variants of it like *sumak kawsay*) and *ubuntu* in recent post-development writing. Likewise, recent decolonial thinking sets out to displace the centrality of the Western canon and to draw more attention to marginalised perspectives (Grosfoguel 2007; Lugones 2010; Mignolo and Walsh 2018; Mignolo 2021). In so doing, such scholars too have referred to concepts such as *buen vivir* and *ubuntu* when imagining decolonial futures.

It is thus fair to say that contemporary post-development and decolonial thinking sets out to promote concepts like *ubuntu* as alternatives to mainstream development. However, as African scholars have played a very marginal role in post-development theory generally, the term *ubuntu* is often referenced very briefly and superficially by non-African scholars as part of a list of supposed alternatives to development. For example, the editors of *Pluriverse* list *ubuntu* alongside *buen vivir* and *swaraj* as part of a 'matrix of alternatives' (Kothari et al. 2019: xxviii) and Mignolo (2021: 54) refers to *ubuntu* alongside *sumak kawsay* as an alternative that can help us break with development. This chapter was motivated by scepticism about the grouping together of such concepts and the assumption that *ubuntu* can serve as an alternative to development. As South African scholars, our sense prior to starting the study was that this is not the way in which South Africans use and think of the term and so we set out to explore the link between *ubuntu* and (post)development thinking. If post-development and decolonial thinkers intend to articulate a constellation of alternative concepts which can be used to counter mainstream development thinking and coloniality, it is important that this be done in a way that is attentive to the origins and general usage of such concepts, rather than one that simply appropriates concepts like *ubuntu* to advance approaches that would not be supported by the people from whom such concepts supposedly originate.

Ubuntu and development thinking

Like development, *ubuntu* is a contested concept. As *ubuntu* has not been discussed in depth earlier in this book, we will spend some time here introducing the concept in some detail. The term '*ubuntu*' is often related to the isiZulu saying '*umuntu ngumuntu ngabantu*' (or similar sayings in other southern African languages). Directly translated, this phrase means 'a person is a person through other people', but Ramose (1999: 52) says that the saying can more generally be understood to mean that 'to be a human being is to affirm one's humanity by recognising the humanity of others and, on that basis establishing human relations with them'. It entails 'a humane, respectful and polite attitude towards others' (Ramose 1999: 52). Anti-apartheid cleric Desmond Tutu, one of the most prominent contributors to shaping the term's current usage, describes *ubuntu* this way: 'My humanity is caught up, is inextricably bound up in yours' (cited in Metz 2007: 323). Similarly, Zondi (2016: 110) describes it as a concept that promotes human solidarity and 'engenders the ethic of mutually enriching co-existence among humans'. Although it is impossible to pin down a single definition of *ubuntu*, the term generally suggests a humane way of relating that emphasises caring, sharing, mutual respect, compassion, group solidarity and collective unity (Letseka 2012: 48; Mokgoro 2010). While *ubuntu* is most often discussed in relation to South Africa, the concept (and related concepts such as the Shona term *hunhu*) is prevalent throughout southern Africa (Manyonganise 2015).

The term *ubuntu* has been taken up by a range of different people for very different ends. In this way, it is much like development which has been used to refer to so many different forms of positive change that it is hard to pin its meaning down. When related to development, *ubuntu* is considered by some as a concept that can help flesh out alternative, more inclusive forms of development or alternatives to development (Boogaard and Van Norren 2022; Metz 2017; Molefe 2011; 2019; Pereira da Silva 2020; Zondi 2016). For example, Molefe (2019: 111) argues that from an *ubuntu* perspective, development cannot be reduced to modernisation and should rather be linked to ideas of broader human flourishing. Similarly, Boogaard and Van Norren (2022: 108) say that the notion of *ubuntu* encourages an approach rooted in the idea that 'mutual sharing is more important than the accumulation of individual wealth, or national growth of wealth'. Zondi (2016: 108) argues that *ubuntu* can be used to counteract the dehumanisation which results from colonial approaches to development and can help bring about a form of development which centres the idea of living well. It is these features of *ubuntu* that encourage post-development thinkers to think that *ubuntu* could be a helpful concept when trying to build alternatives to development premised upon Indigenous concepts.

It is necessary to acknowledge at this point that a range of scholars warn that the term *ubuntu* is being appropriated and misused. For example, Dladla (2017) accuses White scholars of misappropriating the term to advance White supremacist and colonial objectives. Qobo and Nyathi (2016) also believe that *ubuntu* has been appropriated and misused by others, arguing that colonial agents used the term to advance the idea that Africans are 'kind, less prone to materialism and greed', a view which was used to justify racial inequality. Matolino and Kwindingwi (2013) argue that the promotion of *ubuntu* in post-apartheid South Africa is an elitist project that is mobilised to serve the agenda of political elites. They go so far as to suggest that *ubuntu* 'has become anything to anyone who so wishes to deploy it' (Matolino and Kwindingwi 2013: 201). Furthermore, feminist critics point out that the relationship between patriarchy and *ubuntu* needs to be thought through carefully (Cornell and Van Marle 2015; Chisale 2018; Luvalo 2019; Manyonganise 2015). As Gasa (in Suttner 2017) points out, *ubuntu* as a concept has to be understood as 'part of a complex web of a socio-cultural world that is based on patriarchy'.

Thus the meaning of the term *ubuntu*, like the term development, is a much contested one. It is important to recognise how terms like *ubuntu* are contested and how they relate to complex power relations. A failure to recognise such contestation can lead to obfuscation of the power relations that may underlie both attempts to promote development and attempts to advance alternatives to development. Terms like development and *ubuntu* can be appropriated for a range of different ends and by different actors. While the authors in the paragraph above warn that the term has been appropriated by privileged actors within South Africa to advance their interests, it is important to also acknowledge the possibility that scholars from outside South Africa may use the term to advance post-development or decolonial arguments, without being attentive to the ways in which the term is understood and used by the communities from which it supposedly originates. While our chapter is focused specifically on *ubuntu*, it should be noted that similar concerns around appropriation have arisen in relation to the terms *buen vivir* and *sumak kawsay* which are also being given much attention in post-development and decolonial thinking (see for example Domínguez et al. 2017; Ranta 2016; Recasens 2014). These scholars warn against the uncritical celebration of such terms by some affiliated with post-development and decolonial schools of thought.

Post-development, *ubuntu* and alternatives to development

As discussed above, some post-development and other critics of mainstream development believe that the concept of *ubuntu* can be helpful for those trying to find alternatives to development. But what is not so clear is whether alternatives to development are really being widely embraced in the Global South and whether enthusiasm about alternative transformative initiatives based on Indigenous concepts is justified. Even commentators sympathetic to post-development, such as García-Arias and Schöneberg (2021: 867), are concerned that claims that Indigenous communities are widely resisting development risk a 'certain idealisation of traditional societies' and pay insufficient attention to the diversity and internal tensions within such societies. This concern is related to a more straightforward concern about the accuracy of the depiction of such societies: are significant numbers of people in such communities organising to resist development in favour of Indigenous alternatives? The scholarship on post-development and on the relation between *ubuntu* and development does not tend to draw on fieldwork among the communities which purportedly favour alternatives to development. However, some of those who make such claims do provide examples of movements in the Global South that are promoting alternatives to development (see, for example, Kothari 2020).

If we are to try to build upon the post-development critique of development to find alternatives to mainstream development, it is important to find out whether and how people in the Global South use alternative, Indigenous concepts. It is vital to be attentive to the way in which ordinary citizens are engaging with development and what concepts they use to articulate their preferences regarding development. This study hopes to provide a small contribution to such needed research by directly asking some people living in marginalised South African communities how they conceptualise development and relate it to *ubuntu*. While it might be countered that people might 'live' the concept of *ubuntu* without necessarily clearly conceptualising it, it is still the case that by asking people to detail how they relate to concepts like development and *ubuntu*, we will be able to get a better sense of whether and how *ubuntu* can be understood as an alternative to development, rather than by simply taking the way scholars define the term and then extrapolating its relevance to post-development thinking.

Introducing our study

Our study poses two very general questions. Firstly, we wanted to know how South Africans understand development and its connotations and, in particular, whether they understand development in a way that goes against hegemonic views of development. Secondly, we sought to find out whether and how they relate the concept of development to the concept of *ubuntu* and, in particular, whether their way of speaking about *ubuntu* aligns with the way in which post-development thinkers are using the term. We set out to put these questions to some South African citizens living in areas which would be described as 'under-developed' in standard development lingo. While we have no grounds for assuming that participants' views are typical of marginalised South Africans (and of other marginalised communities), in the absence of much research exploring how marginalised communities relate to development and *ubuntu*, this research is a valuable starting point.

This research entailed open-ended interviews with 67 people living in four marginalised South African communities. All participants have been anonymised using pseudonyms and we will also anonymise the names of the places in which they live. The first two sites are situated in the Umzimkhulu municipal region of the province of KwaZulu-Natal (KZN). One site is very rural with residents having to travel more than an hour to reach the nearest town. Residents get water from rivers and streams although there are some community taps installed by government. Residents speak mostly isiZulu, the most spoken language in South Africa and one of South Africa's twelve official languages. The second site is a former informal settlement (now semi-formalised) on the outskirts of the town of Umzimkhulu. The third area is an informal settlement on the edges of Durban, the biggest city in the province of KwaZulu Natal. Residents of the latter two sites are mostly isiZulu-speaking although some respondents preferred to answer our questions in English. The final site is in the Sarah Baartman district municipality in the Eastern Cape (EC) of South Africa and is a remote rural community. Residents of this area speak isiXhosa, one of South Africa's official languages and the language most commonly spoken in the Eastern Cape. The sites were chosen to include a range of communities which mainstream development discourse would deem to be in need of development. These communities would be likely to have some understanding of the concept of *ubuntu* as residents are isiZulu or isiXhosa speakers, two of the sociolinguistic groups commonly associated with the idea of *ubuntu*. All interviews were conducted in the respondents' mother tongue (with English also used by some participants) and subsequently translated by the interviewers. Respondents were chosen using purposive and snowball sampling. Researchers visited the areas concerned and spoke to willing residents they encountered there, while trying to ensure diversity in terms of gender and age.

Commentary on the positionality of the researchers and the process whereby the research was conducted can be helpful in situating the research and understanding its strengths and limitations. The research project arose out of a collaboration between one of the authors, Sally Matthews, who is based at Rhodes University in South Africa, with the Global Partnership Network (GPN). The GPN is an international partnership initiated by Kassel University in Germany, mostly involving researchers based at Global South institutions. As part of a GPN-funded project on alternatives to development, the three authors set about exploring whether and how *ubuntu* is being understood as an alternative to development in South Africa. The first author, Sally Matthews, invited two postgraduate students at Rhodes University, Nhlanhla Mkhutle and Simphiwe Gongqa, to conduct the interviews and assist with the subsequent writing of the article. Nhlanhla Mkhutle conducted, transcribed and translated the isiZulu interviews while Simphiwe Gongqa did the same for the interviews in isiXhosa. Sally Matthews took the lead in the writing of the article in collaboration with Nhlanhla Mkhutle and Simphiwe Gongqa.

All three authors are South Africans: one White English-speaking woman, one Black isiZulu-speaking man and one Black isiXhosa-speaking man. The interviews were conducted in the mother tongue of the latter two researchers. Our positionality brings with it, potential strengths and limitations. Concerning strengths, as South Africans, we already have some understanding of the context. Furthermore, the researchers who conducted the interviews had the linguistic abilities and cultural competency to facilitate the interviews, although they were not members of any of the communities in which the research was conducted. In terms of limitations, this particular study is a very preliminary one which only sought to obtain brief responses to a set of questions about development and *ubuntu*. Respondents were selected using purposive and snowball sampling and so cannot be assumed to be representative of their communities. A further limitation is that the writing up of our findings was led by Sally Matthews (the White academic) in a context where the views of White academics are disproportionately represented. As discussed above, Dladla (2017) critiques White scholars for appropriating and misrepresenting *ubuntu* in ways that reflect and entrench White supremacy. We hope that our way of engaging with the concept *ubuntu* avoids some of the pitfalls described by Dladla (2017) in that we foreground the views of our participants, whereas his critique is mostly directed at philosophers whose interpretations of *ubuntu* are not based on fieldwork. Unlike such work, our article explores how marginalised South Africans, rather than elite scholars, interpret concepts like development and *ubuntu*. We believe our respondents' insights and our discussion of them can make a valuable contribution to broader debates about alternatives to development. However, we must stress that this is only preliminary research and further research is required to corroborate or challenge our findings.

Respondents' views on development

Our research explores how respondents understand the terms *ubuntu* and development and whether and how they relate the two terms. As the interviews were conducted principally in isiXhosa and isiZulu, we used translations of the term development or asked people to provide their own translation of the English word development. Almost all of the respondents who were asked to translate the term development to isiZulu chose to translate it as *intuthuko* which, like the English word development, means positive, continuous change. In isiXhosa, the word most commonly used to refer to development was *uphuhliso* which has roughly the same meaning as development and *intuthuko*. We did not pick up on any respondents insisting that there was a difference between *intuthuko* and development. Rather, they seemed to regard the words *intuthuko* and *uphuhliso* as equivalent to the English word development.

There were some differences in the way in which the communities spoke about development. The KZN communities placed emphasis on infrastructure, education and health, when asked to define how they understand development. Repeated reference was made to roads, 'RDP houses' (by which is meant brick houses built by the state), schools and clinics. Rural respondents also often spoke of farming and agricultural initiatives. Some participants expressed the belief that development is about broadening the mind more generally (rather than only about building schools). Typical responses of KZN residents to the question 'What is development?' are given below:

> We want development … in order to have roads, RDP houses, clinics and farming initiatives.
>
> When we say that a place is developed, we see schools, libraries, roads, churches and clinics.
>
> Things like water, RDP houses, electricity, and sewerage systems … There should be libraries, schools, RDP houses, water, electricity, sewerage systems and hospitals.

In the EC, where only rural respondents were interviewed, residents mentioned infrastructure (roads, houses and schools) less often than those in KZN and placed greater emphasis on income-generation opportunities, employment opportunities and support for farming. Some sample responses are given below:

> Development means the creation of jobs to me.
>
> Development means building. For example, building creches in the village, planting crops and creating jobs.
>
> Development is growth. For example, rearing chickens and other animals for you to grow financially.

Respondents in all four communities were overwhelmingly positive about development, believing it to be desirable and lamenting that the areas they live in are lacking in development. Consider the following comments:

> It [development] is extremely good; it comes with a lot of change even in a way that makes people more informed and their minds broadened.
>
> I say [that development is good] because development helps us as Black people because if there is development there is no hunger, we can farm and be able to take our children to school.
>
> Without development there is poverty, crime, teenage pregnancy and diseases.

The idea of development continues to appeal to these respondents. They relate it to the provision of necessities (food, shelter, sanitation, health care), to the sense of having more opportunities to generate income, and to some extent to the idea of having a broader and more informed approach to life. This understanding of development resonates with some aspects of mainstream approaches to development in that there is an emphasis on the provision of infrastructure, the expansion of formal education and healthcare, and increased opportunities to earn an income. Furthermore – and as will be discussed further below – respondents look to state officials as the key drivers of development, a view which resonates with mainstream development. However, in other ways, the respondents' understanding of development does not align with mainstream approaches to development (as outlined by, for example, Ziai 2016: 57–58). For example, the respondents strongly emphasised small-scale (rather than commercial) farming and, as will be discussed below, spoke of the importance of cooperation and sharing and emphasised the role of the state (as opposed to neoliberal approaches to development which diminish the state's role).

It is also noteworthy that respondents closely associated development with the state and that many suggested that development was something positive that came about (or should have come about) due to the introduction of democracy in South Africa. Consider the following comments:

> … we voted in order for there to be development, and we can see that there is development in other places and we are hopeful that we will also get it.
>
> We use [the word development to refer to] the things that government does for us, that we can see and things that we are able to use. So, it's here we appreciate what the government does for us, so that is development to us.
>
> … we come from the old world where a Black person was oppressed, so the things that are happening now, things that the government does for us, are things that didn't happen before in the old world.

Respondents' views on *ubuntu*

As mentioned above, in some post-development literature, *ubuntu* is being put forward as a worldview which can help us move away from the concept of development. For example, Acosta (2019: 282) says: 'It is crucial to recuperate alternative epistemes like *buen vivir, eco-swaraj, ubuntu*, or communitarianism – to understand and re-organise the world without falling into mandates such as *development*' (italicisation in the original). Our research does not support this view as we found no evidence that people are putting forward *ubuntu* as an alternative to development. Respondents did not spontaneously suggest a connection between *ubuntu* and development or present *ubuntu* as a concept belonging to an alternative value system that they saw as contrasting with development. For example, no one said something like 'We do not want development here; rather, we would like to promote *ubuntu*'. *Ubuntu* was only related to development when we requested respondents to discuss the relation between the two and, when they did so, they overwhelmingly presented the two terms as compatible.

When defining *ubuntu*, participants emphasised care, compassion, cooperation, helpfulness, mutual respect, harmony, consideration, dignity and a willingness to share. Here are some of the typical responses given when people were asked to define *ubuntu*:

> *Ubuntu*? It is being able to live with one another you see. A person is a person because of other people kind of thing, and you must get along with all people and there shouldn't be a person that you hate. You must be able to help another person in need if you can and there must be harmony with everyone.
>
> *Ubuntu* is about unity and empathy and love, yes. If we speak of *ubuntu*, we speak of thinking for each other, and helping each other.

When asked about the relationship between *ubuntu* and development, most respondents suggested that *ubuntu* and development can and should work together. Respondents commonly argued that development could best be advanced if people showed *ubuntu* which was presented as an ethic of care and cooperation. Consider the following comment:

> [Development and *ubuntu*] go hand in hand because when I have something, I have to pull up a person that I see who is struggling and place them at an equal footing with me or maybe higher than me. I don't look down on them because they are struggling, and I shouldn't watch them walk to town everyday whilst I have a car that can help them because they are disadvantaged. If I have food, and a fellow person is hungry; I must give them food for free, yes, that is *ubuntu*.

The strong sense from our interviews is that people want development (understood as the provision of basic services and the general improvement of their lives) and they want it to be brought about in a way that is characterised by an ethics of *ubuntu* (understood as an ethic of care and cooperation).

While respondents support the idea that development should be advanced in a way that is in line with *ubuntu*, many felt that the officials they saw as responsible for development did not implement development in a way that is compatible with *ubuntu*. Respondents reported that *ubuntu* is absent (or at least insufficiently present) in the work of the government officials they believe ought to be promoting their wellbeing. Consider the following comments:

> If the people who are running this country had any *ubuntu*, then there would be development.
>
> I can say that there is *ubuntu*, but it is ambiguous. So, the government shows *ubuntu* but there are people within the government who do not want to show this *ubuntu* to other people.
>
> They [government officials] are taking care of themselves and there is no *ubuntu*.

The residents of the third site – a former informal settlement that has been partially upgraded through various government development projects – were more positive than other respondents about the efforts of the government. Many of these residents reported that the government officials in their area do demonstrate *ubuntu* because they have implemented programmes to improve their lives. They made comments along these lines:

> I could say that our [municipal] councillor has *ubuntu*. …Because the things in this area and the residents of this area have their needs met, now they are fine. They have gotten the care that they wanted through their roads being fixed where there were potholes, and their RDPs [state housing] have now been changed and now these houses are fine.

What these kinds of comments suggest is that the respondents interviewed for this study do not view *ubuntu* as an *alternative* to development. Rather, they appeared to endorse the idea that the values of *ubuntu* (such as care, compassion, generosity and cooperation) should guide the implementation of development. Unfortunately, many feel that the current agents of development (especially government officials) fail to act in ways that show sufficient *ubuntu*.

Alternative livelihoods and agency

One of the hopes of post-development activists is that those marginalised by development will promote alternative livelihoods rather than buying into the idea of development and depending on government and NGO officials to bring economic growth, industrialisation and a 'modern' way of life to them. Post-development advocates argue that while mainstream development is driven by 'experts' with 'the poor' positioned only as recipients of assistance coming from outside their own communities, post-development practice will be different: 'Political agency will belong to the marginalised, exploited, and oppressed' (Kothari et al. 2019b: xxx).

Given this feature of post-development, it is of interest to get a sense of whether and how those in the communities studied here see themselves as agents who can improve their own lives. Our findings suggest that respondents typically identify the state or private sector as the agents who should act to bring about the changes they are keen to see and should guide them in achieving development. Consider the following comments:

> We would like to be supported and helped by being taught to farm. We only know the indigenous way of farming. We want to learn agriculture and be taught about development. We need to be given cows and goats, if that is allowed, because we love to rear cattle. Because we even love to raise chickens, but we sometimes fall short of money when it comes to ordering chicks. But if we had the support that we need, we would be able to raise chickens, sell livestock and see our area being developed.
>
> Development cannot come from us because we do not have money. It must come from the government or the private sector.

One respondent even hoped that our research might lead someone to help her community, saying that 'maybe we can be helped now that we are being interviewed'. When the researcher explained that this was not the purpose of the interview, the respondent replied that perhaps the people who listen to her interview 'might take pity on us and help build us the things that we need as a community that I mentioned here'. These kinds of comments suggest that these respondents did not believe themselves to be in a position to effect the changes they desire to see.

However, some respondents had mixed feelings and did see themselves as playing a role in bringing about the changes they want. One commented that 'The municipality must create the jobs', but then added that 'Citizens here in [our village] can also take initiative and create jobs if they can'. Another person defined development by saying 'It alludes to the youth standing on their own and sustaining themselves. For example, them planting crops and rearing animals, and not depending on the government'. Therefore, at least some respondents could imagine those within their communities playing a leading and important role in bringing about the kinds of livelihoods they would like. However, our overall impression is that respondents view the state as the appropriate entity to drive development.

It should be noted that the respondents' insistence that the state should drive development could be interpreted as an expression of agency rather than as a lack of agency. In a context of deprivation and oppression, such insistence can be interpreted as a way of asserting a particular vision of how the state should function – one that sees the state as owned by and accountable to the people – rather than as an expression of dependence on the state and lack of agency. The comment below implies this kind of orientation:

> By law the government promised us that if we voted … we would get schools and free education and all things like that. They promised us that we will get RDP houses, and they promised that we will get grants. That is why I say that it is mandatory that the government give us development …

Respondents' insistence that the government must be the agent of development can be read both as a lack of agency or as an expression of a form agency, in that they are making demands on a government they believe owes them something and expressing a view on the role the state should play. Nevertheless, however one interprets these comments, there is little resonance between our respondents' insistence that the state should drive development and some post-development theorists' hope that people will reject the role of development experts and exercise agency by putting forward their own alternative ways of improving their lives. Our respondents want government officials to implement development, rather than rejecting the state's development programmes in favour of their own alternative initiatives.

Before continuing, it is worth noting that the South African context is different to many other African contexts, in terms of the size and reach of the South African state, the penetration of modernist development and the longer history of racialised dispossession in the form of settler colonialism and apartheid. This particular context means that South Africans may have different expectations from the state than many other Africans and may interpret exclusion from the 'benefits' of development differently to other Africans.

Challenges for post-development theory's search for alternatives

It is important to preface the remarks that follow with the caveat that our research is a very preliminary research and that more in-depth research using varied methodologies may yield different results. Our preliminary research is based on short interviews with people rather than on longer, ethnographic fieldwork. Critical readers of our chapter have suggested that such research might yield different findings. We acknowledge that this is the case and caution that our conclusions are very tentative.

One thing that does seem clear from our interviews is that the concept of development is a resilient one, but also one that is difficult to pin down in terms of what exactly it means. As many commentators have noted, development is the kind of word that can be used to mean almost anything. As Sachs (2019: xiii) says: '"Development" is a plastic word, an empty term with positive signification'. The word is used in reference to so many things that it is difficult to know exactly what someone means when they claim to be in favour of, or against, development. Our respondents certainly seemed to be in favour of development, but what they mean by 'development' may be different to what some others mean. Those we interviewed generally regard development as a process which should provide them with tarred roads, brick houses, good and easily accessible sanitation, educational opportunities, health care, farming opportunities, business opportunities and paid employment.

Contrary to some strands of post-development thinking that suggest that people are turning their backs on development and embracing alternative Indigenous ways of life, our respondents seemed keen to embrace at least some of the changes they associate with development. Consider the following comments:

> In the olden days, they used horses, people were walking barefoot or with donkeys. It is fine now because we have cars. That's development.
>
> We are speaking of change in circumstances compared to the circumstances we lived under before. We see things happening now. Like before, growing up, we only knew that for you to get water you need to fetch it at the river/stream. You collected firewood in the forest. When people are sick, we used donkey carts to carry them to the hospital, but now we are seeing that the situation is gradually changing. So, I think that is what we call development.
>
> This word that is development means that we as Black people believe in farming, ploughing our fields, planting corn and vegetables. It also means that we raise cattle because these are the things that help us as Black people. When you have extra harvest or extra cattle you can sell them for money. The word development is complex and pregnant with different meanings because we have development now because we have electricity, water, and roads. We did not have things back in the olden days as we were using horses and cows as our mode of transportation.

In the last quote, the respondent emphasises the complexity of the word 'development' and further highlights that complexity in his insistence on maintaining ways of life he sees as important to his identity as a Black person (such as farming and raising cattle, which play important material and cultural roles in the lives of many South Africans), while also embracing things that were not present in the past. This respondent is not keen to abandon all aspects of the way of life of his ancestors, but he also welcomes the arrival of things like electricity, piped water and roads. This kind of position invites post-development thinkers to be clear about what it is that they are rejecting when rejecting development (presumably not piped water and electricity). It reminds post-development and decolonial thinkers who are keen to advance alternatives to development not to underestimate the many attractions of life in the so-called 'developed' world and to realise that for many people, development continues to look like a solution to the ongoing poverty and deprivation they are experiencing. This is especially the case as many state and NGO actors have presented development as a way to address such poverty and deprivation.

As with our respondents, most post-development theorists surely also support the provision of water, electricity, safe housing and the like. However, the anti-development rhetoric that forms part of some post-development writing makes it unclear exactly what is being rejected. As Andrews and Bawa (2014: 929) put it, post-development thinkers 'do not mince words in proclaiming that all development projects are inherently surreptitious and indeed evil', a view they say fails to account for the way in which development plays itself out in Africa. The idea that 'development' should be totally rejected is unlikely to have much purchase in contexts where the term is strongly associated with electricity and piped water. The most valuable aspects of post-development theory – its robust critique of mainstream development and its validation of the lives and ideas of people in the

Global South – can be compromised if post-development thinkers are inattentive to the desire for development expressed by Global South residents such as those interviewed for this study. Post-development approaches that acknowledge and work with this desire for development resonate better with our respondents' views.

Concerning *ubuntu*, our study suggests caution about the idea that *ubuntu* is being widely promoted as an alternative to mainstream development. While our respondents cannot be assumed to be representative of all South Africans and certainly not all Africans, for them (and likely for others positioned similarly), *ubuntu* is something that ought, ideally, to advance development (rather than to serve as an alternative to it). They believe that if those in power had *ubuntu*, they would bring development to marginalised communities.

It could rightfully be objected that our study only looks at what a few individuals in four areas in one country think and that those interviewed here are not part of a social movement or activist group. It may be that other communities and more politically involved individuals may express anti-development views and/or link their views on development to *ubuntu* in a way that presents *ubuntu* as part of the articulation of an alternative vision of social wellbeing. Certainly, this may be so, but our study shows that if this is indeed the case, such activists will need to think carefully about how to approach communities for whom the concept of development has decidedly positive connotations and who do not see a tension between development and *ubuntu*.

Conclusion

After many decades of so-called development, great disparities continue to characterise the lives of those living in the Global North and the Global South. Consequently, it is unsurprising that calls for alternatives to development continue to be articulated. The decolonial turn in theorisation on the Global South has popularised the idea, already advanced for many years within post-development thinking, that Indigenous and marginalised communities may provide conceptual and theoretical resources for building such alternatives to development.

Our study explores how people in marginalised South African communities understand the terms 'development' and '*ubuntu*' and whether and how they relate the two terms. As shown above, our respondents favour development, which they define as a process that will improve their material wellbeing and increase their access to learning, resources and income-generation opportunities. Rather than viewing *ubuntu* as an alternative to development, our respondents suggest that development and *ubuntu* are complementary. They believe that if powerful actors (such as government officials) had *ubuntu* (defined as an ethics of care, compassion and cooperation), they would bring development to marginalised areas. Such a view provides challenges for those keen to use the concept of *ubuntu* to advance development alternatives. Post-development and decolonial critics of development need to carefully clarify exactly what it is they are proposing when advocating alternatives to development – which aspects of development are to be rejected and which, if any, to be retained?

As emphasised earlier, our respondents' views cannot be assumed to be representative of other South Africans and certainly not of others in Africa or the Global South. However, the views expressed here do find resonance in some of the other chapters in this book (see especially Castellsagué and Panthi; Prouchet et al.). The point that we (and others in this book) are making is that there is a diversity of ways of relating to development in the Global South. Researchers interested in alternatives may be drawn to communities which do seem to be building alternatives, but our study (and others in this book) suggest that we need to be very cautious about making easy claims that grassroots communities in the Global South are showing 'open resistance and opposition to development' (Esteva and Escobar 2017: 2560) and that Indigenous concepts like *ubuntu* will 'allow us to divest ourselves from *democracy and development*' (Mignolo 2021: 54, italics in the original). Our research suggests that at least some Global South communities engage with concepts like *ubuntu* and development in ways that do not support such claims. When seeking to articulate alternatives, it is important to be attentive to what people mean by development and *ubuntu* so that activists and scholars from different communities can work together to build better lives for all.

Acknowledgements

This chapter was written with financial support from the Global Partnership Network.

References

Acosta, A. (2012). *Buen vivir. Sumak kawsay: Una oportunidad para imaginar otros mundos.* Quito: Abya-Yala.

Acosta, A. (2017). 'Living Well: ideas for reinventing the future', *Third World Quarterly*, 38 (12), pp. 2600–2616.

Acosta, A. (2019). 'Post-Economia'. In *Pluriverse: A Post-Development Dictionary*, edited by Kothari, A., Salleh, A., Escobar, A., Demaria, F. and Acosta, A.New Delhi: Tulika Books, pp. 280–282.

Alvares, C. (1992) *Science, Development and Violence: The Revolt against Modernity.* Delhi: Oxford University Press.

Andrews, N. and Bawa, S. (2014). 'A Post-development Hoax? (Re)-examining the Past, Present and Future of Development Studies', *Third World Quarterly*, 35 (6), pp. 922–938.

Asher, K. and Wainwright, J. (2019). 'After Post-Development: On Capitalism, Difference, and Representation'. *Antipode*, 51 (1), pp. 25–44.

Boogaard, B.K. and Van Norren, D.E. (2022). '"Development" Perspectives from the Global South: Learning from *Ubuntu* and *Buen Vivir* philosophies'. In *The Politics of Knowledge in Inclusive Development and Innovation*, edited by Ludwig, D., Boogaard, B., Macnaghten, P. and Leeuwis, C.New York: Routledge.

Chisale, S. S. (2018). '*Ubuntu* as care: Deconstructing the gendered *Ubuntu*', *Verbum et Ecclesia*, 39 (1), pp. 1–8.

Cornell, D. and Van Marle, K. (2015). '*Ubuntu* feminism: Tentative reflections', *Verbum et Ecclesia*, 36 (2), Art. #1444, 8 pages. http://dx.doi. org/10.4102/ve.v36i2.1444.

Demaria, F. and Kothari, A. (2017). 'The Post-Development Dictionary agenda: paths to the pluriverse', *Third World Quarterly*, 38 (12), pp. 2588–2599.

Dladla, N. (2017). 'Towards and African Critical Philosophy of Race: *Ubuntu* as a Philo-Praxis of Liberation', *Filosofia Theoretica: Journal of African Philosophy, Culture and Religions*, 6 (1), pp. 39–68.

Domínguez, R., Caria, S. and Léon, M. (2017). '*Buen Vivir*: Praise, instrumentalization, and reproductive pathways of good living in Ecuador', *Latin American and Caribbean Ethnic Studies*, 12 (2), pp. 133–154.

Escobar, A. (2015). 'Degrowth, Postdevelopment, and Transitions: A Preliminary Conversation', *Sustainability Science*, 10 (3), pp. 451–462.

Esteva, G. and Escobar, A. (2017). 'Post-Development @ 25: on "being stuck" and moving forward, sideways, backward and otherwise', *Third World Quarterly*, 38 (12), pp. 2559–2572. Available at: DOI:doi:10.1080/01436597.2017.1334545.

Garcia-Arias, J. and Schöneberg, J. (2021). 'Urgencies and imperatives for revolutionary (environmental) transitions: from degrowth and postdevelopment towards the pluriverse?', *Environmental Politics*, 30 (5), pp. 865–871.

Grosfoguel, R. (2007). 'The Epistemic Decolonial Turn: Beyond Political-Economy Paradigms', *Cultural Studies*, 21(2–3), pp. 211–223.

Gudynas, E. (2011). 'Buen Vivir: Today's tomorrow'. *Development*, 54 (4), pp. 441–447.

Klein, E. and Morreo, C.E. (Eds.). (2019) *Postdevelopment in Practice: Alternatives, Economies, Ontologies*. New York: Routledge.

Kothari, A., Salleh, A., Escobar, A., Demaria, R. and Acosta, A. (2019a). 'Preface'. In *Pluriverse: A Post-Development Dictionary*, edited by Kothari, A., Salleh, A., Escobar, A., Demaria, F. and Acosta, A.New Delhi: Tulika Books, pp. xxi–xl.

Kothari, A., Salleh, A., Escobar, A., Demaria, R. and Acosta, A. (2019b). 'Introduction: Finding Pluriversal Paths'. In *Pluriverse: A Post-Development Dictionary*, edited by Kothari, A., Salleh, A., Escobar, A., Demaria, F. and Acosta, A.New Delhi: Tulika Books, pp. xxi–xl.

Kothari, A. (2020). 'Earth *Vikalp Sangam*: proposal for a Global Tapestry of Alternatives', *Globalizations*, 17: 2, pp. 245–249.

Letseka, M. (2012). 'In Defence of *Ubuntu*'. *Studies in Philosophy and Education*, 31, pp. 47–60.

Lugones, M. (2010). 'Toward a Decolonial Feminism'. *Hypatia*, 25 (4), pp. 742–759.

Luvalo, L.M. (2019). 'Patriarchy and *Ubuntu* Philosophy: The Views of Community Elders in the Eastern Cape Province', *Journal of Social Sciences and Humanities*, 16 (7), pp. 1–10.

Manyonganise, M. (2015). 'Oppressive and liberative: A Zimbabwean woman's reflections on *ubuntu*', *Verbum et Ecclesia*, 36 (2), Art. #1438.

Matolino, B. and Kwindingwi, W. (2013). 'The end of *ubuntu*', *South African Journal of Philosophy*, 32 (2), pp. 197–205.

Metz, T. (2017). 'Replacing Development: An Afro-Communal Approach to Global Justice', *Philosophical Papers*, 46 (1), pp. 111–137.

Metz, T. (2007). 'Toward an African moral theory', *Journal of Political Philosophy*, 15 (3), pp. 321–341.

Mies, M. & Shiva, V. (1993). *Ecofeminism*. London: Zed Books.

Mignolo, W. (2021). *The Politics of Decolonial Investigations*. Durham: Duke University Press.

Mignolo, W. and Walsh, C. (2018). *On Decoloniality: Concepts, Analytics, Praxis*. Durham: Duke University Press.

Mokgoro, J.Y. (2010). '*Ubuntu*, the Constitution and the rights of non-citizens'. *Stellenbosch Law Review*, 21: 221–229.
Molefe, M. (2011). *What can the Socio-Political Ethic of Ubuntu Contribute to Contemporary Conceptions of Development?*University of the Witwatersrand. Unpublished.
Molefe, M. (2019). '*Ubuntu* and Development: An African Conception of Development', *Africa Today*, 66 (1), pp. 96–115.
Ndlovu, M. (2014). 'Why indigenous knowledges in the 21st century? A decolonial turn', *Yesterday and Today*, 11, pp. 84–98.
Ndlovu-Gatsheni, S.J. (2012). 'Coloniality of power in development studies and the impact of global imperial designs on Africa', *The Australasian Review of African Studies*, 33 (2), pp. 48–73.
Pereira da Silva, F. (2020). 'The Community and the Paths of Critical Thinking in the Global Periphery: The cases of *sumak kawsay/suma qamaña* and *Ubuntu*'. In *New paths to development: Perspectives from the Global South*, edited by Bourqia, R. and Sili, M. Switzerland: Springer Nature, pp. 169–178.
Qobo, M. and Nyathi, N. (2016). '*Ubuntu*, public policy ethics and tensions in South Africa's foreign policy'. *South African Journal of International Affairs*, 23 (4), pp. 421–436.
Radcliffe, S. (2012). 'Development for a Postneoliberal Era? Sumak Kawsay, Living Well and the Limits to Decolonization in Ecuador', *Geoforum*, 43, pp. 240–249.
Rahnema, M. and Bawtree, V. (1997). *The Post-Development Reader*. London: Zed Books.
Ramose, M. B. (1999). *African philosophy through Ubuntu*. Harare: Mond Books Publishers.
Ranta, E.J. (2016). 'Toward a Decolonial Alternative to Development? The Emergence and Shortcomings of *Vivir Bien* as State Policy in Bolivia in the Era of Globalization', *Globalizations*, 13 (4), pp. 425–439.
Sachs, W. (2010). 'Preface to the New Edition'. In *The Development Dictionary: A Guide to Knowledge as Power*, (2nd ed.), edited by Sachs, W. London: Zed Books.
Sachs, W. (2019). 'Foreword: The Development Dictionary Revisited'. In *Pluriverse: A Post-Development Dictionary*, edited by Kothari, A., Salleh, A., Escobar, A., Demaria, F. and Acosta, A.New Delhi: Tulika Books, pp. xi–xvi.
Shumba, O. (2011). 'Commons thinking, ecological intelligence and the ethical and moral framework of *Ubuntu*: An imperative for sustainable development'. *Journal of Media and Communication Studies*, 3 (3), pp. 84–96.
Suttner, R. (2017). 'Op-Ed: Decolonising project – what is the place of Ubuntu?' *Daily Maverick*, 27 September. Available at: https://www.dailymaverick.co.za/article/2017-09-27-op-ed-decolonising-project-what-is-the-place-of-ubuntu/.
Villalba, U. (2013). 'Buen Vivir vs development: a paradigm shift in the Andes?', *Third World Quarterly*, 34 (8), pp. 1427–1442.
Viola Recasens, A. (2014) 'Discursos "pachamamistas" versus políticas desarrollistas: el debate sobre el sumak kawsay en los Andes', *Íconos – Revista de Ciencias Sociales*, 0 (48), p. 55. Available at: https://doi.org/10.17141/iconos.48.2014.1209.
Ziai, A. (2014). 'Post-Development Concepts? *Buen Vivir, Ubuntu* and Degrowth'. In B. S. Santos and T. Amal (eds), *International Colloquium: Epistemologies of the South: South-South, South-North and North-South Global Learnings. Other Economies – v. 3.* Coimbra: CES, pp. 143–154.
Ziai, A. (2016). *Development Discourse and Global History: From colonialism to the sustainable development goals.* London: Routledge.
Zondi, S. (2016). 'Ubuntu and sumak kawsay: The Inter-Parliamentary Union and the search for a global South humanist paradigm of development', *South African Journal of International Affairs*, 23(1), pp. 107–120.

3 'Hardware' and 'software' *bikas*

Nepali notions on development and its alternatives

Alba Castellsagué and Injina Panthi

Introduction

Debates on development and its critique have been ongoing in Nepal since the 1990s (Des Chene 1996; Seddon 1998; Shrestha 1995). As in the international academic arena, many researchers on Nepali issues have aligned themselves with post-development thinking (see Ghimire 2009 for a review), strengthening the critique of both development discourses and their practices in the country. More recently, global post-development debates have sought to move beyond development critique and promote the search for new ways of understanding and conceptualising development. To this end, they have explored 'Indigenous' notions around the world that have the potential to become alternatives – not just reformist solutions – to hegemonic development paradigms (Kothari et al. 2019).

Bikas as a concept has been widely explored in research from and about Nepal. However, as we will address in the next section, there are different ways of approaching the notion that are not always consistent, and even contradictory. As we will argue, it is not clear that *bikas* has ever been seen as an 'alternative' or 'oppositional' to hegemonic ways of understanding development.

Bikas and development: meanings, notions and translation

The concept of *bikas* has been widely used in development studies in Nepal. However, its conceptualisation has not always been consistent, ranging from a mere translation of the English word 'development' to a more singular definition of the concept. According to its Sanskrit origin, *bikas* means 'to blossom', 'to flourish', 'to expand' (Gyawali 2017). Its literal meaning relates to biological growth, and according to the Nepali dictionary, *bikas* means 'stage of continuous growth and improvement, progress, expansion, continuous change for betterment' (Nepal Academy 2018).

Shrestha (1995: 268) presented *bikas* as 'the word for development in Nepali language' that became popular during the 1950s and stressed its alignment with wealth, power and education as understood under the ideology of modernisation – economic growth, science and technology-based knowledge, and English.

DOI: 10.4324/9781003477921-4

Shrestha (1995: 268) understood the notion of *bikas* as a part of the colonial apparatus, but one with a more 'neutral tone' and 'euphemistic lexicon'. Reflecting on his personal experience, he saw the adoption of the *bikas* narrative – both at a political and individual level – as an internalisation of the colonial rhetoric.

> When, after decolonization, the indigenous elites acquired control over the state apparatus, they quickly learnt to seek legitimacy in a native version of the civilizing mission and sought to establish a similar colonial relationship between state and society. [...] When I reflect on my own development experience and journey, it is transparent that my mind had been colonized.
>
> (Shrestha 1995: 275)

The 'colonised minds' explanation to development desirability has been previously problematised (Matthews 2017), calling for further and more complex explanations.

Des Chene (1996) distinguished between two definitions of *bikas*. On the one hand, the widespread positive notion related with 'social betterment, increase in well-being and productivity, modernisation, and opportunity' (1996: 260). On the other hand, *bikas* is a 'transnational capitalist enterprise' that allegedly does not aim to help the people, but to make financial and political profits. The author identifies a gap between what is perceived as a 'positive *bikas* culture' in Nepal, and 'the reality of *bikas* industry' (Des Chene 1996: 262).

Pigg (1992, 1993) uses *bikas* as the term through which Nepalis understand their relationship to other places. She distinguishes *bikas* from the theories and models of development discussed in academia or by development agencies, emphasising that *bikas* has a historically and socially contextualised meaning (Pigg 1992). At the same time, however, Pigg's research shows how notions of development have a profound impact on the way Nepalis understand *bikas*, which they don't see as dichotomously different from development. Rather than offering an oversimplified assimilationist perspective, her work shows how notions of development shape social categories in Nepal and provides a meaningful understanding of how Nepalis have integrated *bikas* into their lives and experiences.

Some post-development thinkers, such as Escobar (1995), have referred to Pigg's work on *bikas* as a way of understanding how development representations have an impact at the local level. According to Escobar, different reactions can emerge from such development encounters:

> The impact of development representations is thus profound at the local level. At this level, the concepts of development and modernity are resisted, hybridized with local forms, transformed, or what have you; they have, in short, a cultural productivity that needs to be better understood.
>
> (Escobar 1995:51).

Therefore, *bikas* is not identified as 'resistance' or an 'alternative' at this point, but rather as an example of how development discourse works within local cultures as a process of hybridisation, rather than a simple assimilation of foreign notions of development. Although Escobar's (1995) references to *bikas* precede the attempt to identify Indigenous alternatives to development, the question of why some Indigenous ideas have served as alternatives and others – such as *bikas* – have not seemed significant.

From Shreshta's (1995) perspective based on the idea that development colonises people's minds, to Pigg's (1992) and Escobar's (1995) more hybridising explanation of the relationship between *bikas* and development, research has tended to focus on the relationship between *bikas* and Western ideas of development rather than on the history of the concept of *bikas* itself. Gyawali's (2017, 2018) work is relevant in the sense that it explores pre-*bikas* notions of development to problematise the idea of Nepal as a blank slate before the era of foreign-assisted development. By taking a historical approach, this work shows how the concept of *bikas* itself has changed over time and through societal transformations, and how the equation of *bikas* with development is a rather recent phenomenon.

In the 1940s, although the word development was already established within the Nepali administration, the term *unnati* was most commonly used (Gyawali 2017: 247). *Unnati* refers to dignity, prosperity and elevation. Similarly, the term *sabhyata* (civilisation) was used to refer to the early encounters with the West and the manners of the upper Nepali classes, rather than modernity. While Rana elites[1] embraced the English vocabulary (development, modernity), *unnati* and *sabhyata* were preferred by non-Rana as an attempt to protect the Nepali language. *Unnati* was therefore used to refer to progress and *sabhyata* to the notion of civilisation, but in an ambiguous way, without defining the form in which such progress was supposed to happen.

> Unnati represented an ambiguous assortment of expectations and was not confined to definite goals while development specifically meant 'industrial development'.
>
> (Gyawali 2017: 255)

It was during the 1950s and the establishment of democracy that *bikas* suddenly became visible in political discourse, not only becoming the Nepali translation for development, but also referring to a very specific notion of 'planned development' in line with the international developmentist rhetoric of the time. *Bikas* was thus a response to the presence of new and powerful development agents and the discourses they brought with them. It was not until aid agencies entered the country that *bikas* began to replace the Nepali term *unnati*. Gyawali (2018: 50) explains why *unnati* did not fit the very particular notion of development that was operating at the time:

> Although development was already an ambiguous concept globally, when it was used in the Nepali context in the early 1950s, it referred to planned economic growth aided by technology transfer and bolstered by democratic

> values. These could not accommodate with unnati because unnati had also been the vocabulary of the Ranas whose ethos was different from that of the new agents.

Of particular relevance is the shift from the ambiguity of *unnati* in defining progress to the very particular understanding of progress that *bikas* became: planned economic development aligned with the emergence of foreign aid. This particular elaboration offers a complex vision of *bikas* as an Indigenous term, presenting it as a complex and dynamic 'concentrate of meanings' (Gyawali 2017). Rather than an 'Indigenous' word, *bikas* seems to have gained popularity over *unnati* because of its alignment with hegemonic – rather than Indigenous – notions of development at the time.

Attempts have been made to 'indigenise' *bikas* in Nepal. During the Panchayat[2], a 'native' political system established in the 1960s, the notion of *gram bikas* emerged, in line with the culturally unifying project of the king's policy known as '*Ek Raja, Ek Bhesh, Ek Bhasa, and Ek Desh*' (One King, One Dress, One Language, One Nation). According to Gyawali (2018:77), *gram bikas* was defined as 'village' or 'rural development' and attempted to be an alternative to 'economic development', proposing a singularly Nepali 'decentralised' project:

> Apart from the three decades of the Panchayat, there is no period in Nepali history where *bikās* clearly exhibits the centripetal pull of 'tradition' and the centrifugal push of 'modernity', the former through a Hinduized *grāmbikās* and the latter through planned development. Additionally, the former is pronounced during the incipient years of the Panchayat, while the latter is prominent as the Panchayat consolidates itself.

However, closer explorations of the *bikas* projects at the time showed a more critical view. As Adhikary (1996) argues, *bikas* was used to build a strong and modern national identity, based on the dominant Hindu religion, culture and Sanskrit language. Rather than preserving the diversity of the Nepali people, this process failed to represent Nepal's ethnic minorities. *Bikas* projects, such as the building of bridges and opening of post-offices, were opportunities to deliberately impose Sanskritised names on places. The previous local names (of non-Sanskritic origin) were seen as sounding 'rude', or 'barbarous' (Adhikary 1996: 359), hence the need to replace them with Sanskrit names associated with greater prestige and prominence. Therefore, *gram bikas* was more an ideal than a practice and lost momentum as the Panchayat years passed, as its discourse slowly transitioned towards '*bikas* as modernity'. Such meaning consolidated in the 1990s, with the reinstatement of multi-party democracy, when *bikas* as a concept was democratised too, becoming more popular and used beyond the political language.

The contributions above show the diversity of ways in which *bikas* has been understood at different times, its dynamic meaning and its changing relationship to development. They also show how debates on development and post-development need to move beyond the theoretical and ideological to explore the specific challenges and complexities that the realities of (post)development demand.

Methodology

This chapter situates (post)development discourses in Nepal along two different empirical experiences. First, an ethnographer's account of her fieldwork in the Himalayan region, in the Solukhumbu district. With a background in social and cultural anthropology, the researcher conducted fieldwork (2012–2019) in a rather classical way: long and repeated stays in different rural and urban settings, learning the language and taking a holistic approach to the social phenomena observed. She particularly focused on different analyses: the impact of schooling practices for women and girls (Castellsagué 2023a; Castellsagué and Carrasco 2021a), the experiences of return within the logic of a migration-development nexus (Castellsagué 2023b) and the work-related changes for women with rural-to-urban mobility experiences (Castellsagué and Carrasco 2022), among others. Despite previously exploring discourses and narratives about development and *bikas* (Castellsagué and Carrasco 2021b), her discussions were not quite situated within post-development debates and their growing relevance in Nepal. The second is the first-hand perspective of an author who has worked with an international development organisation in the Lumbini province of Nepal. Her first-hand experience provides valuable insights into the realities and challenges of the development process in Nepal. The author's interactions with various local stakeholders, including politicians, lawmakers, civil society, media, women, youth and marginalised communities, suggest a broad understanding of the diverse dynamics at play in the region. The author has adopted a nuanced approach to information gathering, involving both structured and spontaneous conversations. The observations that emerge from such interactions contribute to a more holistic and contextualised understanding of Nepal's development landscape. The author's engagement with different segments of the population, from politicians to marginalised communities, captures a wide range of perspectives and experiences.

The authors met after the earthquakes that shook the country in 2015, as we were both involved in social and relief projects in the Kathmandu area at the time. We shared research interests and collaborated on Castellsagué's research project at the time. Panthi was involved in translating and transcribing interviews, and we worked closely together for several weeks. After 2015, we kept in touch about our lives and careers. We met several times over the years when we were both in Nepal. On this occasion, the authors have engaged in a series of collaborative reflection sessions to design and develop the analysis for this chapter. In reflecting on their fieldwork, both formal and informal experiences have been considered to highlight different issues relevant to post-development debates in Nepal. While Panthi's experiences are situated within the organisation where she works, the experiences of development workers and their interaction with marginalised communities in Lumbini district, Castellsagué's work has focused on the understandings of *bikas* among Sherpa people, particularly women, living in Solukhumbu district and Kathmandu.

Distance has emerged as a constant in the co-writing of this chapter. First, Lumbini and Solukhumbu are geographically distant, and then our fieldwork experiences were also distant in time. Our positionalities are also quite different, as one of us (Castellsagué) has been more of an 'outsider' to Nepal and development organisations, while the other (Panthi) works within them as a 'local'. At the same time, however, we are aware that positionality is relative to place and social spaces (Bourdieu and Wacquant 2005), and that Nepalis can also be considered 'outsiders' in certain communities, especially if they work in the development sector, have lived in Kathmandu or abroad for a long time, or are not originally from the region where they work, as is the case here[3]. Finally, we were also distant at the time of creating this chapter, which would not have been possible without numerous video calls along the way.

Despite these distances, the authors focus on the similarities in their experiences to reflect on the commonalities in local understandings of *bikas*. In the following sections, the authors will look at similar and different understandings of *bikas* in the field to see how the concept is used, negotiated and signified by the communities they have worked with. This dialogical perspective enhances our analysis in several ways. First, it brings together two different regions of Nepal, revealing differences in addition to many similarities. Furthermore, the chapter looks at how different communities engage with *bikas* through a combination of approaches: from the research angle to the practitioners' point of view.

Bikas understandings from the ground

'Hardware' and 'software' development

The first common issue that arises when looking at *bikas* understandings from the ground is the clear distinction between two types of *bikas*: 'hardware' and 'software' development. The terms 'hardware' and 'software' development are used consistently in casual conversations by politicians, bureaucrats, stakeholders, and local government organisations, as well as among the people.

On the one hand, the 'hardware' notion entails the development of infrastructure, the economy and financial resources enabling the local population's capacity to generate money. Hardware development includes things like building schools, creating roads and providing funds for government agencies to purchase equipment. We found that this notion was prevalent when people referred to *bikas*. For example, in rural communities from different geographical sites, men and women understand *bikas* as material improvements, such as road construction, water supply and electricity. People related the hardships of living in rural areas with a lack of infrastructure and how this affected their living conditions. A woman from the Solukhumbu area noted that 'there's no water supply, no road service, no electricity and no facilities for the children. If we want any new clothes we have to go a long distance to buy it'.

Mobility was one of the most stressed effects of poor infrastructure, as people had to walk long distances to access certain goods and services, such as schools and hospitals. Many of the interviewees said that moving between villages to go to the market or to school on a daily or weekly basis was a 'hard' part of their lives. Another consequence of the lack of basic infrastructure was the burden of work they had to perform in their daily lives, both in the household and in agriculture. It is important to note that this burden is particularly relevant for women, who are the ones who perform these tasks on a daily basis. A woman stated that 'in the village you have to do everything by yourself: carry goods and make all the food'.

People felt that infrastructure development was necessary for the full implementation of *bikas*, hence their insistence on 'hardware' *bikas*. Some people saw themselves as not having *bikas* at all, with statements such as 'there is no *bikas* in any way' or 'in the village there is no *bikas*'. Others noted that *bikas* has only been partially implemented, as one woman pointed out: 'the road service is only half functioning, and every time we have water cuts'. Regarding water, the pipes were usually installed and maintained by the people themselves, which makes for rather precarious facilities. In many rural areas of Nepal, roads have been opened, but they aren't properly maintained and are constantly damaged during the monsoon season, making them difficult and dangerous to travel on. Other areas of the country are still quite isolated in terms of road access. From the local people's views, in both the Solukhumbu and Lumbini regions, tar roads would result in prosperity by facilitating market access and connectivity. Because they think that growth leads to affluence, the locals viewed cement-built buildings, highways and shopping centres as symbols of development.

Infrastructure development is given top priority by the federal and provincial governments in the federal framework since it is an easily quantifiable and observable accomplishment[4]. As part of the reconstruction process following the 2015 earthquake, traditional Nepali homes were replaced with concrete structures. Other infrastructure development projects include the construction of roads, government buildings, view towers, water canals, malls and airports. During our fieldwork, we came across the idea that material *bikas* was a government's responsibility, which was being rather neglected, particularly in rural areas. Therefore, despite the government's efforts to insist on these kinds of improvements, people feel that these efforts are not enough and that the government is failing to provide better living conditions for themselves and their families, and to fully fulfil their material *bikas*.

A second notion found in the field is 'software' *bikas*, which refers to a human and sustainable approach to development[5]. Its main focus is on the empowerment and education of communities so that they are aware of their rights and can claim them. Rather than emphasising material resources, the 'software' *bikas* approach invests in aspects of human development such as education, sustainability and gender equality, and focuses on policy making and implementation.

Software development is the main approach that has been adopted by donor agencies, development partners and organisations in Nepal. A female development worker defined 'software' *bikas* as follows:

> Empowerment, education, and advocacy kind of things. The project that I work on is software *bikas*, because we are focusing on something that results will take long time to occur. Software *bikas* can't be quantified. We are trying to empower.

Another development worker stressed that 'our focus is more on the software part, we want to enable them [the community] so they can fight for their rights'. Upon conversations with development workers, they pointed out the existing gap between policy and implementation regarding rights and resources. 'The law has always criminalised caste-based discrimination, but many Dalits still face discrimination. Many people don't have access to information about their rights and don't go to government offices to ask', explained a project manager in the Lumbini province.

The 'software' understanding of *bikas* was also found in people's views, but with important nuances. Education was a frequently mentioned aspect of *bikas*, as all respondents saw education as a crucial part of *bikas*. For example, one woman stated that 'they [the government] have opened schools which is a sign of *bikas*'. However, education seemed to be a means to material improvement, as the ultimate goal of being educated is to have access to better material conditions. Many respondents reported that education is important for future outcomes by saying that 'If you study hard, you can make a lot of money in the future', and that 'educated people can have better jobs and better money'. Similarly, people tend to refer to schools as infrastructure and equipment, rather than focusing on the quality of education, the teachers or the curriculum. It is true that others emphasised other benefits of education, such as 'becoming good people' and 'behaving well in society', but this vision was significantly less common in our field encounters.

Ambivalent engagement with bikas

The previous section has shown how people see 'hardware' *bikas* as a way to overcome life hardships by investing in material aspects. Therefore, 'hardware' *bikas* is largely seen as a positive thing. '*Bikas* is good. If our [name of village] is developed, it will be good for everyone, not just for us, but for everyone', said a woman from a village in the Solukhumbu region. While the government was most pointedly responsible for 'hardware' *bikas*, NGOs and other development agencies were mentioned more often when referring to education and other areas of 'software' *bikas*. Therefore, the development sector was also seen as an important actor in the provision of *bikas*, particularly for education-related matters.

However, such focus on 'software' *bikas* was not always shared or supported, as we have identified in our fieldwork. First, during a conversation with regional stakeholders in Nepalgunj, a businessman expressed that 'the development sector should support and advocate for infrastructure improvements instead of allocating funds for advocacy. This will create jobs for all communities, especially those extremely marginalised'. A second example is the experience of a development worker leading a project with the Natuwa, one of the marginalised ethnic communities living in the Rupandehi and Kapivastu Districts of Nepal. She noticed a gap between the aims of the project and what the community wanted: 'Our organisation wanted to empower and support Natuwa in networking and advocating for their fight for identity. However, when we reached out to communities for interaction, they wanted us to help with warm clothes, food, education and financial support'. Another example comes from the Rukkum District of Lumbini. A development organisation was trying to implement a civil society and advocacy project. The development worker in charge defined the objectives of the project as follows: 'We are trying to make civil society inclusive enough for women, youth and marginalised communities'. The youth group in the area is critical of the organisation's focus on advocacy and believes that it should invest in the agricultural sector instead. In conversations with one youth leader during meetings with the organisation, he said:

> In our district, there's so much potential in agriculture, and you're investing more in that kind of thing. Why don't you give us money to develop agriculture and create a market?

Instead of focusing on strengthening civil society, they would like the organisation to provide seeds, agricultural technology and facilities so that they can produce and sell their products in the market. Finally, software development was often associated with organising programmes and events rather than taking 'real action'.

As this development worker shared: 'For them [politicians], empowerment is organising big events with banners and all that, instead of doing other things. They think that empowerment means that we organise the events in very fancy hotels just to waste the money'. A mayor from the Lumbini province questioned this approach:

> You are focusing on the marginalised communities and empowerment. Instead of organising a programme in a fancy hotel, if you give this money to the Dalit women to provide them with nutritious food, it would be more effective than organising the programme in the name of empowerment.

Thus, similar experiences were reported by the development workers interviewed, who explained that project objectives did not always match people's aspirations. As one worker put it: 'It's all linked to the livelihood. They want us to focus on livelihood rather than focusing on empowerment and education'. This gap leads to a dilemma widely recognised by development workers:

> We are in a dilemma, because of what communities need. They are in a very poor condition, they don't have even food to eat, or income source. They

> demand us to give them something, to help in livelihood matters, but this is not the scope of our project.

Although they believed strongly in the software approach of their project and organisation, they also recognised the need to address the material needs of the people and communities they were working with. 'We understand that they need warm clothes, but our project won't give that, so at the project level we cannot address that need', another project leader explained. They reported different strategies to overcome this dilemma which they often face in their work. First, they came up with ways to contribute individually with material provisions for the communities, as a worker explains:

> We visited that community last week, and winter is approaching, and they said that they needed warm clothes. And our project doesn't give them warm clothes. And we decided let's contribute individually, at the personal level.

Secondly, they link the communities with other projects that can meet the material needs. Finally, they make efforts to explain the cause of the lack of resources in the community, as well as effective ways to get them from government sources. A development worker explains this strategy:

> We try to tell them that we understand that you need the clothes, and other things, but you are the leader. There are the resources, government has the resources. We are trying to empower your community to get the resources.

In conversations with development workers, they also reported a perception of instrumental compliance with 'software' *bikas.* One development worker said: 'Local governments want more funds to build infrastructure, but they just follow the software approach because of funds. They often talk about that in daily conversations'. Another worker said:

> I think government organisations are reluctant that software development is going to bring any changes. They do it because they cannot say no to the donors, because they think donors are very powerful and they need the money. But they don't actually believe in it.

This was a sensitive issue that arose in our conversations and from our field perceptions of the development sector. However, it is not something that was explicitly mentioned. As a worker elaborates:

> They cannot say this directly to donor agencies, because they need them for support [...] They say that indirectly, it is something that we interpret because what they are doing is that they are just creating obstacles, and they are just reluctant to pass the policies, or they are making false promises. So we understand that, but it's not something that they say directly.

Our findings show, albeit less explicitly, signs of strategic adherence to the goals and scope of software *bikas*, although this approach did not seem to be fully internalised by all development actors in practice. Rather, it points to classic dependency relationships between donors and their local partners, and an unequal power to decide on the scope of projects and the needs to be addressed.

Critical views on bikas

Our results have shown that the material aspects of *bikas* are widely embraced by people in Nepal, while the 'software' development aspects are more often emphasised by NGOs and development agencies. However, people are also critical of the ways in which *bikas* is being implemented. In the following section we will explore these.

First, regarding the model of urbanisation. The district administrator of Rukumkot, the district headquarters of Rukum East, one of the newest federal districts with a remote geographic location, expressed concerns about the urbanisation model being used at the district headquarters. The locals place a high value on the construction of cement-built commercial buildings, believing that these buildings will spur development, but without making the necessary investments to allow such buildings to be used by the people, such as public parks or parking spaces.

Second, regarding the government. Some segments of the civil society criticised the government's *bikas* agenda for not being sustainable in terms of social, cultural or environmental aspects. A first example is the protests of environmentalist groups against the construction of Nijgadh International Airport[6], one of the government's most ambitious projects to date. The legal challenges surrounding the airport's environmental impact and funding problems have caused the project's completion date to be postponed numerous times. Environmentalists have fiercely opposed the project and pressured the government to relocate the airport to a new place with less environmental impact. However, a closer look at the people leading the protests revealed that they were not part of a grassroots movement from the affected communities. Rather, the protests were being led by Kathmandu-based activists, many of whom have studied abroad and are now back in Nepal. Interestingly, the opposition was labelled as 'anti-developmentalist' by the government and the people who support the airport project. They saw environmental protection and sustainability not as the original development agenda, but as a focus promoted by NGOs and Western influence. The voices of the communities potentially affected were not heard much. A resident of the area said the following: 'We are not against development. I think that the airport can provide employment for people in the area. But they have been telling us that it will be built for so many years, and I don't believe it anymore'. The express highway project is another development initiative that encountered opposition from the community. The government's plan to build a national expressway linking Tarai, the southern plain of Nepal, and Kathmandu, was met with opposition from the people of Khokana, an ancient Newari town on the southern edge of the Kathmandu valley. They claimed the project would destroy their arable land and harm their religious and cultural legacy. In this case, protesters were from within Newar communities affected by the project. Despite their focus on heritage protection, the locals also expressed dissatisfaction over the project's insufficient compensation for their land[7]. Thus, there are mixed motives behind the protests, which negotiate between heritage protection and economic interests.

We also found an ambivalent assessment of the importance of foreign aid in Nepal. Field conversations in the Solukhumbu area emphasised the NGO's business orientation, mentioning that 'many NGOs became a business in Nepal. Even during the earthquake, earthquake relief became a business'. Others pointed to corruption as a problem: 'Many social workers and leaders have been appointed by the corrupt politicians. And we can see a lot of big NGOs, they have big cars, and that's a very bad reputation, it's very hard to fight'. Another arising critical aspect was that some people felt neglected because they were not taken into account when decisions were made about how to implement *bikas*: 'Many development budgets have come to our village, but no one has asked us what we think. Our opinion is not important'. Finally, we also noticed a sense of frustration among people, particularly regarding the lack of impact of the projects in their lives. For example, a member of the Natuwa Community stated that 'when people come and talk with us we hope that our situation will change. However we don't find many changes in our life so we get frustrated'. Similarly, locals from Lumbini complained that 'many people come to us and take photos, and then nothing happens. They just want to take advantage of our poor condition, they take photos and sell our name, and earn money out of it'.

Frustration was also noticed among aid workers about such critical views and the questioning of *bikas* impact. They instead, had the feeling that such opposing views came from the difficulty in assessing the non-material impact of 'software' development. A worker shared the following:

> Before, they were not aware, not even that they were also human beings, or of their own citizenship. Because of our work and organisations like ours, they are now aware that they are citizens of this country and they can ask and demand government resources.

The role of development workers is an ambivalent one that does not always fit into the post-development binaries, where they have mainly been characterised as 'agents of governmentality' (McKinnon 2008).

Critical views of *bikas* described in this section are in line with a wider questioning of the effectiveness of foreign aid in the country, which has been found to be rather ineffective and even counterproductive in terms of impact (Dangi et al. 2021; Ghimire 2009; Prasain 1998).

Discussion: *Bikas* as an 'Indigenous alternative'?

> So, it appears development is a bad word after all. Five development plans and as many zones later, we are being told that progress is a pain in the neck and we

> should slip back to subsistence farming. It seems to me that now is a rather late juncture to come to this realisation.
>
> (Dixit 1986: 134)

Discourses and social categories of *bikas* are deeply embedded in the Nepalese society, not only at a macro-level but also meaningfully for the people (Pigg 1992). This chapter has explored different conceptions of *bikas* on the basis of the authors' field experiences and encounters with people and communities in two regions of Nepal. As the results have shown, a tension exists between two notions of *bikas*.

First, the most common way of understanding *bikas* is through the idea of 'hardware' *bikas*. It is based on quantifiable and short-term outcomes and focuses on infrastructure and facilities. The prevalence of a notion of 'hardware' *bikas* is consistent with previous research highlighting the centrality of the material aspects of *bikas* (Gellner 2015; Gyawali 2017; Shrestha 1995). Such material understandings of *bikas* are closely linked to the figure of the government and people hold it responsible for providing 'hardware' *bikas*. This finding is in line with Pigg's (1993:49) idea that '*bikas* has become synonymous with the services that people think the government should provide'.

Despite the fact that this is the most widespread notion of *bikas*, people show an ambivalent assessment of the 'hardware' *bikas*. On the one hand, people demand proper implementation based on the perception that *bikas* has only been partially implemented and that material improvements are still needed, especially in rural areas, where they could significantly help overcome the hardships of life and work. Our findings are consistent with other research showing that people desire infrastructure improvements, both in Nepal (Leve 2007), and in other parts of the world (Matthews et al. in this volume). On the other hand, there are critical voices about certain government-led infrastructure projects and urbanisation models. People seem to embrace 'hardware' *bikas* as a solution to their everyday problems and to improve their quality of life, while more critical voices emerge when it comes to larger infrastructure projects. Although the opposing views explored in this paper are often expressed within the discourse of sustainability, they tend to come from a privileged section of the population (as also noted by Matthews 2017), and it is not so clear that such an orientation is shared by the local people and communities affected by the projects.

The second notion of *bikas* that we found was referred to as 'software' development. It addresses issues that are more difficult to quantify and more long-term oriented in terms of outcomes. Approaches to development underwent a shift in the 60s and 70s, with the intention of moving away from the economic-centred ways of understanding development and focusing on poverty and inequality, sustainability, gender equality, and human rights (Unceta 2012). In Nepal, development has also moved from 'servicing needs' to 'building capacities to understand, claim, and fulfil their rights' (Sharma et al. 2014: iii). In Gellner's (2015: 8) words, 'the development fashion had moved on. Now it was about targeting disadvantaged groups, enacting pro-poor policies, encouraging gender sensitization, and above all, spreading something called empowerment'.

Education was repeatedly mentioned by people as an important part of *bikas*, in line with previous and current research highlighting the centrality of education in *bikas* discourses in Nepal (Pigg 1992; Valentin and Pradhan 2020). As argued elsewhere, the social status of *bikasi* (the developed) is closely linked to the notion of the educated person in Nepal (Castellsagué and Carrasco 2021b). However, other aspects such as gender equality and sustainability were not as prevalent in people's visions. Instead, the notion of 'software' *bikas* was more common among development practitioners and NGOs and their projects. If Robinson-Pant (2000) has previously suggested a gap in vocabulary between development professionals and local discourses, our findings suggest that it is more a question of conceptual difference than only a matter of wording. Moreover, our fieldwork shows how this gap in understanding of *bikas* often leads to frustration among different actors. While people expect *bikas* to solve their material problems in the short term ('hardware' *bikas*), the projects and aid they receive are more focused on the long-term outcomes of 'software' *bikas*.

Bikas was repeatedly equated with development in our findings, as we saw it used as the main word to translate the term 'development' in Nepal. But this has not always been the case (Gyawali 2017; 2018) and this chapter helps to show the complexity of the ways in which *bikas* is understood. Complexity has to do with development actors, who are diverse and may not always share the same visions, and with the ambivalent engagement with *bikas* by the people who live in the midst of development practices. Similarly, Robinson-Pant (2000: 147) noted that '*local* cannot be generalised as one dominant Nepali ideology of *bikas* (as Pigg suggests), but needs to be seen from varying perspectives of caste, gender and geographical differences'. By highlighting complexity and internal diversity, this chapter contributes to challenging the ways in which post-development discourse has tended to simplify and homogenise both mainstream development and its 'alternatives' (Pieterse 1998; Ziai 2004)[8].

As seen throughout the chapter, 'hardware' *bikas* is aligned with a classical way of understanding development typical from the 1950s, rather than being seen as an alternative to traditional development. People seem to embrace some aspects of it that are more related to improving material living conditions, but at the same time are sceptical about other aspects such as macro-infrastructure projects. Instead, 'software' *bikas* is widely used by development practitioners and NGOs, and is consistent with human and sustainable development. However, it does not represent an opposition to the dominant model, nor does it seem to be in line with what communities want. As previously noted, the appeal and desire of certain aspects of development has been underestimated by the post-development discourse (Matthews 2017; Pieterse 1998). Rather than a clear acceptance or rejection of any development model or idea, we found a strategic assessment of what development should – or should not – be based on the needs and priorities of each actor. In a country like Nepal, where *bikas* – in all its nuances – is completely embedded in the way people think and live (Pigg 1992; Sharma et al.

2014), we argue that the 'rejection' claimed to be the singularity of the 'alternatives to development' (Demaria et al. 2023; Escobar 1995) is one that is difficult to imagine in practice.

Our findings contrast with the 'alternatives' to development suggested by post-development scholarship. First, because they tend to be presented as uncontroversial and consistent concepts rather than changing notions that condense diverse meanings and understandings. The historical perspective taken by Gyawali (2017; 2018) shows that the popularity of *bikas* was not free from political tensions regarding its meanings. The findings in this chapter demonstrate the diversity and dynamism of ways in which people are critical to development, rather than identifying a single way forward or alternative. For this, it calls for a (re)assessment of the notion of 'Indigenous' alternatives, which are also political, and should be seen as internally diverse and in constant debate and transformation.

Furthermore, 'development alternatives' are claimed by some post-development thinkers to be the result of 'a rejection of the entire development paradigm altogether' (Escobar 1995: 215) and the result of a 'radically new ethic' (Kothari et al. 2019: xxix), in contrast to the ambivalence found in this research. Although *bikas* is a unique way of understanding development in Nepal, it has rarely been presented as an 'alternative', probably because it is in some ways aligned with classic development approaches. It is time to revisit Escobar (1995: 223), with his own question: 'Where then, lies "the alternative"?', and further interrogate: which ethnographic realities 'serve' as examples of alternatives and which not? Post-development research's strategic selection of singular case studies and focus on particular – and limited – 'alternatives' from Latin America, India and South Africa (Kothari et al. 2019) may obscure other, more ambivalent ways of engaging with development from other parts of the world.

As this chapter has shown, acceptance or desire for some aspects of development does not necessarily mean that there are no critical views. At the same time, critical views of some development ideas or projects do not mean that others can be viewed positively by local communities. In fact, critical voices were found at the individual and collective levels, from personal opinions to mobilised groups. But even the criticism is diverse in terms of actors and discourses. Some of them seem to reinforce the need for 'hardware' development, while others are certainly more in line with 'software' development and ideas of sustainability. The latter are led by well-educated activists and supported by NGOs rather than by marginalised communities and individuals. Therefore, we cannot claim that the existing critical voices on development represent a 'development alternative', but rather an amalgamation of different actors' diverse understandings of what *bikas* is and should be.

Finally, this chapter has shown how nuances emerge when *bikas* is studied in its implementation, in a contextualised setting. Beyond the political and academic settings, development and post-development discourses exist and operate in the everyday lives of people and organisations. It is in the ordinary experiences that tensions and contradictions arise. The dynamics of development in Nepal is, above all, an ongoing process where multiple and diverse actors take part.

Without underestimating the power of the global and hegemonic development discourses (Sharma et al. 2014), we must continue to seek to understand the complexity of local actors and people and consider them as active producers of specific cultural forms (Willis 1981). Despite Escobar's assertion that 'conceptualizing alternatives must include a significant contact with those whose "alternatives" research is supposed to illuminate' (Escobar 1995: 223) in reference to ethnography as a method for post-development research, its body of knowledge has tended to be methodologically limited to discourse analysis and the rhetorical aspects of (post)development (Pieterse 1998). As this chapter, and others in this book, have noted, such an approach may be limited or inappropriate when 'taken to the field' (McKinnon 2008; Sharma et al. 2014). It is therefore crucial to continue empirical research on (post)development practices in order to capture the ambivalences and complexities embedded in notions of development and its alternatives.

Notes

1 From 1846 to 1951 Nepal was ruled by an authoritarian and autocratic aristocracy: The Rana. This period was characterised by a strong traditional Hindu orientation, which 'had the backing of the law and the state's repressive machinery' (Gellner 2007: 50).
2 Period of the Nepalese history (1960–1990) characterised by a partyless political system that placed all governmental power with the King of Nepal, who was seen as 'the guarantor of democracy, equality, and development for all' (Gellner 2007). *Panch* (five) and *yat* (assembly) The *panchayat* (*panch*=five *yat*=assembly) was extolled as an Indigenous form of governance, as a form of government that was 'native to the soil of Nepal' (Gellner 2007). Simultaneously, Hindu values and beliefs were reiterated to bolster the centrality of the king and the institution of monarchy in the political and cultural arena (Gyawali 2018: 59).
3 Castellsagué (2023b) has previously questioned the clear distinction between outsiders and insiders in development projects, and how Nepalis have often played the role of negotiators between 'locals' and 'foreigners'.
4 A recent review of the Nepal national plans (1956–2019) shows their primary focus on developing infrastructure (roads, communication, railway, electricity), promoting the increase of national income and GDP, and poverty reduction (Dangi et al 2021).
5 Such concepts encompass a wide range of approaches to development, from more reformist to more transformative. They have also been criticised and contested, and are therefore not closed paradigms, but are constantly being discussed. See Hopwood et al. (2005) for an overview of notions on sustainable development.
6 Approved in 1995, the planned hub airport is situated in Kolhabi, the Madhesh federal province, next to the town of Nijgadh, 68 kilometres south of Kathmandu.
7 Financial compensation for land acquired for infrastructure projects is a common practice in Nepal. At the same time, the amount of compensation is the most frequently contested issue by local communities (Prasai et al. 2021).
8 Escobar claims that 'cultural difference is at the root of post-development' in the sense that 'cultural differences embody possibilities for transforming the politics of representation' (Escobar 1995: 225). However, he seems to be referring to differences *between* cultures rather than differences *within* cultures.

References

Adhikary, K.R. (1996). 'Naming Ceremonies As Rituals of Development', *Studies in Nepali History and Society*, 1 (2), pp. 345–364.

Bourdieu, P. and Wacquant, L.J.D. (2005). 'El propósito de la sociología reflexiva', *Una Invitación a La Sociología Reflexiva*, Siglo Veintiuno Editores: Argentina, pp. 101–300. Available at: Doi:doi:10.1017/CBO9781107415324.004.

Castellsagué, A. and Carrasco, S. (2021a). 'Development, Education and Gender: challenging the empowerment rhetoric from an ethnographic study in rural Nepal', *Ethnography and Education*, 16 (1), pp. 92–108. Available at: Doi:doi:10.1080/17457823.2020.1764856.

Castellsagué, A. and Carrasco, S. (2021b). 'Schooling and development: global discourses and women's narratives from Nepal', *Compare: A Journal of Comparative and International Education*, 51 (7), pp. 1058–1076. Available at: Doi:doi:10.1080/03057925.2019.1709803.

Castellsagué, A. and Carrasco, S. (2022). 'The "City" and "The Easy Life": Work and Gender among Sherpa in Nepal'. In *Gendered Lives: Global Issues*, edited by Fernandez, N.T. and Nelson, K. SUNY Press: Albany, pp. 116132.

Castellsagué, A. (2023a). 'The Relevance of Gender in the (Re)production of Education, Training and Work (Dis)continuities', NORRAG Special Issue *The Education-Training-Work Continuums: Pathways to Socio-Professional Inclusion for Youth and Adults*, 8, pp. 31–33.

Castellsagué, A. (2023b). 'The rhetoric of return: Mingma or the contradictions of development in Nepal', *Mobilities*: Routledge, pp. 1–16 Available at: Doi:doi:10.1080/17450101.2023.2232947.

Dangi, M.B., Schoenberger, E., Boland, J.J. and Chaudhary, R.P. (2021). 'Quest for development: An examination of more than a half-century of national planning and foreign aid practice in Nepal', *Sustainable Futures*, 3, pp. 100051. Available at: Doi:doi:10.1016/j.sftr.2021.100051.

Demaria, F., Kothari, A., Salleh, A., Escobar, A. and Acosta, A. (2023). 'Post-development: From the Critique of Development to a Pluriverse of Alternatives'. In *The Barcelona School of Ecological Economics and Political Ecology*, edited by Villamayor-Tomas, S. and Muradian, R. Studies in Ecological Economics, pp. 59–69. Available at: Doi:doi:10.1007/978-3-031-22566-6_6.

Des Chene, M. (1996). 'In the Name of *Bikas*', *Studies in Nepal History and Society*, 1 (2), pp. 259–270.

Dixit, K. (1986). 'The Development Industry'. In *Bikas-Binas? Development-Destruction? The Change in Life and Environment of the Himalaya*, edited by Tüting, L. and Dixit, K. Ratna Book Distributors: Kathmandu.

Escobar, A. (1995). *Encountering Development. The Making and Unmaking of the Third World*. Princeton University Press: Princeton, NJ. Available at: Doi:doi:10.2307/j.ctv11g96cc.22.

Gellner, D. (2007). 'Democracy in Nepal: Four Models', *Seminar Publications*, 576, pp. 50–56.

Gellner, D.N. (2015). 'Rituals of Democracy and Development in Nepal'. In *Governance, Conflict and Development in South Asia: Perspectives from India, Nepal and Sri Lanka*, edited by Hettige, S. and Gerharz, E. Sage: Delhi, (6), pp. 99–127.

Ghimire, S. (2009). 'Macro Development and Micro Social Processes: Development as Discourse in Nepal', *Occasional Papers in Sociology and Anthropology*, 11, pp. 221–243. Available at: Doi:doi:10.3126/opsa.v11i0.3038.

Gyawali, B. (2017). 'Nepal's Pre-*bikas* encounters with the west: Sabhyata and Unnati as precursors to Development', *Studies in Nepali History and Society*, 22 (2), pp. 227–260.

Gyawali, B. (2018). *Ambiguous Bikās: History of the Concept of Development in Nepal 1900–2006*. Doctoral Dissertation. University of Helsinki.

Hopwood, B., Mellor, M. and O'Brien, G. (2005). 'Sustainable development: Mapping different approaches', *Sustainable Development*, 13 (1), pp. 38–52. Available at: Doi: doi:10.1002/sd.244.

Kothari, A., Salleh, A., Escobar, A., Demaria, F. and Acosta, A. (2019). *Pluriverse. A Post-Development Dictionary*. Tulika Books: Delhi. Available at: Doi:doi:10.4324/9781315542126-3.

Leve, L. (2007). '"Failed Development" and Rural Revolution in Nepal: Rethinking Subaltern Consciousness and Women's Empowerment', *Anthropological Quarterly*, 80(1), pp. 127–172.

Matthews, S. (2017). 'Colonised minds? Post-development theory and the desirability of development in Africa', *Third World Quarterly*, 38 (12), pp. 2650–2663. Available at: Doi:doi:10.1080/01436597.2017.1279540.

McKinnon, K. (2008). 'Taking post-development theory to the field: Issues in development research, Northern Thailand', *Asia Pacific Viewpoint*, 49 (3), pp. 281–293. Available at: Doi:doi:10.1111/J.1467-8373.2008.00377.X.

Nepal Academy. (2018). *Brihat Nepali Sabdhakosh*. 10th ed. Pragya Pratisthan: Kathmandu.

Pieterse, J.N. (1998). 'My paradigm or yours? Alternative Development, Post-Development, Reflexive Development', *Development and Change*, 29, pp. 343–373.

Pigg, S.L. (1992). 'Inventing Social Categories Through Place: Social Representations and Development in Nepal', *Comparative Studies in Society and History*, 34(3), pp. 491–513. Available at: Doi:doi:10.1017/S0010417500017928.

Pigg, S.L. (1993). 'Unintended Consequences: The Ideological Impact of Development in Nepal', *Comparative Studies of South Asia, Africa and the Middle East*, 13(1–2), pp. 45–58.

Prasai, S., Arjal, N. and Tiwari, R. (2021). *Politics and Processes of Local-Level Dispute Resolution in Infrastructure Development Projects in Nepal: A Rapid Assessment*, The Asian Foundation.

Prasain, D. (1998). '"In the name of the people": Writing Bikas in Post-1990 Nepal', *Studies in Nepali History and Society*, 3(2), pp. 341–394.

Robinson-Pant, A. (2000). *Why Eat Green Cucumbers at the Time of Dying, Women's Literacy and Development in Nepal*. Unesco Institute for Education: Hamburg.

Seddon, D. (1998). 'Association for Nepal and Development in Nepal: Issues and Approaches', *Himalaya, the Journal of the Association for Nepal and Himalayan Studies*, 18 (2), pp. Art. 6.

Sharma, S.R., Upreti, B.R., Manandhar, P. and Sapkota, M. (2014). *Contested Development in Nepal: Experiences and Reflections*. School of Arts: Kathmandu University and Nepal Centre for Contemporary Research, Kathmandu.

Shrestha, N. (1995). 'Becoming a development agent'. In *Power of Development*, edited by Crush, J. Psychology Press: London, pp. 266–277.

Unceta, K. (2012). 'Desarrollo, Subdesarrollo, Maldesarrollo y Postdesarrollo: una mirada transdisciplinar sobre el debate y sus implicaciones'. In *Antropología y desarrollo: discurso, prácticas y actores*, edited by Galán, B.P. Catarata, Madrid, pp. 415.

Valentin, K. and Pradhan, U. (2020). 'Anthropological Perspectives on Education in Nepal', *Anthropological Perspectives on Education in Nepal*, pp. 2–27.

Willis, P. (1981). 'Cultural production is different from cultural reproduction is different from social reproduction is different from reproduction', *Interchange*, 12(2–3), pp. 48–67. Available at: Doi:doi:10.1007/BF01192107.

Ziai, A. (2004). 'The ambivalence of post-development: Between reactionary populism and radical democracy', *Third World Quarterly*, 25 (6), pp. 1045–1060. Available at: Doi: doi:10.1080/0143659042000256887.

4 Development as nostalgia and reverie in Eastern Rwanda

Justin Dodd Mullikin

Ambivalence and agrarian change

It was late morning and everyone could feel the rain coming, so we started hustling down the mountain toward shelter. It was early 2020 in Gatsibo District, in Rwanda's Eastern Province, and I was with Steve and Etienne – two former colleagues working on my research team – and an older farmer who was showing us around his small eucalyptus plantation, two of his curious friends in tow. It started pouring before we could reach the truck, so we all ducked into a neighbour's compound to wait things out. Etienne disappeared to look for some water and Steve and I took a seat in one of the houses where three older gentlemen were each working their way through large 500 ml bottles of Primus, one of the most ubiquitous commercial beers in the Great Lakes region.

Though widely popular, Primus and other 'modern' alcoholic drinks are starkly different from the thick, almost porridge-like sorghum beer, *ikigage*, that has been brewed in the country for centuries (Ezeanya-Esiobu 2019). *Ikigage* has long been an important element of Rwandan culture: sorghum appears on the national seal, *ikigage* is a central component of wedding and harvest rituals, and home brewing was once an important source of income for many households. Despite its socio-cultural importance and popularity, recent agricultural policies have actively discouraged sorghum cultivation and home brewing of any alcohol has been banned in most places. These changes are intertwined manifestations of the Government of Rwanda's (GoR) national development vision, discussed below, that seeks to 'modernise' nearly all aspects of Rwandan society (Mann and Berry 2016; Ansoms et al. 2018). National agricultural priorities have shifted away from staple crops like sorghum to focus on higher-value market crops. Myriad policies, programmes and laws target other aspects of society deemed insufficiently modern or too disorderly. Many GoR officials told us that, in addition to being unhygienic, home-brewed sorghum beer encourages drunkenness, sloth, and that people who miss it simply have 'backwards mindsets'. Incidentally, the prohibitions on home brewing have created a gap that national, and multinational, beer and alcohol companies are quickly filling. As a result, *ikigage* is disappearing from daily life.

Steve and I idly chatted with the men for a while, but the conversation soon petered out as it became clear they were mostly just being polite and that we had

DOI: 10.4324/9781003477921-5

interrupted an intimate moment. As the rain let up and we prepared to leave, I asked the men if they preferred the 'new' beer or *ikigage*. The most loquacious of the group, a dapper man seemingly in his 70s, dressed in a suit jacket and felt hat, leaned in and jabbed playfully at me with an *inkoni*, a traditional walking stick that the Eastern Province had once tried to ban from public use (Times Reporter 2008). 'Because of development we *have* to drink this', he said. Then, referring to me (a White foreigner asking questions about development) he added, 'You brought us money, but you took our beer' (2020, personal communication, 5 March). This quote struck me as emblematic of a wider connective theme that was just coming into focus during our research: an ambivalent, sometimes contradictory relationship to all of the ways life in rural Rwanda is rapidly changing. These men were not necessarily angry about the changes brought about by the government's agrarian 'modernisation' schemes, nor were they entirely sanguine about the promises of prosperity that accompany these changes, however.

Our conversation with the three men continued for a while longer, until the rain eased a bit and we left them to their chatter.

Agrarian development in Rwanda

Our research was focused on the connections between vanishing agrarian rituals – poems, songs, mutual aid and celebrations – and GoR policies that had transformed cultivation practices. These rituals were intimately connected to the seasonal rhythms of staple crops such as sorghum. Poetry and songs about sorghum were once abundant. People knew these by heart, learned through years of communal labour and celebration where they would be recited. Sorghum was a powerful symbol and its various products valuable gifts. 'Sorghum was very important to us', one woman explained, 'the reason being, sorghum united a family and a community' (2019, personal communication, 19 November).

Over the course of the project, my team and I conducted dozens of small focus groups in three different areas of Gatsibo. Additionally, we interviewed dozens of individual farmers, local leaders, agronomists and officials at all levels of the GoR bureaucracy. The focus groups were facilitated by two members of the team and myself, with one person leading the discussion and another helping me with real-time translation, so the conversations could flow more smoothly. Our recorded conversations were transcribed by two research assistants; first into the original Kinyarwanda and then into an English translation. Due to the free-flowing nature of the focus groups, we felt it was important to edit the transcripts and words as little as possible. Where the direct translation was unclear, or if there were no suitable English equivalents, the translators would include clarifying commentary, seen here in the endnotes.

At the time of our conversation about beer with the three gentlemen in Gatsibo, the GoR was preparing the release of Vision 2050, the successor to Vision 2002, both master plans that outline Rwanda's strategic development commitments, metrics and goals. The stated ambition of Vision 2050 is to 'lead the country to the living standards of upper middle income by 2035 and high-income countries by 2050' (Republic of Rwanda 2020: 5). These ambitions are totalising; 'focused on transformation of the entire economy and society' (Republic of Rwanda 2020: 8). Making its priorities clear, agrarian transformation is addressed under the heading 'Agriculture for Wealth Creation'. 'Going into 2050', the document states, 'the agricultural sector is expected to be totally transformed with professional farmers and commercialised value chains' (Republic of Rwanda 2020: 6). This transformation will entail a focus on market and global value chain integration, access to finance, production at scale and the increased 'use of modern inputs and technologies to maximise productivity' (Republic of Rwanda 2020: 25).

Many of the priorities in Vision 2050 are not new. For over two decades the GoR has used various tactics to push rural landscapes toward a 'productivist mode of agriculture – a system oriented towards productivity maximisation on the basis of "modern" techniques that regulate – or try to regulate – natural diversity' (Collier 2010 cited in Nyenyezi Bisoka and Ansoms 2020: 244). The main pillar of Rwanda's agricultural development policies is the Crop Intensification Programme (CIP). Launched in 2007, CIP incentivises and subsidises the use of chemical fertiliser and 'improved' seed for over a dozen 'priority crops' (predominantly maize, rice and Irish potatoes) that the state has deemed to have major food security and export potential (Hakorimana and Akcaoz 2018). Many people linked the disappearance of agrarian rituals to the homogenisation of agricultural practices due to a subcomponent of CIP, land use consolidation (LUC). The main goal of LUC is to 'harmonise' production between neighbouring plots of land, some owned by different farmers, effectively creating monocultures of CIP's priority crops.

While participation in CIP is technically voluntary, participation is mandatory in sites specifically targeted for LUC, which includes all cooperative land and fertile marshlands. Owners of consolidated plots retain legal titles to their land, but their decision-making power over how to use it is effectively removed since each LUC site must conform to a handful of general rules: grow the same crop from a list of two to four priority crops deemed suitable for the region, use inputs approved by the GoR, and conform to Ministry of Agriculture (MINAGRI) (2019) cultivation guidelines and timetables. While farmers on an LUC site can technically choose which crops to grow each season, in reality there is rarely an option. A common situation is a hillside LUC site in a cell where the suitable priority crops are maize, beans, rice and soy. Rice cannot be grown on the hillside, and MINAGRI (2019) guidelines for their area state that maize is most suitable for the A Season and must be rotated with beans in the B Season. At a seasonal planning meeting, agronomists present this information to farmers on the site who then 'choose' to grow maize and beans.

At the inception of LUC, the GoR also made several commitments to 'provide assistance' to land-users in the form of 'understanding and participating in market-based agriculture', appropriate crop selection, financial services, 'agricultural sensitisation services' and 'facilitation of the sale of the crops to buyers' (Republic of Rwanda 2010: 22–23). The commitments represent an expansion of state control over land-use decision-making tacitly framed as farmer support.

With the legal possibility of land expropriation for noncompliance (Republic of Rwanda 2010) ever-looming, promises of 'assistance' in areas such as crop selection and the vaguely-worded 'sensitisation services' can reasonably suggest coercion. Yet, importantly for the expectations of farmers, the *promise* of support, markets and prosperity remains.

Year by year, district and local leaders are pushed to expand the total number of hectares under consolidation in their area. As a result, LUC has expanded well beyond cooperatives and marshlands over the past decade to encompass anywhere between 25% and 59% of all agricultural land as of 2019 (MINAGRI 2019; National Institute of Statistics Rwanda (NISR) 2020). In Gatsibo, what had been a patchwork landscape of small, mixed-cropped plots has, in the most 'successful' LUC areas, transformed into homogenous stretches of maize, rice and a handful of other market-oriented crops. Where sorghum is still cultivated in any meaningful sense it is often against the wishes of local leaders and, sometimes, undertaken covertly.

The GoR's development ideal doesn't see smallholder agrarianism as a viable form of employment in a 'modern' economy. This became clear when one high-level MINAGRI official (2020, personal communication, 11 February) expressed his frustration that the GoR couldn't simply buy off smallholders, 'give them... a pension, move them off the land and let business take over'. This wasn't possible because 'We are too many farmers. Farming is still more than a business'. This last statement concedes that, as currently lived, farming is still much more than a way to make money and, in order for Rwanda to 'develop', this must change. People should view their land and their labour not as livelihoods and communities, but as parts of an economic transaction that prioritises little else but the production of wealth. This is also why 'that old sorghum culture' must end – it is too expansive to be captured and managed by market or state; it (re)produces too many other things, much of which cannot be commodified in any meaningful sense – before it comes around to producing the 'increased incomes' or 'job opportunities' prioritised in Vision 2050. In this space, facing the rapid erasure of the past while being promised the elusive benefits of development as 'modernisation', an ambivalence fluctuating between nostalgia and reverie has bloomed.

The losses and promises of development

The changes brought about by LUC and other 'modernisation' policies are more than just material; the new crops, technologies, labour requirements and market economies have radically changed the way people relate to the land and to each other, and affected the quality of their lives. As the agrarian economy has shifted to market crops and wage labour, the communal labour practices and celebrations that revolved around crops like sorghum have also disappeared.

A common refrain when we discussed these changes with farmers, as exemplified by one older woman's (Kabarore farmer 2020, personal communication, 17 February) lament, was 'The culture has changed, there are no songs. Only money matters today; if someone harvests five sacks of maize or twelve sacks of beans [they] think of themselves as rich and can't party with that one who worked for them. You cannot sing with people who are working for money'. In this sense, the materiality of the new crops and their required cultivation methods have made it difficult to engage in farming as anything other than a wealth-maximising enterprise. Most of these crops will be sold for consumption elsewhere. The old crops didn't have songs because of their economic value; they had songs because they were entangled *in place*, as one farmer (2020, personal communication, 5 February) expressed:

> In the past, people would dance excitingly, encouraging others to grow sorghum in a way of friendship ...Those sweet potatoes, that sorghum, those beans; they would stay where they were grown. They would be eaten there or drunk there. But today, taking maize as an example, it is grown and then it is delivered to different provinces in the country, and even abroad. So, the artist who makes the song will show that that crop earns money. That is the difference.

Vision 2050's promises of modernity and wealth are highly alluring and often equally elusive. Yet, all too often the promises of modernity are deferred or unseen. 'The grand narrative of progress is, in part, vulnerable simply because so much is expected from it. The idea is crowded with so many aspirations that disappointment and disillusionment are inevitable' (Bonnett 2010: 34). This makes nostalgia not simply a yearning for the past, but a powerful critique of the present. Nostalgia as a critical practice is also not confined to those with direct memories of what has been lost. When facing 'day-to-day paradoxes of wealth and nothingness ...', Molemo Moiloa (2012: 338) argues, nostalgia is a powerful way for youth on the continent to 'take ownership of memory and mold it according to their needs, producing tools and strategies for negotiating what is an incredibly difficult political and ethical arena'.

Yet, when our focus group conversations turned from the past to how people experience LUC in the present, many of the same people (and especially younger farmers) spoke of all the ways 'modernised' agriculture and a market-productivist approach to farming had given them hopes of a better future. As one man (2020, personal communication, 27 February) explained, it had now become possible to access all sorts of material goods undreamed of in the past:

> In the past, they would [cultivate] so that they can eat and get satisfied. But in this new century, a person cultivates with the goal of progress; to buy a motorcycle, or to buy a car. In the past you would only see few of those, but today, the number of motorcycle and car owners grows continuously. And for most of them, it is because of agriculture.

At the same time, very few of the people we spoke with had seen that sort of dramatic prosperity themselves. Rather, they dreamed about the lives that younger generations might someday have. One woman (2020, personal communication, 20 February) put it this way:

> For us, even as we work, we work for our children. Those who are to study, we send them to study, those who want to do technical professions the same; but all that comes from that agriculture. Because we don't have any scholar knowledge, we only know the hoe. Which means that I don't wait for any other salary that is going to solve my problems. The salary will come from waking up early to go to cultivate.

The demands and promises of 'modernity' are, for better or worse, a repudiation of the past and a sometimes-violent realignment of the future. Capitalist 'modernity' in particular is also a rejection of 'everyday practices that produce without capitalising, that is, without taking control over time' (de Certeau 1988: xx). It is what Mbembe (2001: 16–17) described as an *emerging time,* particular to the post-colonial African experience, that mixes together 'absence of those presences that are no longer so and that one remembers (the past), and absence of those others that are yet to come and are anticipated (the future)'. What is distinctive about this mixture is the constant struggle for agency and control that is the hallmark of the postcolonial period; an experience of time in which, 'the future horizon is apparently closed, while the horizon of the past has apparently receded' (Mbembe 2001: 17).

With such uncertain futures, reverie is a natural way to imagine how things might be better. I understand reverie as more than dreaming of a better future, however; it is also a form of claim-making. I take the concept of 'reverie' from Nancy Rose Hunt (2015: 19) for whom 'reverie comprises the poetic, material imagination ... Neither hallucination, delusion, or trance, reverie may be aspiration or suggest a claim'.

Many people, especially older farmers, felt unmoored in the *now*, unable to fully see themselves at home in the present moment. Their attitude toward change seemed to be occupying an ambivalent space 'between longing and despair' (Secor 2007) where it was unclear if the assurances of a better life would be worth losing much of what they had known and loved about their old life; or, in fact, if that imagined life was even attainable in their lifetimes. The tension here, perhaps never to be resolved, is that people want *both* of these things. Many people in Gatsibo seem to locate themselves in what Mudimbe (1988: 18) has called an 'intermediary space', characterised by a 'strong tension between a modernity that often is an illusion of development, and a tradition that sometimes reflects a poor image of a mythical past'. In this space, nostalgia plays a crucial role in maintaining a sense of subjectivity and connection to place, even if the tension is sometimes between an idealised past and uncertain future.

Nostalgia

It cannot be overstated how important stories – transmitted through oral poetic histories and popular songs – were, and in some ways still are, to Rwandan identity, culture and state-building (Nzabatsinda and Mitsch 1997; Vansina 2004; 2000). Agriculture, especially sorghum and cattle, were primary subjects of Rwanda's poetic landscape and as such, central components of Rwandan placemaking (Kagabo 2005). A traditional poet (2020, personal communication, 20

March) in Kigali put it this way: 'If there is no sorghum, Rwanda culture doesn't exist … Rwanda was made from agriculture and entertainment'. Control over the poetic tradition has been contested ground for centuries, playing important functions in state formation, the legitimisation of power (Newbury 1994; Vansina 2004) and in knowledge reproduction. The stories told through poetics and song are not simply productive of place, they are also productive of tensions about how to interpret the past, present, and future *in* place: what the oral historian Jan Vansina (2000) described as their 'etiological' functions.

Much of what we discussed with rural folks in Gatsibo revolved around a tension between the leisure time they had in the past and the new aspirations of the present: nostalgia in conversation with different interpretations of 'development' and 'progress'. For example, after the standard opening question during a conversation in (2020, personal communication, 18 February), Steve asked if the crops that have replaced sorghum, such as rice and soya, have songs of their own:

MUGISHA ALICE: The only song is that we eat and pay school fees for our kids; the [old songs] were lies, [pretending] that people were happy.[1]

UWITONZE DIANE: They were not lies, it was their time. And, again, it was the norms and rituals of then and seeing your ten children working in your field would bring songs and happiness.

ISHIMWE ALFRED: That was before the development, there were no jobs, and people had time to meet and talk for hours at someone's place, drinking local beer and kids who're getting to know about the past from them. But today there is no time to waste; people have work, and even when some people decide to sit and talk, we end up calling them lazy. Everyone goes to work and when they get back home it is only resting, and getting back to work again. That's the reason those songs have vanished.

UWITONZE DIANE: In the past there were parties where people could drink and sing, but today there are no parties.

ISHIMWE ALFRED: Today many people are Christians. In the past we used to have beer parties but today people think of drinking as a sin. We sing salvation songs, we visit each other after church, but no traditional songs and poems. Also we don't do *ubudehe* anymore; people use money to pay workers. I can call it development.

Like Ishimwe, most people connected the disappearance of songs to the gradual disappearance of an agrarian form of 'mutual aid' known as *ubudehe*. While there were regional variations in how *ubudehe* operated, in its simplest form neighbours would come together each day during busy seasons to work in a particular person's field, using songs (and sometimes dance) to both pass the time and to coordinate their labour. At the end of the day, the host would serve sorghum or banana beer and food – swapping stories, poems, 'brags' and songs – often dancing and celebrating 'in all-night revels', as a number of people reminisced. *Ubudehe* would rotate in this manner throughout the community until planting (or whatever work was at hand) was finished for everyone. Sorghum was essential to *ubudehe*, both as the crop being cultivated and for the beer that was used as payment and to 'facilitate' the work. Much more than a simple transaction, '*Ubudehe* was a sign of unity, partnership and love. Before cooperatives, people settled on a same hill worked together, they prepared drinks and farmed one person's farm only one day and it made them love each other even stronger' (Rugarama farmer 2020, personal communication, 5 March).

The term *ubudehe* is now used as the name of a GoR programme that assigns each household a number based on their level of poverty. Those in the poorest *ubudehe* category are eligible for more government assistance and aid from state-imposed community workdays. Thus, the substantive, commonplace meaning of the idea of *ubudehe* itself has transformed along with the changing agrarian landscape; from something like 'mutual aid' to something more like 'state charity'. This shift in *ubudehe* mirrors the GoR's vision for both agrarian and national 'modernisation'. The 'backwards mindset' of collective farming and celebration needs to be replaced with a more 'serious mindset' of farming as a business. If people come together to help one another, it must be related to specific development goals, have measurable outcomes and operate discretely in time (present-day *ubudehe* usually lasts for a few hours during the day) so that people can get back to work rather than work spilling into 'all-night revels'.

A Rwandan musician and friend (2018, personal communication, 27 July) once told me that in Kinyarwanda there is an aphorism that some still repeat – 'if it's in a story it must have happened'. Without a doubt, *ubudehe* was not perfect, nor universally beloved. I am not interested, however, in resolving these tensions or finding the truth in these stories; their repeated retelling by so many people in Gatsibo is illustrative in its own right. Most people analysed agrarian change as if the stories of *ubudehe* were universally good and true. In this sense, I understand the past-narratives of folks in Gatsibo along the same lines as Laura Ogden (2011: 25–26), who views nostalgia as 'remembering as a critical practice' where, rather than searching for 'truth', 'we should look to what the tensions these practices of remembrance produce.'

The reminiscences of folks in Gatsibo were certainly sanitised in various ways, recovered from the layered retellings of the past through the haze of all the *presents* in between. Geographer Alastair Bonnett (2010: 10) has observed that:

> One can hardly dispute that nostalgia distorts, that it offers a rose-tinted view of the past… Why are the backward-looking called 'misty-eyed' but not the forward-looking? The point is reinforced by the simple fact that nostalgia is often based on acquired information, on memory.

Memory and remembering, even when imperfect, is an essential component to grappling with how the present has arrived in such a way and what is to be done with it. Even when, or if inherently, idyllic, 'sense-making is at the heart of nostalgic practice' (Kitson and McHugh 2015: 503). Far from an idle practice, the storytelling that is inherent to nostalgia is productive of place-making and is necessary to a community.

Even when not overtly treated as such, nostalgia can be a radical, provocative act that inverts power relationships. One productive element of nostalgia is projecting an element of control in a fast-changing world. Nostalgia is an especially critical practice, as Bode Omojola (2009: 250) argues, for 'marginalised societies whose task of interpreting the past often becomes more challenging as a result of the social and political developments arising from … domination'. Domination, in Omojola's (2009) framing, includes the loss of localised artforms which entails a violent alienation from one's past, subjective present, and sense of agency over the future. Nostalgia, in this understanding, rekindles the ability to make-place.

In a place as heavily surveilled (Purdeková 2011) and quickly changing as Rwanda, it is not only agrarian practices but entire lifeworlds represented by disappearing songs and their attendant practices that are vanishing in the face of globalised capitalism. The old songs are a recollection of *home*, the archetypical object of nostalgia, as complicated as home can be. Kofi Agawu (2003: 241) observed that 'Singing in one's language is an invitation into an intimate space, home …', but cautions that, even as this can bring 'solace and assurance … home is a contested space … For many postcolonial subjects, home is linguistically constituted as a set of fragments; home is the sum of (necessarily) partial competence in indigenous and colonial languages.' A poet and friend (2018, personal communication, 2 August) in Rwanda expressed something similar when I first told her I was interested in the old songs and poems, saying that 'all the socio-cultural practices that were done away with – even if they perpetuated the patriarchy and gender stereotypes – at least they imparted [to people] a sense of worthiness, independence, in charge of their own identity and proud of it. And now, that's all gone'. This echoes what one man in Gatsibo (2020, personal communication, 5 February) told us:

> Those songs were so important because they helped bring people and culture… someone would invite them to come and help them harvest sorghum. They all woke up happily and joined their hands to help them, singing those songs. It was a good culture, and also was a sign of love, and if you were absent you felt like you have missed something very important. But today things have changed. Maybe it is because of development and civilization, but it seems like everyone is just busy with themselves.

What folks seem to be nostalgic for is not only the celebration, but the affective, *living* aspect of community. Many of the most popular traditional songs and dances are still remembered and learned, but in a calcified form and disconnected from communities and places. They are now performed by organised troupes, many sponsored by the GoR. Rather than an organic form of communal celebration, however, these troupes now mostly perform at state functions, large NGO events, domestic and international conferences and hotels, and are ubiquitous in Ministry of Tourism promotional videos. Much like *ubudehe*, this tradition has been captured, abstracted even, serving a different social function while maintaining some remnant of its form.

Yet, any effort to 'preserve culture' only results in culture's death. When it is removed from its roots in a place – in situated, visceral practice – it loses its life-force and it dies. As one woman (Rugarama farmer 2020, personal communication, 7 February) lamented, 'Sometimes they ask your child things relating to culture, and the child comes to you and ask you, "Mum, what is culture? Can you give me a definition of culture?" and then you explain how culture was in the past'. In the past, she continued, children would 'would hear the song here, then the next day they hear it being sung in another place…'. Only now, children are hearing these songs from the same places, the state or media; not as reproductions of place, but as the reproduction of market or nation.

These abstractions also have the effect of dividing and ordering people according to market logics of value, as these women (2020, personal communication, 19 February) discussed:

RURANGWA PACIFIQUE: So, in the time of ***ubudehe***, they would sing while digging. They would be happy with the digging because they would be singing; and it would give them energy to go on also because they would be many. They would brew some booze, drink and then go back to their digging … But that is over. It is over. It eventually ended, and then came looking out for oneself.

UWIMANA FLORENCE: Times have changed.

RURANGWA PACIFIQUE: There came self-centeredness. If you didn't have money to look for workers, you would cultivate late.[2] And then you would harvest later than that person who had money. Because the person with money gets the work done fast, but for the person who doesn't have any… it would be a problem. They wouldn't harvest anything. Last things come last.[3]

'Last things come last' reflects a person's 'poverty' onto the person themselves. 'People loved each other, they knew the value of a person, more than today. Today everything is about money', as one man (2020, personal communication, 5 February) put it. This is a very similar analysis to the idea of the invention of poverty where 'only after… the monetisation of society that the poor were defined as lacking what the rich could have in terms of money and possessions' (Rahnema 2019: 175). A state of 'lack' comes to define people who previously were more or less capable of providing for themselves, their families and their communities. 'Development' brings many things, including new problems. Speaking with one young farmer in (2020, personal communication, 4 March) – who, importantly, was highly approving of GoR agricultural policy – about how things have changed, he responded:

> How can I explain this? Look, that time they didn't have many problems. For example, these days people need sheet metal roofing but that time they

> used grass for roofing; and they didn't need vehicles or moto bicycles for transport because that time they walked on foot. The needs have changed … Before people didn't have problems as they do now, so they were happier that time.

There were certainly problems in the past, and much lack, but the solution to these issues were typically not 'become wealthier'. The problems of the past were generally collective problems of social reproduction. If someone could not afford to host their own *ubudehe*, a wealthier farmer would often slyly host it for them. As one woman told us (2020, personal communication, 7 February), 'Even though people weren't the same, they gave what they had'. She then related a story about her father who had a poor neighbour who couldn't afford to make beer for *ubudehe*. On the day the community was working in the poorer farmer's fields, her father said, 'We are going to dig for [me] tomorrow. Let's go drink there' and served his own beer instead. She concluded that 'they had already dug for the other person who didn't have anything. No trouble arose because they knew that they couldn't blame him'.

Collective stories, songs and labour – organised around the *whole* lifecycles of crops like sorghum (and not just their path to the market) – sustained continuity between generations through a deep well of experience for understanding how to handle problems, make places and navigate change. The nostalgia we witnessed was expressed as a loss of love, cohesion and commonality within a community, as much as it was an elegy to present and future loss. The songs, poems and brags connected people to those who performed them in the past, to the people with whom they were performed in the past-present and to the future generation, the children who would learn them and continue the (re)appropriation of the meaning, belonging and place-making that were inherent in the act of recitation in community. Now, as repetitive performances for 'important' events or to promote Rwandan tourism, they have become generic, calcified and (re)productive of a homogenous Rwandan-ness that represents an entire country but no *place* in the everyday sense.

In observing an old bucket that had served as a landmark on his farm for years, Wendell Berry (2017: 17) noted the accumulation of soil within that spoke to the 'slow work of growth and death, gravity and decay, which is the chief work of the world'. This, he continued, was:

> irresistibly metaphorical … A human community, too, must collect leaves and stories, and turn them to account. It must build soil, and build that memory itself – in lore and story and song – that will be its culture. These two kinds of accumulation, of local soil and local culture, are intimately related.
>
> (Berry 2017: 103)

Without the slow, shared accumulation of soil, stories and histories – without the agency to name place, to *make* places rooted in collective, if contradictory, ideas of who a community was, is, and hopes to be – nostalgia and reverie are a natural refuge and the present is too easily defined by how efficiently landscapes and communities can be exploited.

One portion of our first conversation about *ubudehe* (Rugarama farmers 2020, personal communication, 27 January), is still the most memorable for me. In many ways, it encapsulates the entwined spirits of nostalgia and reverie I am trying to translate:

> Another thing we can add is that you must understand that if back then fifty people would come to cultivate for you, and now you are getting like one or three people and you agree that they will come and cultivate for you, while being only three of them. They are just coming to get money. They will not have that time to dance. They are only focused on cultivating. And you will also be focusing on other necessities. There are even those who are more advanced and who are using machines to cultivate. Can the machines dance or ....

In asking 'can the machines dance?' this man was expressing a mixture of nostalgia and reverie. Later in the conversation many people specifically asked for more technology such as 'cultivating machines' and mechanical irrigation. This suggests something of a 'cyborg logic' (Haraway 1991: 181) where 'reconstructing the boundaries of daily life' is built on both the destructive and creative potential of technology; 'it means both building and destroying machines, identities, categories, relationships, space stories'. As inherently cyborg, then these narratives were not uniform.

Reverie

While sad for what they had lost, many people hoped GoR policies would result in better lives for their children. These dreams for the future were usually quite reasonable, given all that had been promised to them. Yet responses to the nostalgic mindset of many farmers and their reticence to change, often invoked a mixture of paternalism and wild flights of fancy regarding what the future might hold. When I asked one GoR official why, according to a recent newspaper article, MINAGRI was training farmers on the use of drones, she replied 'So that [farmers] can move with this world. Sometimes they are saying the robots will be doing things!' (2020, personal communication, 7 February). The ambition and scale of the changes planned by the GoR are so staggering as to be nearly unbelievable, even by those in charge of implementing these policies. As one MINAGRI Extension Specialist (2020, personal communication, 7 February) expressed when I asked how long she thought it would take to achieve the Vision 2050 ambitions she responded, 'Decades, it will take decades … 2050 if the country stays stable, if we have good leadership as we do now. Maybe 2050'.

As mentioned previously, Vision 2050 was the successor to Vision 2020 which had also pledged to 'fundamentally transform Rwanda into a middle-income country by the year 2020' (Ministry of Finance and Economic Planning 2000:

9). Even accounting for its wild ambition, Vision 2020 had very obviously not resulted in the promised wholesale transformation of the country (Ansoms and Rostagno 2012; Uwizeyimana 2019). Despite the lack of transformative progress, agrarian communities are constantly inundated with new policies and agrarian 'modernisation' schemes they have no choice but to comply with, all in the service of developing the nation. Understandably, this creates tension within agrarian communities, especially in a place like Rwanda where state surveillance is pervasive and dissent against the government is frequently (and often violently) repressed (Ansoms and Cioffo 2016; Desrosiers and Thomson 2011; Freedom House 2024; Purdeková 2011). Still, people can take only so much. Another agricultural Extension Specialist (2020, personal communication, 7 February) explained this tension:

> Sometimes you find the policies are not consistent. One Minister or [Director General] has an idea, but then they are removed … and you change from this to this. It affects the extension work. In it was 2003, specialised crops, then it was 'The industries are coming!'. When the policy changes, we must follow the policy. [Farmers] are waiting to see the success of one thing, and we come with another. And they say, 'We are tired of your words'.

Vision 2050, rather than offering something new, simply deferred these promises another 30 years. The tension that is produced here is that many folks are still hopeful for the opportunities and promises afforded by 'development' and 'progress', especially in relation to younger (or future) generations.

A particular conversation with older farmers in Muhura, Gatsibo (2020, personal communication, 27 February) illustrated this tension by pointing to the ways in which gatherings have changed. One of the participants addressing the research team, said 'Let me give you an example; you came here early; since you got to this place, did you see anyone with a drink in their hand?!' His friend chimed in, 'Or seen anyone [idly talking like] this?! Nope!' The first man, laughing and with a wink, said to the group, 'He will tell me if he saw anyone'. As everyone laughed a third man interjected, 'At this time in the past, you would have found us drinking sorghum beer –' to which the most excited of the bunch exclaimed, 'Right now, this ceremony would be epic!'. The conversation continued:

TUYISENGE CHARLES: Let me tell you the celebrations that are there nowadays. Our children study. After studying, they bring us good things of the development. For example, they brought us these coffee factories. It is no longer foreigners who come and work in those factories.

UWAMAHORO CLEMENT: To invest in them …

TUYISENGE CHARLES: Our children are working in those factories; those investors hire them. You no longer find that those people from Tanzania or Uganda are the ones who come to work in those factories. Our children studied, and those factories gave them work. Which is good.

Considering the urgency of plans like Vision 2020 and 2050, there is no room in 'modernising' Rwanda for those with 'ignorant' or 'backwards' mindsets who cling to past ways. Even people's personal ambitions must change to align with those of a middle-income future, no matter how far-flung they might seem. This is in stark contrast to the past, as one older farmer in Muhura, Gatsibo (2020, personal communication, 17 February) explained:

> I think things change with time and again think it is because of development. In the past, there was love and freedom but today life is more planned. However, today people know how to write and to read, to speak foreign languages like English and French; those are the only better things for today. And you have your own vision, which is different from what people in the past had.

As Tania Li (2017: 18) has noted, high-modernist schemes are inherently idealistic projects: 'Being "irreducibly utopian", governmental interventions can never achieve all they seek'. Things escape, reality overflows. Top-down development interventions like LUC, that seek homogenous transformations create difference even as they claim not to see, or want, difference. These schemes draw boundaries that put some things *in place* while designating others *out of place* – land, ideas, behaviour, people. Like the racialised modernities perpetuated through colonialism (Quijano 2007), Rwanda's development *others* and excludes. As Stuart Hall (1996: 55–57) expressed, 'This is not an external function, operative only against those whom it disposes or disarticulates (renders silent). It is also pertinent for the dominated subjects … who come to experience themselves as "the inferiors"'. One woman in Muhura, Gatsibo (2020, personal communication, 18 February) expressed this as a combination of personal marginalisation and reverie for her children:

> In the past, parents kept their children from schools; today we have parents who never got in school even for once, because of our parent's mindsets. They told us to go look after goats and cows instead of going to school until we end up not going to school at all. Today… we send our children to school telling them to go that they may not live as we are. That is the difference.

People who *want* money and opportunity can also mourn the things that 'have' to be sacrificed. This is especially the case if one's aspirations are placed in the future of children, not yet fully realised in the present for oneself. This, to me, seems to be partially about agency. Many people express both a desire for the unseen promises of modernity *and* 'an aspiration to overcome categorical subordination' (Ferguson 2006: 20) that will allow for more agency to shape that desired future. As Ferguson (2006) argues, people's desire to be included, on their own terms, in the increasingly visible prosperity of globalised modernisation should be taken seriously in large part because of the historical inequality that has accompanied 'development':

> 'Globalisation'... has brought an increasingly acute awareness of the semiotic and material goods of the global rich, even as economic pauperization and the loss of faith in the promises of development have made the chances of actually attaining such goods seem more remote than ever.
>
> (Ferguson 2006: 21)

What I believe Ferguson misses here is that, at least for people in Gatsibo, faith in the promises of 'development' has not so much been lost as transferred to younger generations. As the present seems increasingly alien to older generations it becomes similarly difficult to imagine what the future will be like, requiring an almost fantastical leap of imagination that remains alive with hope for the possibility of a prosperous life for younger generations. Reverie becomes relevant again here as a claim-making. Perhaps, by reinvesting hope in the deferred promises of 'development' to future generations, farmers are reinforcing their claims to recompense for all they have lost. Reverie, then, is a political act; an attempt to make the future *thus,* even if the present cannot be. Reverie has 'the potential to shape what citizens expect and how they engage (or disengage) the state' (Gallagher et al. 2024: 5).

This loss of agency over both the past and present generates nostalgia as a critical practice while inspiring dreams of the future, expressed through reverie. The GoR's high-modernist policies and promises of prosperity generate 'ongoing claim-making' (Gallagher et al. 2024), while their dismissal of nostalgic reluctance and disengagement with the social reproductive needs of communities might only push farmers further into reverie. This interplay is 'neither positive nor negative but ambivalent, as partial state responsiveness, combined with the crucial nature of claimants' needs, propel ongoing engagement even when the rewards of such action are sporadic' (Gallagher et al. 2024: 5).

An elegiac life

When explaining the difference between the past and the present, many people expressed ambivalence regarding the shifting aspirations of 'development'. As one woman (2020, personal communication, 19 February) explained:

> You see the way people from the past were seeking development, is not the same as today. Today the need for development has increased. A farmer from the past would grow crops so as to fill the granaries and store a lot ... He wouldn't think, 'Let me use these crops to maybe build a nice house, let me see if I can get out of this hut, let me take my child to school'. Cultivating in the past didn't have a goal.

Even as people embrace the goals of money and material opportunity, they come at a cost. These ambivalent narratives emerged in nearly every conversation we had with agrarian communities, especially among the older farmers. I came to understand this 'polysemic enthusiasm for development' (Klenk 2004: 57) as produced in an affective space where nostalgia and reverie are closely entangled. It was true that 'development' had brought closer the possibility of accessing 'formal' education and material goods previously unavailable, and, in some cases, more money. Many people in Eastern Rwanda are, in fact, happy to have money to improve their houses, send their children to school and buy new agricultural inputs. Yet, there also seemed to never be *quite* enough money for everything – the high cost of inputs and labour, along with low market prices for crops, were ubiquitous points of conversation, even in informal settings.

The overriding sentiment regarding the past, and the tensions that remembering evoked, embodied a common story of rural communities everywhere encountering modernity, as expressed by Wendell Berry (2017:107):

> They were poor, as country people have often been, but they had each other, they had their local economy in which they helped each other, they had each other's comfort when they needed it, and they had their stories, their history together in that place. To have everything but money is to have much.

As one Rwandan scholar (2020, personal communication, 18 March) observed, when talking about development in the country, most observers 'only talk about the things Rwanda has gained and not what we have lost'. To that I can add, '*nor do we talk enough about how people feel about these changes.*' This is a problem in much of the critical development literature, where even if there is a focus on 'resistance', damage done to livelihoods, ecosystems and local knowledges, or the loss of agency, rarely does analysis treat as anything but peripheral 'the lives, hopes, and fears of the subaltern' (Gupta 1998: 25). Rather than analysing development in a flatly critical way – and, in the process, tacitly appropriating the same homogenising work they are critical of – people in Gatsibo 'constructed development as a contested process, rendered meaningful through their own situated constraints, experiences, and hopes' (Klenk 2004: 76). The focus on material gain – yields, market access, machines – as the predominant concern of mainstream 'development', and the opposing impulse for critics of 'development' to *disprove* development's ability to adequately provide these things, is itself a legacy of racialised colonialism. 'One of the great tools of colonisation has been pushing the assumption that poor people (especially black people) have neither the inclination nor the time to be concerned about the substantive quality of their lives' (hooks 2019: 213). Perhaps we have misplaced the critique: what many people in the Global South are actually expressing through nostalgic practices or reverie as claim-making is a discontent with uneven modernity in general, not any particular mode of development.

The sense of nostalgia described by people in Gatsibo who, at the same time, dreamed of (or claimed) a better life cannot be disconnected from the process by which ever-increasing spheres of life are abstracted into a capitalist logic, captured by 'the engine of modern civilization… money, which aggressively unhinges itself and sweeps up everything from other social formations', (Saldanha 2017: 72). While 'modernity', and money can meet many desires – a child's education, a new roof, a motorcycle, food, etcetera, other desires – love, community, reciprocity, respect – are not wholly reproduced in *place*. In that tension is twined nostalgia and reverie, an 'elegiac life' (Whyte 2016).

Understanding this could shift the focus of critical development research and the focus of those in power who truly want to understand development to help deliver the promises that people truly do want made good. People, after all, *do* make claims. They *do* want their local leaders and economies and governments to do right by them, to deliver (or at least make possible) prosperity and security. We can't write those people off. If we learned to care as much about making space for parties as we do about creating jobs; as much about ensuring people have enough leisure time as we do about ensuring they have enough money; as much about social reproduction as we do about material production; and if education could focus as much on learning histories and skills that reproduce place as on learning skills that produce wealth, then nostalgia and reverie will have done their work well.

Notes

1 Translator's note: 'They mean real singing is achieving family goals today, like paying school fees and getting food. But that other kinds of happiness before achieving family needs wasn't true happiness. To sing or praise things without being able to meet family needs, like in the old days, wasn't true happiness'.
2 Translator's note: 'In above statement the farmer is trying to explain how these days there is almost no working together in fields for free/helping each, it is more personal than community working together in fields as it used to be'.
3 Translator's note: 'A farmer is trying to explain how without money to hire people to help her in her field, she may end up harvesting late compared to someone with money, hence farming today needs someone to have money to invest in it so as to get output/harvest on time compared to the past where people would help just because you have made local beer for them'.

References

Agawu, V. K. (2003). *Representing African music: postcolonial notes, queries, positions.* New York: Routledge.

Ansoms, A., Cioffo, G., Dawson, N., Desiere, S., Huggins, C., Leegwater, M., Murison, J., Nyenyezi Bisoka, A., Treidl, J. and Van Damme, J. (2018). 'The Rwandan agrarian and land sector modernisation: confronting macro performance with lived experiences on the ground', *Review of African Political Economy*, 45 (157), pp. 408–431.

Ansoms, A. and Cioffo, G. (2016). 'The exemplary citizen on the exemplary hill: the production of political subjects in contemporary rural Rwanda', *Development and Change*, 47.

Ansoms, A. and Rostagno, D. (2012). 'Rwanda's Vision 2020 halfway through: what the eye does not see', *Review of African Political Economy*, 39 (133), pp. 427–450. Available at: https://doi.org/10.1080/03056244.2012.710836.

Berry, W. (2017). *The World-Ending Fire: The Essential Wendell Berry.* Counterpoint.

Bonnett, A. (2010). *Left in the Past: Radicalism and the Politics of Nostalgia.* Bloomsbury Publishing USA.

de Certeau, M. (1988). *The Practice of Everyday Life.* University of California Press.

Desrosiers, M.E. and Thomson, S. (2011). 'Rhetorical legacies of leadership: projections of 'benevolent leadership' in pre- and post-genocide Rwanda', *The Journal of Modern African Studies*, 49 (3), pp. 429–453. Available at: https://doi.org/10.1017/S0022278X11000279.

Ezeanya-Esiobu, C. (2019). 'The role of rural women in making home brew: a Rwandan case study', *The Conversation*, 05 May. Available at: URL https://theconversation.com/the-role-of-rural-women-in-making-home-brew-a-rwandan-case-study-76805 (Accessed 01 June 2022).

Ferguson, J. (2006). *Global Shadows: Africa in the Neoliberal World Order.* Durham and London: Duke University Press.

Freedom House. (2024). *Freedom in the World 2024: Rwanda.* Available at: URL: https://freedomhouse.org/country/rwanda/freedom-world/2024 (Accessed 29 February 2024).

Gallagher, J. K., Kruks-Wisner, G. and Taylor, W.K. (2024). *Claim-making in comparative perspective: everyday citizenship practice and its consequences.* Cambridge University Press.

Gupta, A. (1998). *Postcolonial developments: agriculture in the making of modern India.* Duke University Press.

Hakcrimana, F. and Akcaoz, H. (2018). 'The Functional Analysis of Maize Production and the Effect of Land Consolidation on the Productivity in Rwanda', *The Journal of Animal & Plant Sciences*, 28 (1), pp. 280–289.

Hall, S. (1996). 'Race, Articulation, and Societies Structured in Dominance'. In *Black British Cultural Studies: A Reader*, edited by BakerJr., H. A., Diawara, M. and Lindeberg, R. H. The University of Chicago Press, pp. 16–60.

Haraway, D. J. (1991). *Simians, Cyborgs, and Women: The Reinvention of Nature.* New York: Routledge.

hooks, bell. (2019). *Belonging: a culture of place.* Routledge.

Hunt, N. R. (2015). *A Nervous State: Violence, Remedies, and Reverie in Colonial Congo.* Durham and London: Duke University Press.

Kagabo, L. (2005). 'Alexis Kagame (1912–1981): Life and Thought'. In *A Companion to African Philosophy*, edited by Wiredu, K.Oxford, UK: Blackwell Publishing Ltd, pp. 231–242. Available at: https://doi.org/10.1002/9780470997154.ch17.

Kitson, J. and McHugh, K. (2015). 'Historic enchantments – materializing nostalgia', *cultural geographies*, 22 (3), pp. 487–508. Available at: https://doi.org/10.1177/1474474014549946.

Klenk, R. M. (2004). '"Who is the developed woman?": women as a category of development discourse, Kumaon, India', *Development and Change*, 35(1), pp. 57–78. Available at: https://doi.org/10.1111/j.1467-7660.2004.00342.x.

Li, T. M. (2017). 'Rendering land investible: five notes on time', *GEOFORUM*, 82, pp. 276–278. Available at: https://doi.org/10.1016/j.geoforum.2017.04.004.

Mann, L. and Berry, M. (2016). 'Understanding the Political Motivations That Shape Rwanda's Emergent Developmental State', *New Political Economy*, 21 (1), pp. 119–144.

Mbembe, A. (2001). *On the Postcolony.* Univ of California Press.

MINAGRI. (2019). *Ministry of Agriculture and Animal Resources Annual Report 2018–2019*. Republic of Rwanda, Kigali.

Ministry of Finance and Economic Planning. (2000). *Rwanda Vision 2020*. Republic of Rwanda, Kigali.

Moiloa, M. (2012). 'Youth in Khutsong, South Africa: nostalgia for a different political present', *Peace and Conflict: Journal of Peace Psychology*, 18 (3), pp. 329–340. Available at: https://doi.org/10.1037/a0029074.

Mudimbe, V. Y. (1988). *The invention of Africa: gnosis, philosophy, and the order of knowledge, African systems of thought*. Bloomington: Indiana University Press.

Newbury, D. (1994). 'Trick Cyclists? Recontextualizing Rwandan Dynastic Chronology', *History in Africa*, 21, pp. 191–217. Available at: https://doi.org/10.2307/3171886.

NISR. (2020). *Seasonal Agricultural Survey*. Republic of Rwanda, Kigali.

Nyenyezi Bisoka, A. and Ansoms, A. (2020). 'State and local authorities in land grabbing in Rwanda: governmentality and capitalist accumulation', *Canadian Journal of Development Studies / Revue canadienne d'études du développement*, 41 (2), pp. 243–259. Available at: https://doi.org/10.1080/02255189.2019.1629884.

Nzabatsinda, A. and Mitsch, R. H. (1997). 'The Aesthetics of Transcribing Orality in the Works of Alexis Kagame, Writer of Rwanda', *Research in African Literatures*, 28, pp. 98–111.

Ogden, L. A. (2011). *Swamplife: People, Gators, and Mangroves Entangled in the Everglades*. University of Minnesota Press.

Omojola, B. (2009). 'Politics, Identity, and Nostalgia in Nigerian Music: A Study of Victor Olaiya's Highlife', *Ethnomusicology*, 53, pp. 249–276. Available at: https://doi.org/10.4324/9781315090986-16.

Purdeková, A. (2011). '"Even if I am not here, there are so many eyes" surveillance and state reach in Rwanda', *The Journal of Modern African Studies*, 49(3), pp. 475–497.

Quijano, A. (2007). 'Coloniality and Modernity/Rationality', *Cultural Studies*, 21(2–3), pp. 168–178. Available at: https://doi.org/10.1080/09502380601164353.

Rahnema, M. (2019). 'Poverty'. In *The Development Dictionary: A Guide to Knowledge as Power*, edited by Sachs, W. Zed Books, pp. 174–194.

Republic of Rwanda. (2010). Ministerial Order No 14/11.30 of 21/12/2010 Determining the Models of Land Consolidation and its Productivity, Official Gazette No 52 of 27/12/2010. Republic of Rwanda.

Republic of Rwanda. (2020). *Vision 2050*. Republic of Rwanda, Kigali.

Saldanha, A. (2017). *Space after Deleuze*. Bloomsbury Academic.

Secor, A. J. (2007). 'Between longing and despair: state, space, and subjectivity in Turkey', *Environment and Planning D: Society and Space*, 25 (1), pp. 33–52. Available at: https://doi.org/10.1068/d0605.

Times Reporter. (2008). 'Local leaders enforce ban on traditional walking sticks', *The New Times*, 12 October. Available at: URL: https://www.newtimes.co.rw/section/read/45058 (Accessed 01 June 2022).

Uwizeyimana, D. E. (2019). 'Progress made towards achieving Rwanda's Vision 2020 key indicators' targets', *International Journal of Management Practice*, 12 (1), pp. 4–46.

Vansina, J. (2000). 'Historical Tales (*Ibitéekerezo*) and the History of Rwanda', *History in Africa*, 27, pp. 375–414.

Vansina, J. (2004). *Antecedents to Modern Rwanda: The Nyiginya Kingdom*. The University of Wisconsin Press.

Whyte, D. (2016). David Whyte: Seeking Language Large Enough [Podcast]. On Being with Krista Tippett. Available at: URL: https://onbeing.org/programs/david-whyte-seeking-language-large-enough/ (Accessed 29 February 2024).

5 CAMPFIRE and the politics of ambivalence

Attitudes towards development in Kanyemba, Zimbabwe

Neil Maheve

Introduction

As I stood with Kanyemba residents waiting for the meat from a slaughtered 'problem animal' to be shared, we were conversing about different things, from soccer to politics. 'Problem animal' is a phrase that is used to refer to an animal that is wreaking havoc in the area, either destroying gardens or attacking people. When such animals are killed, the meat is distributed to community members. One elderly man said he anticipated getting this morsel of meat which was barely enough for his family. Another one complained that the value of the meat did not cover even a fraction of the losses incurred through the animals' misdeeds. I asked them if they wanted the CAMPFIRE programme through which they had received the meat, to continue, and they said no. Then, after some time, they said they did, however, want the houses, clinics and projects promised to them as part of CAMPFIRE. This expression of ambivalence towards development makes up the crux of this chapter. The chapter is set in the Mbire district in Zimbabwe, in a small ward called Kanyemba, where two ethnically distinct groups of people reside. The residents of Kanyemba are recipients of development in the form of CAMPFIRE, a conservation-for-development programme. As this chapter will show, the community displays complicated and ambivalent attitudes towards this development initiative.

Post-development theory rejects development as a Westernised discourse, a culturally imperialistic and unrealistic concept (Ziai 2017; Sachs 2010). What the post-development school of thought dismisses is not only the discourse but also the practices of development. However, it is not an easy task to define development. As Sachs (2010: x) puts it, '...development can mean just about everything, from putting up skyscrapers to putting in latrines, from drilling for oil to drilling for water, from setting up software industries to setting up tree nurseries'. Similarly, Esteva (2023: 26) asserts that 'development today is an amoeba-word that is applied indiscriminately to anything'. Development is an ambiguous and far-from-clear concept (Ziai 2017). It is a complex concept with different meanings and implications for people and contexts. In this chapter, the diverse and context-specific definitions and descriptions of development provided by the Kanyemba residents, based on their knowledge, values and aspirations, are

DOI: 10.4324/9781003477921-6

presented. I contextualise development in relation to the Communal Areas Management Programme For Indigenous Resources (CAMPFIRE), a programme introduced in rural Zimbabwe in the late 1980s. The programme sought to empower local communities by giving them control over resources. The CAMPFIRE initiative was introduced in the 1980s to promote wildlife conservation and rural development by giving local communities the right to manage and benefit from wildlife resources. The people's responses to CAMPFIRE and the alternatives to it they propose demonstrate their ambivalence to development.

Kanyemba

Kanyemba is a 300-square-kilometre area in the mid-Zambezi Valley (Jani et al. 2023; Jani 2022; Bola et al. 2014; Hasler 1991). Kanyemba is in Mbire District, Mashonaland central province. As of 2023, Zimbabwe had ten provinces with 67 districts. Mbire district has 17 wards and Kanyemba is Ward 1. The population of Kanyemba now stands at 3773 (Zimstats 2022). Kanyemba is divided into five Villages Development Committees (VIDCOs hereafter). The villages are Chiruhwe, Chansato, Nyaruparo, Chiramba and Mariga. These five VIDCOs are made up of 40 villages (2022 census). Kanyemba is a border community with Mozambique to the East and Zambia to the North, along the Zambezi River. Kanyemba falls in Zimbabwe's Agroecology Region Five, characterised by high temperatures and low erratic rainfall patterns. The high temperatures, the low erratic rainfall patterns and the vegetation make the region best suited for animal ranching, both for domestic and wild animals. Kanyemba is situated between two animal safaris: the Chewore Safaris Areas to the west of Kanyemba and the Dande Safari Area on the south-eastern side of Kanyemba. In addition to the game reserves, part of Kanyemba now falls within the Chitsere Conservancy, established in 2017. The latter is a non-hunting conservancy that aims to replenish the low wildlife population.

The ethnic composition of Kanyemba

The Kanyemba community consists of two main groups: the Tembo Mvura and the Chikunda. The history of these groups is intertwined, and there is a dispute about their origins and autochthony, although both are known to have migrated from present-day Mozambique. Oral histories highlight a long-standing rivalry from the Portuguese plantation era in Mozambique when the Chikunda armies raided weaker and fragmented groups (Isaacman 1972; 2000; Marizane 2016). The Tembo Mvura was one of the affected groups and the raids by the Chikunda led to the tension between the groups, with this tension continuing today. These two groups' settlements are divided by the Mwanzamtanda River. The Tembo Mvura predominantly inhabit the western side, and the Chikunda inhabit the eastern side. This river physically separates the two groups and symbolises the contrasting perspectives and attitudes towards development, thereby revealing a significant impact on the progress achieved in the area.

The Tembo Mvura, also known as the Doma/Dema people, claim they originally came from Tete province in present-day Mozambique. Tembo Mvura's oral accounts assert that their arrival pre-dated the Chikunda. Narratives depict various migration patterns leading to their ultimate settlement in the Kanyemba area, which the dominant Chikunda later occupied. Oral traditions offer the Songo Mountains, in present-day Mozambique, as a place of 'origin' of the Tembo Mvura (Claudio 2005). In an interview, the elder Prugia[1] highlighted that the people migrated from Tete, Mozambique, under the guidance of a diviner known as Chiyambo. Oral traditions estimate that the people settled in Kanyemba between 1850 and 1870. The people crossed Zimbabwe using a narrow stretch along the Zambezi River known as *Kavharamanja* (Gate). After crossing into Zimbabwe, the group settled in the mountains and moved between Karuwaya, Katsuuku Karemwa, and the Chirambakudomwa mountains in the present-day Chitsere Conservancy and Chewore game reserve in search of honey and tubers. Marindo and Zaba (1995) emphasise that people preferred Karemwa Mountain because of its proximity to Tunsa Hotsprings, which had abundant fish that the people could catch and dry for the rainy season (Hasler 1999). Present-day Tembo Mvura stay on the western side of the Mwanzamtanda River in the Mariga, Chiramba and Chagurika villages.

The most populous group found in Kanyemba are the Chikunda people. The name Chikunda loosely translates to 'conquering', and it refers to a group of warriors that worked for Mozambican-Portuguese plantation owners (*Prazeiros*) in the 18th and 19th centuries (Isaacman 1972; 2000; Marizane 2016). The *prazo* system was a land tenure that granted large estates to Portuguese settlers who employed African labourers and soldiers. The system contained a rigid social hierarchy of leaders (Portuguese), enslaved soldiers (from whom the Chikunda are descended) and labourers (Claudio 2005). One of the most prominent Chikunda leaders was José Rosario de Andrade, popularly known by his African name Kanyemba. According to Selous (1970 [1881]), who met him in 1874, Kanyemba held an official position under the Portuguese governor of Tete, a town in Mozambique. The position referred to by Selous was that of a *capitao* (captain) at Zumbo, a town in present-day Zambia (Isaacman 2000). In the late nineteenth century, Portuguese and British pressure to acquire and control colonies increased and threatened the power of many living in the region. After several insurrections from his lieutenants and pressure from colonial concessioners, Kanyemba led his people to settle in the area between the Mwanzamtanda and Zambezi Rivers and named their settlement after himself. The Chikunda, who came to Zimbabwe with Kanyemba, have maintained relationships with those in Zambia and Mozambique. The Chikunda are settled in the Chansato, Chiruwe and Chapoto villages on the eastern side of the Mwanzamtanda River.

CAMPFIRE

This chapter is interested in people's ambivalent attitudes towards CAMPFIRE, and for this reason, I briefly explore the programme's origins to set the context.

In 1989, the Zimbabwean government launched the Communal Areas Management Programme For Indigenous Resources (CAMPFIRE) in response to the failure of a project called Wildlife Industries New Development For All (WINDFALL hereafter). In 1975, the Southern Rhodesian government[2] introduced the Parks and Wildlife Act. The Act transferred the authority over animals on private lands from the state to private owners (Peterson 1991). Whilst this Act empowered White private landowners, it disenfranchised the Black landholders. The people in the communal (rural) areas could not benefit from the animals in the vicinity. To rectify this, the colonial government introduced the WINDFALL project in 1978 (Matzke and Nabane 1996). Murindagomo (1990) argues that this project was an attempt to include the local communities and make them benefit from the wildlife. The WINDFALL project necessitated the provision of meat and money from culled and trophy-hunted elephants to the local communities living in the buffer zone (Derman 1996). The programme did not succeed due to various reasons, chief of which, was that there was insufficient local participation and decision-making was not localised (Murindagomo 1990; Dalal-Clayton and Child 2003; Shereni and Saarinen 2021). In response to the failure of WINDFALL, in 1982 the government of Zimbabwe amended the 1975 Act, among others, to pave the way for new programmes. The Department of National Parks and Wildlife Management (DNPWLM), in collaboration with different Non-Governmental Organisations (NGOs), academics and ecologists, came up with the idea of CAMPFIRE (Murphree 2004; Child 1993; Mashinya 2007; Balint and Mashinya 2008). The replacement of WINDFALL can be understood as part of the post-independence Zimbabwean government's decolonisation process.

Murindagomo (1990) posits that the introduction of CAMPFIRE was based on a combination of three principles: sustainable development, community empowerment and conservation. CAMPFIRE aimed to empower rural communities in Zimbabwe to manage their resources by devolving authority to the local people (Child 1993). CAMPFIRE is managed through the Rural District Councils (RDCs), which negotiate the lease agreements with safari operators and distribute the revenue to the wards (Child 1993; Murombedzi 1992; 1999; Murphree 1998). On paper, CAMPFIRE accorded communities rights over the resources (animals, trees, groves, caves and water sources) in their area (Murombedzi 2001; Balint 2009). CAMPFIRE is one of the first programmes that considered wildlife as a renewable natural resource, while addressing the allocation of its ownership to local people in and around conservation-protected areas primarily arid and unsuitable for agriculture (Balint and Mashinya 2008; Gandiwa et al. 2013). Conceptually, CAMPFIRE includes all resources, but its focus is wildlife (Taylor 2003). Until recently the assumption was that CAMPFIRE is concerned with animals, but of late there has been interest in maintaining tree species that are becoming extinct. The programme was meant to allow rural communities to earn an income from tourism contracts (lease agreements with safari operators), wildlife safari hunting and the sale of animal products (Neumann 1995). CAMPFIRE was touted as a key to poverty reduction and a buffer against drought-induced hardships that mainly affected the areas where it was implemented (Logan and Mosley 2002). In exchange for protecting animals and not hunting them, local people were supposed to gain benefits from the revenue earned through tourists coming and paying to see or to hunt animals.

It could be said that CAMPFIRE rose as a response to the failure of a mainstream conservation and development programme, WINDFALL. For this reason, CAMPFIRE can be understood as being influenced by alternative development thinking. Nederveen Pieterse (1998; 2010) argues that alternative development was concerned with redefining the goals of development through participatory and people-centred practices. It is against this that this chapter contextualises CAMPFIRE as a development initiative born out of alternative development theory. As Murindagomo (1990) highlighted, the programme was envisioned to promote sustainable development in areas near animal sanctuaries, benefiting local communities for their role in protecting natural resources. I use the term 'development', acknowledging that CAMPFIRE was widely perceived as a development project capable of fundamentally transforming people's lives. Framing the programme within the development context enables me to engage with ambivalent attitudes within the broader development discourse.

Post-development theory

This edited book is influenced by post-development thinking, and likewise, this chapter critically examines the development of Kanyemba from that perspective. Post-development theory emerged in the 1980s as a response to the failures and negative impacts of mainstream development policies and practices (Esteva 1985; Escobar 1992). Post-development thinking dismisses development for being a vehicle of cultural imperialism, which is environmentally destructive and denigrates non-Western ways of being.

Post-development thinking is varied, with Ziai (2004) differentiating between two approaches: neo-populist post-development and sceptical post-development thinking. Neo-populist post-development idealises traditional cultures, depicting them as unchanging and resistant to modernisation. This discourse romanticises the notion of a static cultural identity while simultaneously rejecting the principles of modernity. It advocates for a return to subsistence agriculture to reclaim a perceived authenticity that is believed to be lost in the development process (Ziai 2004: 1053). Ziai (2004) identifies Rahnema and Bawtree (1997) and Alvares (1992) as the proponents of this perspective. The sceptical post-development perspective takes a more critical view of local communities and cultural traditions. This viewpoint carefully scrutinises the implications of modernity, embracing a constructivist understanding of culture (Ziai 2004: 1054). It scrutinises modernity, adopts a constructivist view of culture, and refrains from prescribing specific models for societal transformations in the future. Ziai (2004) associates this form of post-development with scholars such as Escobar (1995), Esteva and Prakash (1998), and Apffel-Marglin (1996) and argues that this variant of post-development thinking fits with the notion of radical democracy as laid out by Lummis (1996) and Laclau and Mouffe (2001).

This chapter resonates more with the sceptical post-development variant because the ambivalent attitudes to development expressed by those in Kanyemba can best be understood using that variant. The chapter joins Matthews (2017) in highlighting how aspects of development are viewed as desirable and by exploring its contested nature and challenging its assumed benefits. Andreasson's (2017) work on post-development in Africa provides valuable insights into the African context and supports the critical examination of development in Kanyemba. By acknowledging and valuing diverse perspectives, this chapter contributes to a more comprehensive understanding of development in Kanyemba and elsewhere.

Methodology

'What is development? Has development changed your life? Would you like the development initiative to continue?' These are the questions that I asked as part of this study. This chapter is a product of an ethnographic study for my PhD, which sought to understand local people's attitudes towards CAMPFIRE. Clifford and Marcus (1986) argued that ethnography pays attention to human groups, institutions or cultural settings. Ethnography focuses on how people interact and collaborate in everyday life in a natural setting (Gill and Johnson 2002). Ethnography involves immersing oneself in a community to observe, document and interpret its members' cultural norms, practices and beliefs, and to explore how the local people perceive and respond to these issues (Njie and Asimiran 2014).

Positionality is a critical concept in qualitative research that examines how researchers and participants construct and relate to each other in the field. One aspect of positionality is the insider-outsider distinction, which reflects how participants perceive the researcher's identity and cultural proximity to them (Sultana 2007). On one hand, we have insider research which is when researchers study their social group based on shared characteristics (Liu and Burnett 2022). Insider researchers have direct experience and deep familiarity with the phenomena they study (Heath et al. 2009). On the other hand, outsider research can have benefits, such as bringing neutrality and a new outlook to research and observations, as outsiders may be less affected by prior beliefs or interests (Brannick and Coghlan 2007). This neutrality allows them to approach the subject matter with openness and interest, without the biases and assumptions that insiders may have. Outsiders tend to conduct a more thorough and detailed investigation of a research topic as they do not know much about the participants' world (Al-Makhamreh and Lewando-Hundt 2008). In Kanyemba my positionality oscillates between an insider with some limitations and an outsider, depending on the side of the river I stayed on. I am neither a member of the Tembo Mvura or Chikunda community. However, despite not being a member of the Tembo Mvura, on the western side of the Mwanzamtanda River, I am considered as a quasi-insider because I have spent much time there over several years doing academic and non-academic work with the community, thus some consider me as an extended community member. The Chikunda consider me an outsider, and this was necessitated by my choice of accommodation during my 2017 stay during my Master's research. At that time, I was hosted by a member of the Zimbabwe Republic Police who was a friend, and this made people associate me with the security sector and which made them wary of me. However, during my 2022 research the people gradually warmed up to me and they were willing to share some information. My positionality in Kanyemba can be construed as both insider and outsider and this proved to be an important aspect. The cons associated with being an insider were countered by being an outsider and vice versa. This chapter is a product of my PhD research and I stayed with the people for six months, a period in which I conducted interviews and observed people's everyday interactions with each other and with the CAMPFIRE development programme in order to get a better understanding of their attitudes towards development.

This chapter relies upon semi-structured interviews with the residents of Kanyemba villages to gather detailed information about individuals' attitudes, beliefs, and experiences with CAMPFIRE. Magaldi and Berler (2020) described semi-structured interviews as exploratory interviews used in qualitative research. The participants were identified using snowball and purposive sampling methods. Snowball sampling involves the researcher asking initial respondents to refer them to other knowledgeable individuals (Naderifar et al. 2017). This method was advantageous within the Tembo Mvura community, known for its wariness of outsiders. A referral made it easier to secure an interview. Polit and Beck (2010) highlight that snowball sampling simplifies accessing respondents from private communities where key members may be hard to reach. Purposive sampling was also employed, specifically within the Chikunda community. Robinson (2014) avers that purposive sampling enables the researcher to use their knowledge and judgment to select individuals who are expected to provide the most valuable information, thereby contributing to the achievement of the study's goals. I interviewed residents from various age groups, genders, and professions. To protect their privacy, all participants' names have been altered.

Development: Kanyemba definitions

Since the mid-20th century, the concept of development has consistently carried the connotation of escaping from the undignified state referred to as under-development (Esteva 2023: 10). Development has been defined and described in many ways and has no universal definitions or descriptions. Nevertheless, the term is usually associated with economic growth, improvements in infrastructure and the introduction of 'modern' technologies. Schoneberg et al. (2022) point out that the term development is notoriously ambiguous, able to morph into anything depending on who defines it. In this chapter, I concur with Esteva's (2023) characterisation of development as an amoeba word, as I present a varied understanding of development from a local perspective. Shona is the widely used language in Kanyemba, and the language cuts across the social divide. Development, when translated into Shona, means two closely related but broad interpretations. *budiriro* and *vandudzo*. *Budiriro*, when loosely translated, refers to progress. To provide the reader with clarity, the term *budiriro* can be used thus: '*Budiriro inoreva kudya chikafu chakanaka chine hutano*' ('Development means having enough quality and healthy food'). The term development has also been used to mean *vandudzo*, which can be loosely translated to mean improvement. Used in a statement '*Vandudzo inoreva kugara mudzimba dzakanaka dzine marata, inoitawo mwenje*' ('Development means having a house with an iron sheet roof where you can have lights inside'). While I am cognisant of the differences between the English translations of the two Shona words referring to development, in this chapter, I use the two development translations interchangeably because the narratives used are translated from the vernacular and people would use both *budiriro* and *vandudzo* in such narratives.

My study explored how Kanyemba residents understand development. Simon,[3] a Tembo Mvura man, defined development as 'the ability to put food on the table and have three meals a day without worrying about the future'. His definition reflects one of the core objectives of many development interventions in the Global South: eradication of poverty. Interviews with Mavhuto[4], and Maidei[5] substantiated the view that food provision is a key development indicator. In a closely related definition of development, Maidei defined development as having enough food with meat as a relish. Jivasi[6], a Tembo Mvura man, defined development as:

> ... having fresh and dried meat in his wife's kitchen. Development means not eating these greens you see our wives preparing for us. The animals roam around, yet we do not have relish in our pots. Development means having meat like we used to do when CAMPFIRE was introduced.

This description of development as the ability to have food stems from the way in which CAMPFIRE was introduced. People were promised money that would help them acquire food in exchange for giving up hunting for their own meat. Jivas referred to the abundance of meat in the early years of the CAMPFIRE programme. There was a drought in 1992, and animals were culled. The people received much meat and dried most of it, lasting through 1993. The dried meat was supplemented by the fresh meat, which was still being disbursed by then. This availability of meat is strongly associated with development for Kanyemba residents.

Access to clean and safe drinking water is also important in the description of development. Mavhuto described development as having easily accessible boreholes with clean, drinkable water. His description is prevalent among Chagurika, Chansato, Mariga and Chiramba villagers. These villages have little to no access to clean drinking water. Matinetsa[7], viewing development as *vandudzo* (improvement), shared what development means.

> Having boreholes close to our settlements and not forcing us to walk three kilometres to access the closest borehole. Most of the time, we drink the water from the *mufuku* (riverbed) because walking to the borehole in the sun and on an empty stomach is not easy. Development should mean fetching water closer to your home. We have dangerous animals here.

Most residents of the villages on the western side of the Mwanzamtanda River continue to rely on traditional water sources such as *mufuku* (holes dug in riverbeds). It is against this that their definitions of development (*budiriro* or *vandudzo*) are closely associated with having boreholes that produce clean and safe drinking water.

Infrastructural innovation has influenced the way in which the Kanyemba residents define development. Tichaona,[8] a member of the Tembo Mvura community, views development as building houses with corrugated iron sheets, cement floors and windowpanes, not the pole and mud homes most Tembo Mvura currently live in. Moses, a middle-aged Tembo Mvura man who was a young boy when CAMPFIRE was introduced, described development as owning 'proper houses'. He said, 'Development means having a house with a cement floor and iron sheet roof where you can have lights inside. Houses that you can enter with a lamp and not be afraid of setting it on fire'. Descriptions of development related to the construction of proper houses are better understood when we factor in the promises made when CAMPFIRE was introduced. Zvanyadza,[9] a Tembo Mvura woman, recalled how development was introduced to them:

> When they [conservationists, ecologists and development experts] came here, they showed us bioscopes showing the effects of burning forests, cutting down trees and killing animals [not conserving the resources]. After that, they showed us films showing different types of food we could eat. They showed us nicely built schools, clinics, and houses. They claimed we could own such houses and eat good food as long as we did not kill the animals, cut down trees or burn the forests. They showed us what development is – staying in a nicely built and proper house, having easy access to schools and clinics.

The present condition of the houses on the western side of the river does not match the expectations of people who benefit from the animals in their vicinity. The Tembo Mvura, mostly, still do not have 'proper' structures. People use the lack of houses as a sign of CAMPFIRE's failure to live up to its promises.

Different contexts and perspectives may influence how development is understood and measured. Some Tembo Mvura and Chikunda members believe that development involves them having control over animals. Daniel[10] posed questions about the development:

While this is neither a description nor a definition of development, it drives home the point that people like Daniel do not believe that development has achieved its stated intentions. The people still await authority over the animals and the power to make decisions. The decision pertaining to the control of the animals exudes a top-down approach.

Human well-being can be understood as an indicator of development. In this regard, having access to medical facilities and medicine can be seen as an indicator of development, as it reflects the level of healthcare provision and the population's quality of life. Tony[11] defined development as:

> … having clinic closer to our homesteads. Walking 18 kilometres to get to a clinic dissuaded many people from visiting the clinic. We ended up using herbs, and most of us were born at home because our mothers could not walk to the nearest clinic. Now we have a clinic closer, and I can say we are developed.

Having a clinic as a form of development, is a sentiment shared by many Tembo Mvura members. This description comes from people who did not have a functional clinic for 27 years after the promise of constructing one was made.

While the Tembo Mvura community members define development as having a functional clinic built in their area, the Chikunda members, who have had a clinic for many years, describe development as having a properly equipped clinic. In an interview, Samuel[12] claimed that:

> Development means having a clinic with all medications, where we are not asked to buy bandages and other necessities for a patient to be helped. Development means having a clinic that can treat people attacked by animals and not have them travel to Zambia. Development means having a clinic that does not only write prescriptions but also dispenses the medicine.

Additionally, Aaron,[13] a Chikunda man, agrees that development is not just about the clinic building. He believes it entails having clinics staffed by competent nurses and stocked with essential medicines. Aaron questions the value of beautifully constructed buildings that ultimately serve as empty shells without the necessary resources to benefit the community. In his view, functional and purposeful infrastructure is the hallmark of genuine development.

The absence of a school on the western side of the river until 2014 (officially opened in 2017) influenced how people defined development. In an interview, Brian[14] argued that development should entail the presence of a school within the community that is inclusive and accommodating, regardless of one's background or possessions. Closely related to this, Taurai[15] described development as the ability to read and write, emphasising the vital role of literacy in personal and societal progression. The Mariga Primary School was built in 2014 in collaboration with the Seventh Day Adventist Church. The school was, however, only officially opened in December 2017. The absence of a school compelled Tembo Mvura children to endure an arduous 18-kilometre journey to Chapoto Primary School. The school-going age among the Tembo Mvura was slightly delayed until one could walk back and forth to school, and many learners dropped out of school because of the distance. Many Tembo Mvura adults lack basic literacy skills, severely limiting their employment prospects and hindering their participation in economic, social and political activities.

Whilst the Tembo Mvura associate development with factors such as being food secure, having access to education, and the ability to build brick houses, the Chikunda have higher aspirations. Their multifaceted view of development reflects the nuanced nature of their understanding. Education emerged as a prominent development aspect in the interviews with the Chikunda community. The Chikunda no longer perceive mere access to education as the sole indicator of development. For instance, Maria, a Chikunda member who has completed tertiary education, expressed that development encompasses equal access to education and the acquisition of new skills that can enhance their overall quality of life. By emphasising the importance of skill acquisition, Maria's viewpoint signifies a broader understanding of development beyond conventional educational attainment.

Development for some Chikunda residents entails achieving self-sustainability in different domains of life. This broad definition encompasses the diverse perspectives expressed by Jackson,[16] who regards the establishment of fisheries and horticulture ventures as development. These income-generating projects reflect the aspirations and agency of individuals who seek to improve their living conditions and social status. Alternatively, Peter,[17] a young Chikunda man, presents a different perspective on development, highlighting the importance of electricity and improved internet connectivity. This perspective transcends basic needs and encompasses desires that may differ depending on one's situation and background. However, for individuals grappling with food insecurity, contemplating access to electricity and reliable mobile reception remains an intangible aspiration beyond their immediate comprehension.

This section highlighted that development is not a monolithic or universal notion but a context-specific and dynamic one that varies across time and space. Contrasting viewpoints emerge among the Tembo Mvura and Chikunda communities, shedding light on the multifaceted nature of development (progress and improvement). These definitions and descriptions of development pave the way to understanding the ambivalence some feel towards development.

Attitudes towards CAMPFIRE

In its early years, CAMPFIRE provided people with dividends locally known as *mari yemakanda* (money from animal hides). This money was disbursed by the Rural District Council to the people every year, and the people used the money to buy groceries. Every elderly member of the Kanyemba community remembers the days when they got the money. The money was not enough to sustain them throughout the year, but the people appreciated it as a token of their effort to protect the animals. The dividends system was later discontinued and replaced with the project system, which prioritised infrastructure development in the area. The Chikunda celebrates the construction of additional buildings at schools and clinics as another positive. The Tembo Mvura, however, view this as a form of marginalisation as they did not have a school or a clinic and yet the animal funds were being used to improve existing structures serving the Chikunda. The effects of the shift from dividends to the projects systems presented an interesting aspect. The effects of the changes proved to be different depending on the people's material conditions and their aspirations. This is closely linked to the notions of development not being universal in meaning.

Despite the positives, many Kanyemba residents have come to reject CAMPFIRE and development more generally. The definitions and descriptions of development serve as the foundation for understanding people's dismissal of CAMPFIRE and development. The Tembo Mvura view development as food security and having three meals daily without worrying about the future. The inability to be food secure has made people feel disillusioned about development. CAMPFIRE had promised to ensure the state of food security for the people, but the way in which this food security was to be achieved was not adequately spelt out. In an interview, Tichaona dismissed CAMPFIRE, saying that:

> CAMPFIRE was supposed to bring us food, not relief we get from donors. We thought the sale of our animals would mean us getting money to buy food, and we would not be hungry. However, we have been more hungry because of CAMPFIRE. If we cannot have enough food on our tables, what is the point of having a development programme in our community?

The sentiments expressed by Tichaona are widely shared within the Tembo Mvura community. The community members were dissuaded by CAMPFIRE from their traditional practices of hunting and gathering, which had been their primary means of sustenance. The people's hunting and gathering cultures were viewed as unstainable. This kind of approach is what post-development thinkers refer to as 'culturicide' (Esteva 2023: 137) or the consequence of development's replacement of existing systems through cultural imperialism (Sachs 2010: 319). Some neo-populist post-development thinkers tend to view Indigenous communities as being in balance with nature and ecologically sustainable. In return for quitting hunting and gathering, the Tembo Mvura were promised a more reliable food supply. The community accepted that they had to adopt this new approach advocated by the ecologists and development experts. However, they still await the food security that the ecologists and development experts promised them. Interviewees made references to the period before CAMPFIRE, indicating that they had a better way of living than the present situation. It is important not to misconstrue this as implying that the community was food secure before the introduction of CAMPFIRE. I am aware of the utopianism and nostalgia that may influence the accounts of the elderly Tembo Mvura: the hunger they are facing today may seem worse than the hunger they experienced in the past, and as a result, they end up portraying a picture of an idyllic past.

The dismissal of development for its failure to ensure food security should be examined from a dual perspective. On the one hand, CAMPFIRE offered the promise of food security through revenue generated from animal hunts and lease agreements. The meat provided by safari operators supplemented the income generated from the programme. This arrangement allowed community members to purchase other food items, relying less on traditional relishes as they were assured a supply of meat from the hunted animals. On the other hand, community members claim that CAMPFIRE has failed to ensure food security by inadequately managing the wildlife population in the area.

Following the prohibition of hunting and gathering, community members turned to subsistence farming as an alternative. Agriculture is practised through two main methods: upper terrace farming (***kuminda***) between November and March and riverbed gardening (***goba/gova***) between March and September, primarily along the Mwanzamtanda River. The Chikunda and Tembo Mvura communities cultivate crops such as maize and sorghum, with a few still cultivating cotton and some exploring sesame seed farming. Both the Tembo Mvura and Chikunda community members express their discontent with CAMPFIRE due to the destruction of their gardens and fields by animals, particularly elephants and buffalos. While the founding principles of CAMPFIRE assert that the animals belong to the community, this claim is disputed by the people, who argue that the CAMPFIRE programme owns the animals. They point out their lack of authority to eliminate or take necessary measures to deter animals from their fields, which undermines their status as owners of these animals. Consequently, the community regards the development initiative (CAMPFIRE) as exacerbating hunger in the region. The animals' encroachment results in decreased agricultural yields, especially in gardens, with no compensation provided to the affected individuals, further fuelling rejection of the development initiative.

The Tembo Mvura community dismiss development for its failure to transition them from being underdeveloped to developed. Their situation brings to mind Nanda Shrestha's (1995: 261) comments: '…So, poor and hungry, I certainly was. But underdeveloped? I never thought – nor did anybody else – that being poor meant being "underdeveloped" and lacking human dignity.' Prior to the introduction of CAMPFIRE, the Tembo Mvura did not perceive themselves as underdeveloped. The state of being underdeveloped has been described and defined in many ways, but it all comes down to being in an unworthy and undesirable condition (Esteva 2023). Prior to CAMPFIRE, the residents of Kanyemba, particularly the Tembo Mvura, did not see their condition as unworthy or underdeveloped. Their housing seemed to them adequate, their food supply sufficient, and their education system satisfactory for survival. However, the introduction of CAMPFIRE highlighted the unhealthy condition of their houses, food, medicines, and education systems, by introducing them to other possibilities. In an interview with the Fosho husband and wife,[18] they said:

> We were born and raised in the mountains you see before you. Our way of life was simple, relying on hunting, gathering, and barter trading. Occasionally, my father and I would embark on hunting trips, setting snares and bringing back the meat to Chiruhwe, a village across the Mwazamtanda

> River, for trading. We never went hungry as we sustained ourselves through hunting, gathering, fishing, and trading, with a constant supply of abundant food. I recall an occasion when our lives took a different turn. The year when our second child was born, a White man accompanied by council members visited us, along with the Chief. They explained the significance of animals, not only for the country but particularly for our community. Through bioscope [film] presentations, they showcased how animals could transform our lives. The films depicted the abundance of food we could afford, the improved houses we could construct, and the clothing we could purchase with the money earned from selling animals.

CAMPFIRE, arguably, was their first contact with 'western modernity'. Prior to being shown the films described above, the people did not view their everyday lives as being lacking or missing something. Development experts and ecologists presented them with the prospect of 'modern' housing, improved education and Western medical facilities, distant from traditional herbal remedies. Consequently, the community ceased relying on traditional (regular) systems and awaited the promised improvements, but these did not materialise. Benjamin[19] articulated, 'If we cannot afford brick houses, what is the essence of claiming development? We want decent housing like everyone else. Animals are killed every year, but our living conditions remain unchanged.' The Tembo Mvura community dismisses CAMPFIRE for its failure to improve their circumstances. They continue to inhabit the same dwellings as they did three decades ago, now feeling underdeveloped due to their awareness of the 'better' amenities they could access.

Access to healthcare facilities in Kanyemba has significantly improved, but not due to CAMPFIRE. The opening of the Mariga clinic in 2017 means that people no longer have to trek eighteen kilometres for medical assistance. However, the effectiveness of these facilities is undermined by the absence of essential medicines. The clinics in Kanyemba lack full equipment, contributing to the community's ongoing dismissal of development (CAMPFIRE). The dismissal of development for its failure to ensure adequate medical supplies is particularly significant in cases of human-wildlife conflicts, which are common in the area. When animals attack individuals, prompt access to local medical assistance is crucial and is more convenient if help is secured locally. Unfortunately, the clinics in Kanyemba lack necessary medicines and cannot adequately treat injured individuals, compelling victims to seek medical help across the border in Zambia. Crossing the border to seek medical attention underscores the community's dissatisfaction with development efforts. The failure of CAMPFIRE to financially assist victims of such attacks further strengthens the community's resolve to dismiss development initiatives. They expect CAMPFIRE to have a dedicated fund for incidents of animal-induced injuries. Yet, its absence in many cases, coupled with the lack of medical supplies at the clinic, reinforces the community's dismissal of development efforts. This sentiment is echoed by Jani et al. (2023), who argue that residents of Kanyemba are convinced that CAMPFIRE prioritises animals over human welfare. The insufficient provision of medicines and funds for animal attack victims has played a significant role in the community's rejection of development initiatives.

Ambivalence in Kanyemba

Criticism and rejection of the CAMPFIRE programme in Kanyemba should not be understood to mean that people do not want to achieve the state of being 'developed'. It means that they want to achieve status, but they believe that the current initiative has failed. The people do desire development. However, they have issues with some aspects of the initiative that are supposed to bring about development, resulting in feelings of ambivalence. Ambivalence can be a source of creativity, adaptability and problem-solving, but also of confusion, frustration and indecision.

The Tembo Mvura dismiss CAMPFIRE for failing to ensure that they build 'proper' houses. As promised to them, the people expected to be able to construct houses from the funds generated by the leases and the hunts. The people want 'modern' houses, which represent a state of being developed; however, they are convinced that the current initiative cannot deliver them. While they dismiss CAMPFIRE, the people still want to own modern houses. However, they are critical of the failure of the programme to deliver development.

The people dismiss development for its failure to equip the clinics with proper medication. Some community members, especially the Tembo Mvura, appreciate the clinic even though it is poorly equipped. Child mortality has been reduced, people no longer walk long distances to the clinic and are no longer wholly reliant on herbs. Once again, it should not be assumed that herbs are 'archaic or old fashioned', but due to the movement restrictions enacted by the conservancy and game parks, getting the herbs has been a challenge. In addition, the preparation of the herbal remedies took longer than ingesting the readily available modern medicine. Having this as a background, one can understand the ambivalence pertaining to the dismissal of development. The people appreciate the positives associated with development and want modern houses, clinics and electricity, but they still dismiss CAMPFIRE because it has failed in some areas.

Discussion

Post-development theory has not sufficiently engaged with the ambivalent choices that often accompany development. Matthews (2017) highlights how post-development falls short in understanding African experiences with development. She argues that there is a need to acknowledge that people can embrace the goods associated with development and, at the same time, reject other aspects. The complexity is exacerbated by the assumption that people dismiss development because they do not desire it. The positives that development brings are appreciated; however, some issues overshadow them. Some post-development thinking dismisses development in toto because it is believed that the negatives far outweigh the positives. However, Corbridge (1998) criticises post-development for its failure to appreciate the positives that development has done. In my analysis of the Kanyemba attitudes, I can assert that people appreciate the positives associated with CAMPFIRE. The meat from the animals killed, the building of additional blocks at the school and even the extension of the maternity section of the clinic are appreciated.

Despite the positives, people still dismiss CAMPFIRE and some aspects of development. To adequately capture the people's ambivalence, I use a proverb that an elderly Tembo Mvura man used. He said, '*matakadya kare haanyaradze mwana*', loosely translated to 'the past glory days cannot be used to pacify a crying baby'. I will unpack this further. When CAMPFIRE was first introduced, people were sure that the programme was the right one and that the path it was taking would take them from their state of 'underdeveloped' to the other side. They were willing to give up hunting animals in exchange for receiving dividends and meat from the CAMPFIRE programme. At first, the people received meat and money quite often, which enabled them to buy household goods and groceries. Any 'problem animals' (which attacked people or destroyed crops) were dealt with decisively, and there was notable infrastructural development. However, the halcyon days came to an end with the stopping of dividends, which coincided with the reduced amount of meat shared. The argument put forth by the proverb is that people cannot continue basking on the past and hope to forget the current issues. People have been alienated from their past ways of life through CAMPFIRE but have not received the benefits promised by the development programmes that encouraged and enforced this alienation.

Conclusion

In conclusion, the discourse surrounding the dismissal of development in Kanyemba reveals a nuanced perspective. While initial impressions might suggest a blanket rejection of development initiatives, closer examination uncovers a complex interplay of grievances and aspirations among the residents. Their discontent stems from a multitude of unmet expectations, ranging from food security to wildlife intrusion protection and economic empowerment through programmes like CAMPFIRE. However, it is crucial to recognise that their dismissal of specific initiatives does not equate to a rejection of development as a whole. Ultimately, the residents of Kanyemba seek tangible improvements such as 'proper' housing, clean water and enhanced livelihood opportunities, but they are no longer convinced that CAMPFIRE will bring these improvements. CAMPFIRE has alienated them from their previous livelihoods while not bringing the 'development' it promised.

Notes

1 Interview with Prugia Chiambo August 2017, Chiramba Village.

2 Zimbabwe attained its independence in 1980. Prior to 1980 it was known as Southern Rhodesia. It was a British colony, although from 1965 to 1979 it was under the control of a White-dominated settler government which unilaterally declared independence.
3 Interview with Simon, 22 April 2022, Mariga village.
4 Interview with Mavhuto, 24 April 2022, Mariga village.
5 Interview with Maidei 12 May 2022, Mariga village.
6 Interview with Jivasi, 19 April 2022, Mariga village.
7 Interview with Matinetsa, 11 May 2022, Chagurika.
8 Interview with Tichaona, 26 April 2022, Chiramba village.
9 Interview with Zvanyadza, 14 May 2022, Chagurika village.
10 Interview with Daniel, 6 May 2022, Chiramba village.
11 Interview with Tony 21 April 2022, Mariga village.
12 Interview with Samuel, 20 May 2022, Chiruwe village.
13 Interview with Aaron, 18 April 2022, Majaya Business Centre.
14 Interview with Brian, 18 May 2022, Chapoto.
15 Interview with Taurai 16 May 2022, Chiramba village.
16 Interview with Jackson, 6 June 2022, Chiruwe village.
17 Interview with Peter, 10 June 2022, Chapoto.
18 Interview with Mr and Mrs Fosho, 16 June 2022, Chagurika.
19 Interview with Benjamin, 26 June 2022, Mariga primary school.

References

Alvares, C.A. (1992). *Science, development and violence: The revolt against modernity.* Delhi: Oxford University Press.

Al-Makhamreh, S.S. and Lewando-Hundt, G. (2008). 'Researching "at home" as an insider/outsider: Gender and culture in an ethnographic study of social work practice in an Arab society', *Qualitative Social Work*, 7 (1), pp. 9–23.

Andreasson, S. (2017). 'Fossil-fuelled development and the legacy of post-development theory in twenty-first-century Africa', *Third World Quarterly*, 38 (12), pp. 2634–2649.

Apffel-Marglin, F. (1996). 'Introduction: Rationality and the World'. In *Decolonizing Knowledge: From Development to Dialogue*, edited by Apffel-Marglin, F. and Marglin, S. A. Oxford, online edn: Oxford Academic.

Balint, P.J. and Mashinya, J. (2008). 'CAMPFIRE through the Lens of the 'Commons' Literature: Nyaminyami Rural District in Post-2000, Zimbabwe', *Journal of Southern African Studies*, 34 (1), pp. 127–143.

Balint, P. (2009). 'CAMPFIRE During Zimbabwe's National Crisis: Local Impacts and Broader Implications for Community-Based Wildlife Management', *Society and Natural Resources*, 21 (9), pp. 783–796.

Bola, G., Mabiza, C., Goldin, J., Kujinga, K., Nhapi, I., Makurira, H. and Mashauri, D. (2014). 'Coping with droughts and floods: a case study of Kanyemba, Mbire district, Zimbabwe', *Physics and Chemistry of the Earth*, 67, pp. 180–186.

Brannick, T. and Coghlan, D. (2007). 'In defence of being "native": The case for insider academic research', *Organisational Research Methods*, 10 (1), pp. 59–74.

Child, B. (1996). 'The status of wildlife-based', *CAMPFIRE 1991 report.*

Child, B. (1993). 'Zimbabwe's CAMPFIRE programme: using the high value of wildlife recreation to revolutionise natural resource management in communal areas', *The Commonwealth Forestry Review*, 72 (4), pp. 284–296.

Claudio, F.M. (2005). *Domination, Development, and Drought: A Study of Two Chikunda Settlements in Dande, Zambesi Valley, Zimbabwe.* Doctoral Dissertation. Department of Anthropology: London School of Economics and Political Science.

Clifford, J. and Marcus, G.E. (1986). *Writing Culture: The Poetics and Politics of Ethnography.* 2nd edn. Berkeley, CA: University of California Press.

Corbridge, S. (1998). 'Beneath the pavement only soil: The poverty of post-development', *The Journal of Development Studies*, 34 (6), pp. 138–148.

Dalal-Clayton, B. and Child, B. (2003). 'Lessons from Luangwa: The Story of the Luangwa Integrated Resource Development Project, Zambia'. *Wildlife and Development Series*, 13, International Institute for Environment and Development: London, England.

Derman, B. (1995). 'Environmental NGOs, dispossession, and the state: the ideology and praxis of African nature and development', *Human Ecology*, 23 (2), pp. 199–215.

Escobar, A. (1992). 'Imagining a Post-Development Era? Critical Thought, Development and Social Movements', *Social Text*, (31/32), pp. 20–56.

Escobar, A. (1995). *Encountering development: the making and unmaking of the Third World.* New Jersey: Princeton University Press.

Esteva, G. (1985). 'Development: Metaphor, Myth, Threat', *Development, Seeds of Change*, 3, pp. 78–79.

Esteva, G. (2023). *A critique of development and other essays.* London: Routledge.

Esteva, G. and Prakash, M.S. (1998). *Grassroots post-modernism: remaking the soil of cultures.* London: Zed Books.

Gandiwa, E. and Heitkönig, I.M.A. (2013). 'CAMPFIRE and Human-Wildlife Conflicts in Local Communities Bordering Northern Gonarezhou National Park, Zimbabwe', *Ecology and Society*, 19 (3), pp. 1–12.

Gill, J. and Johnson, P. (2002). *Research methods for managers.* 3rd ed. Sage Publications.

Hasler, R. (1991). *The political and socio-economic dynamics of natural resource management: the Communal Areas Management Programme for Indigenous Resources (CAMPFIRE) in Chapoto Ward 1989–1990.* University of Zimbabwe: Centre for Applied Social Sciences.

Hasler, R. (1999). 'An overview of the social, ecological and economic achievements and challenges of Zimbabwe's CAMPFIRE programme', *Evaluating Eden Series*, Discussion Paper No 3: I.I.E.D.

Heath, S., Brooks, R., Cleaver, E. and Ireland, E. (2009). *Researching young people's lives.* Sage publications.

Isaacman, A. (1972). 'The Origin, Formation and Early History of the Chikunda of South-Central Africa', *Journal of African History*, XIII (3), pp. 443–461.

Isaacman, A. (2000). 'Chikunda trans frontiersmen and transnational migrations in pre-colonial south-central Africa CA 1850–1900', *Zambezia*, 27 (11).

Jani, V., Webb, N. L. and de Wit, A. H. (2023). 'Community-based natural resource management and social exclusion in Zimbabwe', *Development Southern Africa*, 41 (1), pp. 225–242.

Jani, V., Webb, N.L. and de Wit, A.H. (2022). 'Evaluating the Relevance of the CAMPFIRE Principles to Wildlife Utilisation in Northern Zimbabwe', *African Journal of Wildlife Research*, 52(1), 57–71.

Laclau, E. and Mouffe, C. (2001). *Hegemony and Socialist Strategy: Towards a Radical Democratic Politics.* 2nd edn. New York: Verso.

Liu, X. and Burnett, D. (2022). 'Insider-outsider: Methodological reflections on collaborative intercultural research', *Humanities and Social Sciences Communications*, 9 (1), pp. 1–8.

Logan, B.I. and Moseley, W.G. (2002). 'The political ecology of poverty alleviation in Zimbabwe's Communal Areas Management Programme for Indigenous Resources (CAMPFIRE)', *Geoforum*, 33, pp. 1–14.

Lummis, C.D. (1996). *Radical Democracy.* Cornell University Press.

Magaldi, D., Berler, M. (2020). Semi-structured Interviews. In: Zeigler-Hill, V., Shackelford, T.K. (eds) *Encyclopedia of Personality and Individual Differences (4825–4830).* Springer, Cham.

Marindo-Ranganai, R. and Zaba, B. (1995). *Animal conservation and human survival: A case study of the Tembomvura people of Chapoto Ward in the Zambezi Valley Zimbabwe.* University of Zimbabwe: Centre for Applied Social Sciences.

Matthews, S. (2017). 'Colonised Minds? Post-Development Theory and the Desirability of Development in Africa', *Third World Quarterly*, 38 (12), pp. 2650–2663.

Matzke, G.E. and Nabane, N. (1996). 'Outcomes of a community-controlled wildlife utilisation program in a Zambezi Valley community', *Human Ecology*, 24, pp. 65–85.

Mashinya, J. (2007). *Participation and devolution in Zimbabwe's CAMPFIRE programme: findings from local projects in Mahenye and Nyaminyami.* Doctoral Dissertation. University of Maryland College Park, Maryland, U.S.A.

Marizane, A.S. (2016). *Religious change in the trans-frontier Nyungwe-speaking region of the middle Zambezi c1890-c1970.* Doctoral Dissertation. Department of History, School of Oriental and African Studies (S.O.A.S.), University of London.

Maveneke, T.N. (1995). 'ZIM CAMPFIRE programme: Community initiatives in natural resources management', Paper presented at a regional workshop.

Murindagomo, F. (1990). 'Zimbabwe: WINDFALL and CAMPFIRE'. In *Living with Wildlife: Wildlife Resource Management with Local Participation in Africa*, edited by Kiss, A. Washington, D.C: World Bank Technical Paper No. 130, pp. 123–139.

Murombedzi, J.C. (1992). *Decentralisation or Recentralisation? Implementing CAMPFIRE in the Omay Communal Lands of the Nyaminyami District.* University of Zimbabwe, Harare: Centre for Applied Social Sciences.

Murombedzi, J.C. (1999). 'Devolution and Stewardship in Zimbabwe's CAMPFIRE Programme', *Journal of International Development*, 11 (2), pp. 287–293.

Murombedzi, J.C. (2001). 'Committees, Rights, Costs and Benefits: Natural Resource Stewardship and Community Benefits in Zimbabwe's CAMPFIRE Programme' In *African Wildlife and Livelihoods: The Promise and Performance of Community Conservation*, edited by Hulme, D. and Murphree, M. Oxford, U.K: James Currey.

Murphree, W.M. (1993). *Communal Land Wildlife Resources and Rural District Council Revenues.* C.A.S.S Occasional Paper. (Series Number – 51/93).

Murphree, W.M. (2004). 'Communal approaches to natural resource management in Africa: from whence and to Where?', *Journal of International Wildlife Law and Policy*, 7, pp. 203–216.

Naderifar, M., Goli, H. and Ghaljaie, F. (2017). 'Snowball Sampling: A Purposeful Method of Sampling in Qualitative Research', *Strides in Development of Medical Education*, 14 (3).

Pieterse, J.N. (1998). 'My Paradigm or Yours? Alternative Development, Post-Development, Reflexive Development'. *Development and Change*, 29(2), 343–373.

Pieterse, J.N. (2010). *Development Theory Deconstructions/Reconstructions.* 2nd edn. London: Sage.

Neumann, R.P. (1995). 'Ways of Seeing Africa: Colonial Recasting of African Society and Landscape in Serengeti National Park', *Ecumene*, 2 (2), pp. 149–169.

Njie, B. and Asimiran, S. (2014). 'Case Study as a Choice in Qualitative Methodology', *IOSR Journal of Research and Method in Education*, 4, pp. 35–40.

Peterson, J. (1991). *CAMPFIRE: A Zimbabwean Approach to Sustainable Development and Community Empowerment through Wildlife Utilization. University of Zimbabwe*, Harare: Centre for Applied Social Science.

Polit, D.F. and Beck, C.T. (2010). 'Generalisation in quantitative and qualitative research: myths and strategies', *International Journal of Nursing Studies*, 47 (11), pp. 1451–1458.

Rahnema, M. (1997). 'Towards Post-Development: Searching for Signposts a New Language and New Paradigms'. In *The Post-Development Reader*, edited by Rahnema, M. and Bawtree, V.London: Zed Books.

Robinson, R.S. (2014). 'Purposive Sampling'. In *Encyclopedia of Quality of Life and Well-Being Research*, edited by Michalos, A.C.Dordrecht: Springer.

Sachs. W. (2010). 'Development'. In *The Development Dictionary: A guide to knowledge as power*, edited by Sachs. W. (2nd ed.). London: Zed Books.

Schoneberg, J., Haudenschild, D., Darvishi, H., Momeni, S. and Ziai, A. (2022). 'The many faces of Post-Development: alternatives to development in Tanzania, Iran and Haiti', *Sustainability Science*, 17, pp. 1223–1234.

Selous, F. C. (1970 [1881]). *A hunter's wanderings in Africa*. Bulawayo: Books of Rhodesia.

Shereni, N. C. and Saarinen, J. (2021). 'Community perceptions on the benefits and challenges of community-based natural resources management in Zimbabwe', *Development Southern Africa*, 38 (6), pp. 879–895.

Shrestha, N. (1995). 'Becoming a development category'. In *Power of development*, edited by Crush, J.C. Routledge.

Sultana. F. (2007). 'Reflexivity, Positionality and Participatory Ethics: Negotiating Fieldwork Dilemmas in International Research', *ACME: An International E-Journal for Critical Geographies*, 6 (3), pp. 374–385.

Taylor, R. (2003). From Liability to Asset: Wildlife in the Omay communal land in Zimbabwe. *Wildlife and Development Series* (No.8).

Ziai, A. (2004). 'The ambivalence of post-development: between reactionary populism and radical democracy', *Third World Quarterly*, 25 (6), pp. 1045–1060.

Ziai, A. (2017). 'Post-development 25 years after The Development Dictionary', *Third World Quarterly*, 38 (12), pp. 2547–2558.

2022 Population and Housing Census, Zimbabwe National Statistics Agency (Zimstats), Harare.

Part II

Buen Vivir, Living Well And Wellbeing

In this section, we bring together chapters that reflect critically on the concept of buen vivir and related concepts, highlighting some of the ambivalent features of contemporary attempts to build alternatives to development

DOI: 10.4324/9781003477921-7

6 The *vivir bien* rhetoric and Afro-Bolivian women's struggles for recognition and inclusive citizenship

Eija Ranta and Cecilia Zenteno Lawrence

Introduction

On 22 January 2024, Bolivia celebrated the fifteenth anniversary of the founding of the plurinational state. Legally established in the 2009 constitution, plurinationalism signalled – in principle – the recognition of diversity and interculturalism, and a shift away from colonial, republican and liberal state traditions (Nuñez del Prado 2015; Postero 2017; Radhuber 2012). According to some Indigenous scholars, the plurinational state would, ideally, imply 'the incorporation of Indigenous institutions and political practices to the new institutional map of the state for the self-determination and self-government [of Indigenous peoples]' (Choque Mamani 2014: 14). The organising life philosophy behind the plurinational state is considered to be *vivir bien*, a notion referring to 'good life or living well', holistically, and in solidarity and harmony with nature and the community (Burman 2017; Huanacuni Mamani 2012; Kunstek 2021). With its decolonising aims and community orientation, *vivir bien* – or *buen vivir*, its Ecuadorian equivalent – can be perceived as an example of the post-development paradigm put into (state) practice (Gudynas 2011; Lang 2019; Ranta 2016a, see also Cordova Suxo, in this volume).

However, at the time of the highly publicised and televised celebrations of the plurinational day on January 22nd at the Casa Grande del Pueblo in the city of La Paz, a disturbing incident occurred, demonstrating cracks in the idyll of inclusivity. While the presidential palace turned into a site for performing Indigenous rituals and celebrating the plurality of Indigenous cultures (including close zoom-ins by TV cameras of the face, figure and dress of an Afro-Bolivian woman amongst the audience) a video of a protest by Carmen Angola Campos, the executive director of the Afro-Bolivian National Council (Consejo Nacional Afroboliviano, CONAFRO), outside the gates of the presidential palace began to circulate in social media. In a video clip distributed by the Afro-Bolivian journalist Omar Torrez, the CONAFRO executive tried to gain access to the celebrations, fiercely criticising the decision not to invite her, even though she had been democratically elected as the supreme representative of the Afro-Bolivian people. 'We are not recognised in our own country,' she declared, and asked,

DOI: 10.4324/9781003477921-8

disillusioned, 'What kind of plurinationality is this?' '[Politicians] exploit us all the time,' Angola Campos continued, finally asking, 'Is it because I am Black?'[1]

In this chapter, we examine the complex positionalities and perceptions of Afro-Bolivian women of their struggles for recognition and inclusive citizenship in plurinational Bolivia, which is often associated with post-development and decolonial alternatives in international scholarship. By focusing on women's own views of development and the desirable life, we discuss the gaps between romanticised *vivir bien* rhetoric, as employed by state authorities, and the concrete struggles of Afro-Bolivian women for dignified and good lives. In the face of government neglect and multiple discrimination in increasingly polarised and racist public spheres and political spaces, we demonstrate the value of, and the support by, fellow Afro-Bolivian women and their autonomous organising, particularly as manifested in *saya*, an Afro-Bolivian singing, dancing and music assemblage. We conclude that *saya* creates spaces for resistance and alternative visioning and practices.

Due to the overwhelming dominance of Indigenous peoples in academic scholarship about Bolivia, little is yet known about the locally grounded development alternatives, life philosophies, and opportunities of the Afro-Bolivian ethnic minority. In fact, as Busdiecker (2009: 121–122) describes, Afro-Bolivians have often been invisibilised vis-a-vis indigeneity and *mestizaje*:

Afro-descendants have been present in the territory that is now Bolivia for well over four hundred years, and yet they have been rendered virtually invisible by a numerically dominant Indian and *Mestizo* [Mixed-Race] population, by a politically and economically dominant *Mestizo* and White minority elite and by popular visions of Bolivian history, society, culture and national identity that focus on negotiating degrees and kinds of 'Indianness' and distances from Indianness (for example, in '*mestizoness*') to the exclusion or marginalisation of interrogations of other types of social identities.

This division between Afro-descendants and Indigenous peoples has been common throughout Latin America (Wade 2010). While both Afro-descendants and Indigenous peoples suffer from poverty, unemployment and lack of social services, Indigenous peoples have mobilised politically and achieved several legislative and territorial gains, particularly during the multicultural reforms of the 1980s and 1990s (Hooker 2005). Afro-descendants, in contrast, have been generally seen as 'systematically ignored, marginalised, and belittled' (Wade 2010: 36). Research on them has often focused on race and racism, while Indigenous peoples have been studied through the prisms of ethnicity, indigeneity and Indigenous rights. Indigenous peoples have more visibly represented the anthropological cultural Other, while Afro-descendants have often seemed mere ordinary (poor) citizens (Wade 2010). In Bolivia, race and racism have not been the key topics in social sciences, but when racism is discussed, the literature focuses predominantly on Indigenous peoples (Loayza 2014; Macusaya 2022; Zegada 2023), and not on Afro-Bolivians, with the exception of Busdiecker (2019).

According to the most recent National Census in 2012, 41 per cent of the Bolivian population over the age of 15 self-identifies as being of Indigenous origin: the Aymaras (42,5 per cent) and the Quechuas (45,7 per cent) comprising the vast majority of them (Mamo 2022: 339). Defining indigeneity in Bolivia is complex, and Indigenous peoples are usually called *pueblos indígenas originarios campesinos* (Indigenous, native and peasant peoples), including in the current constitution.[2] According to the 2012 census, 23,330 persons self-identified as Afro-Bolivians (Instituto Nacional de Estadísticas 2015: 29). While that is only 0,58 per cent of those self-identifying as Indigenous, peasants, or Afro-Bolivians, and only 0,13 per cent of the total Bolivian population, Afro-Bolivians were still the seventh largest non-Hispanic population group in the country (Machaca Benito and Ballivián 2016: 37–39).

This chapter is based on focus group discussions and individual interviews with Afro-Bolivian women in the cities of Cochabamba, La Paz, and Santa Cruz. Most of the women were leaders of various Afro-Bolivian associations and councils, but their ages, educational backgrounds, and political stances varied. We conducted the first focus group discussion with seven women in November 2022. In 2023, Zenteno Lawrence conducted four in-depth interviews, and during fieldwork in January-February 2024 Ranta conducted four in-depth interviews and one focus group discussion with three women. Additionally, Ranta interviewed four Bolivian academic scholars of racism. Finally, we conducted two focus group discussions collaboratively in February 2024. Zenteno Lawrence herself belongs to the Afro-Bolivian community, which facilitated access, trust and continuous lived reciprocity. Besides her research, she is an activist and protagonist of Afro-Bolivian affairs. In addition to having lived in Bolivia in 2001 and 2002, Ranta conducted fieldwork there from 2008 to 2009, in 2018, 2020, 2022 and 2024, on several topics, including *vivir bien* politics.[3]

We begin the chapter by exploring the complex dynamics between post-development paradigms in Bolivia. After that, we move into the empirical chapters by first focusing on the legislative and policy advances that the *vivir bien* politics have brought for Afro-Bolivian women. Second, we examine women's perceptions of key contemporary societal challenges, thus exposing the chasms between everyday lived realities and the *vivir bien* rhetoric as an arguably local alternative to 'Western' development. The final empirical section introduces the Afro-Bolivian community's own alternative visionings and organising, as manifested in the Afro-Bolivian dance and music – *saya*. We do not represent *saya* as an Afro-Bolivian alternative to mainstream development nor as an expression of *vivir bien* policies, but rather as an intrinsic component woven into women's agency, serving as a cultural medium that both reflects and shapes Afro-Bolivian belonging and social organising. We also suggest that the practice of *saya* has been a crucial tool for Afro-Bolivian women in their struggles for recognition and inclusive citizenship.

Post-development, *vivir bien*, and *saya*

In post-development and decolonial scholarship, Bolivia has become known for its critique of 'Western' development and elaborations of locally grounded societal alternatives. Alongside southern African *ubuntu* and Indian *swaraj*, the notion of *buen vivir/vivir bien* has become one of the most promising alternative paradigms, emerging from the Global South and circulating all over the world amidst scholars and activists. In many parts of Latin America, the concept of living well has been presented as an alternative life philosophy beyond individualistic, economistic and 'Western' development. Academic and activist debates about b*uen vivir* and *sumak kawsay* (a Kichwa term for 'good living') in Ecuador are the most well-known (Cubillo-Guevara and Hidalgo-Capitán 2015; Lalander 2014; Radcliffe 2012). In Bolivia, the conceptualisation of a good life as human and more-than-human conviviality is perceived to originate from, and bring together, diverse Indigenous peoples' cosmologies and life philosophies, including '*suma qamaña*' ('living well' in Aymara language) and '*ñandereko*' ('harmonious life' in Guaraní language) (Farah and Vasapollo 2011; República de Bolivia 2008; Schavelzon 2015). It is closely interwoven with Indigenous peoples' struggles for land rights and territories, as well as water, forests and other living environments (Choque Mamani 2014; Huanacuni Mamani 2012; Ranta 2023; Yampara 2001).

Although pushed forward by Indigenous scholars and social movements, the rhetoric of *vivir bien* was popularised by the Bolivian government as an anti-neoliberal and anti-colonial policy principle (Ranta 2016b), during the presidency of the coca union leader Evo Morales (2005–2019) and the rule of the Movimiento al Socialismo (Movement toward Socialism, MAS) party, which continues to this day. Through the symbolic figure of Evo Morales (whose indigeneity is much debated in Bolivia, as he is often seen as representing peasants rather than Indigenous peoples), Bolivia succeeded in profiling itself internationally as the proponent of radical anti-imperialist alternatives of Indigenous origin. Furthermore, it has been labelled an 'Indigenous State' (Postero 2017).

While such conceptualisations as *sumak kawsay/suma qamaña* have been intimately tied to Indigenous peoples' cosmologies, land relations and territories (Alonso González and Macías Vázquez 2015; Cubillo-Guevara and Hidalgo-Capitán 2015; Yampara 2001), some conceptualisations similar to *vivir bien/buen vivir* have also recently emerged in Latin America among Afro-descendant populations. Such is the case with the discourse of '*vivir sabroso*' ('living joyfully') in Colombia, pushed forward by the Afro-Colombian Vice-President Francia Márguez, who is an award-winning environmental activist and Afro-Colombian rights advocate (Caicedo Sarralde 2023). In Bolivia, the Afro-Bolivian ethnic minority held high hopes and expectations for the concept of *vivir bien*, as pushed forward by their own social movements, most particularly The Cultural Movement of Afro-Bolivian Saya (Movimiento Cultural Saya Afroboliviana, MOCUSABOL) and the Bolivian Center for Integral Development (Centro Boliviano para el Desarrollo Integral, CADIC). The *vivir bien* rhetoric about the importance of community and decolonisation resonated well with their African diaspora experience and long-term struggles for recognition and rights. However, according to Afro-Bolivian scholars, *vivir bien* is first and foremost an Indigenous peoples' concept, and there is no direct Afro-Bolivian equivalent to it (Ballivian 2012: 271). In Bolivia, it was mostly the Aymara intellectuals, NGOs, and politicians, as well as Quechua organisations, who propagated the notion of *Suma Qamaña* (Burman 2017; Yampara 2001), while in Ecuador it was the Sarayaku Indigenous communities and anthropologists that elaborated the idea of *Sumak Kawsay* (Alonso González and Macías Vázquez 2015; Cubillo-Guevara and Hidalgo-Capitán 2015).

Afro-Bolivians' own organising and cultural and political mobilisation has revolved around *saya*. *Saya* is an Afro-Bolivian dance, music and singing assemblage, which is often perceived as 'the supreme manifestation of the Afro-Bolivian cultural expression' (Angola Maconde 2010: 196). As Ponce Vargas et al. (2014: 216) put it: '[A]s a cultural manifestation, as a demand, [and] as a mechanism of resistance and visibility, [*saya*] is the means through which Afro-Bolivians express their feelings, denounce their oppression, claim their rights'. According to Rey Gutierrez (1998), the term *saya* derives from the Central African Kikongo word *nsaya*, which refers to collaborative work in which all members of the community work and sing together under the direction of a lead singer. In *saya*, both men and women participate in singing verses and choruses. Traditionally, only men played percussion instruments, such as drums, metal bells and bamboo sticks as part of the dance, but recently women have also started to do so. The choreography of the performance is led by women and accompanied in the background by the musicians. While *saya* dance has always been part of Afro-Bolivian life, our interlocutors observed that it has been revitalised over the last 30 years within the Afro-Bolivian communities both in rural and urban areas. Many noted that *saya* songs have lyrics that relate to their identities and socio-political issues in their everyday lives.

Afro-Bolivians are predominantly descendants of enslaved Africans brought to the Potosí silver mines during the 16th century by the Spanish colonialists (Crespo 1995). The approximately 10,000 Spanish men who conquered Upper Perú, as Bolivia was called at the time, were accompanied by a nearly equal number of enslaved Africans (Klein 2003: 47). When the silver economy collapsed during the 18th century, the agricultural large estates (*hacienda*) in the Yungas valleys became the sites for further enslavement of the Black population (Angola Maconde 2010). They also laboured in gold mining and coca leaf cultivation (Ballivian 2012: 64). It was at the haciendas where the *saya* was articulated 'as resistance to the system of oppression' (Ballivian 2012: 87). When the patrons held celebrations for the Catholic saints, *saya* offered spaces for autonomous social and cultural expressions and a temporary sense of 'liberation from the sufferings' (Ballivian 2012: 87).

Due to the histories of slavery, enslaved Afro-Bolivian populations have experienced 'territorial uprooting' and 'deterritorialisation' (Tejerina Vargas 2014: 36), which makes their historical and contemporary experience different from those of many Indigenous peoples, who can claim guardianship of lands and territories on the basis of their indigeneity.[4] While slavery was officially abolished in 1851, in practice the Afro population continued to work at the haciendas in the form of forced labour, called *ponguaje* and *mitanaje*, as they had no land nor alternative means of making a living: men worked in agriculture (*pongos*) and women in domestic labour (*mitana*) (Bridikhina 1997; Machaca Benito and Ballivián Vásquez 2016: 20–21). When the 1952 nationalist revolution and the 1953 agrarian reform finally abolished the forced labour system, many Afro-Bolivians stayed in Los Yungas as small-scale farmers (peasants). Until the nationalist revolution, Black Bolivians were not allowed to attend schools, and therefore those belonging to the oldest generations are nearly illiterate even today (Sessarego 2009: 109). This changed from the mid-1950s onward with the expansion of rural education. After the nationalist revolution, when Afro-Bolivian families gained some access to land, they started to practice patrilineal land ownership and heritage practices. As women moved to the houses and communities of their husbands, investing in girls' education was often seen as a waste of money (Zambrana Balladares 2014: 114). Outside of *saya* events, women's and girls' spheres were restricted to homes, domestic chores and raising children. They did not have economic or political autonomy and they were vulnerable to multiple abuse and violence. Today the school attendance of the Afro-Bolivian population is a bit lower than the country average, but in terms of higher education, their numbers are higher than those of minority Indigenous groups (Machaca Benito and Ballivián Vásquez 2016: 75–76). Apart from primary education, there is still a significant gender gap in education (Machaca Benito and Ballivián Vásquez 2016: 74).

While the nationalist revolution significantly changed Afro-Bolivians' citizenship status and labour conditions, its political agenda aimed at social, cultural and linguistic homogenisation, through universal education and the dominance of the Spanish language (Zambrana Balladares 2014: 105). The state did not recognise Afro-Bolivians as a collective, a distinct people (Komadina and Regalsky 2016: 39). Indigenous and Afro-descendant traditions, cosmologies and cultural expressions were not allowed, and they were instead considered to signal backwardness and a hindrance to modernity. Currently, most Afro-Bolivians speak Spanish as their mother tongue, but also Indigenous languages such as Quechua (8 per cent) and Aymara (4 per cent) (Machaca Benito and Ballivián Vásquez 2016: 77–78). In the Yungas, the Afro-Bolivians and the Aymaras have lived side by side for centuries, facing similar practices of forced labour during the republican era and state-led peasant unionism (*sindicato*) since the revolution. Their relations often rely on interethnic conviviality, although competition over limited resources has recently risen (Zambrana Balladares 2014: 118). According to Spedding (2008), the peasant unions are peoples' main forms of political organising and mobilisation in the Yungas, even if Afro-Bolivian organising based on racial identity and as a distinct people, has grown, particularly amidst the urban-educated Afro-Bolivians.

Legislative and policy advances for Afro-Bolivians

When Bolivia transitioned from decades-long military dictatorships (1964–1982) to representative democracy during the early 1980s, the first culturally driven Afro-Bolivian movements arose around *saya*. During this period, many young Afro-Bolivian women started to migrate from the Yungas region to the cities of La Paz, Cochabamba and Santa Cruz, among other places, in search of better economic opportunities. They emerged as key advocates in revitalising the *saya*, transforming it into public spaces for social interaction and fostering political engagement (Zambrana Balladares 2014: 115). The first *saya* group emerged in Coroico at the Guerrilleros Lanza school during the early 1980s. One of the senior Afro-Bolivian female leaders told us about the revitalisation process and its gendered dimensions in the following way:

> I became the first Afro-Bolivian woman to leave my village to study at school in Coroico, where I was not under the control of my parents. For the community it was a taboo. How could a woman go to study? The people in the community did not want me to do it. They told my father that, 'if your daughter goes out to study, she will come back pregnant'... I was also the first Afro woman who did not wear a pollera [long skirt typical for the Aymara women], because, for me, the skirt was imposed by the Spanish [colonialists] ... In school, I understood that everyone else had culture. My [female] friend and I were the only Black people in the school. 'There is no culture for us,' we noticed. 'There is no history for us,' there was nothing that was ours. Then one of the teachers suggested, 'Why don't you dance *saya*?' I grinned, because at the time *saya* was always *tundiqui* [a Bolivian folklore dance performed by Whites and *Mestizos* with a blackface], but the teacher said no, 'it should be the *saya* that your grandfathers and grandmothers always danced.'
>
> (interview in Santa Cruz, 3 February 2024)

The *saya* dancers – under the leadership of women – started to perform in different cities and to occupy public spaces with their voices, sounds, instruments and their own traditional attire: white *pollera*. The *saya* dress includes a skirt (*pollera*) with a red horizontal ribbon in the middle for women, white trousers with a vertical red ribbon for men and a multicoloured ribbon decorating the white blouse (for women) and shirt (for men). Even if the dress that Afro-Bolivian women use for the *saya* encounters has changed slightly over the years, it remains the same in all the regions of the country. While the dress could be perceived to have some colonial influence, it differs – and has different meanings – from the dresses used by the Aymara or the *criollo/mestizo* (White/Mixed-Race) (Ponce Vargas et al. 2014: 212). This is due to the attributes that are given to it, as one of the interviewed women explained:

> … the white colour represents our integrity, the red ribbon both in the skirt and trousers signifies the spilled blood of our ancestors, and… both the blouses and the shirt are adorned with ribbons of different colours, which can be interpreted as our longing for diversity and acceptance.
>
> (interview in Cochabamba, 23 September 2023)

In this sense, the *saya* promoted the Afro-Bolivian culture and presence in the country. It also created and reactivated connections and collaborations among Afro-Bolivians from different municipalities, cities and towns, succeeding in promoting the formation of the MOCUSABOL in the city of La Paz, in 1988. Several other organisations followed, and currently there are more than ten Afro-based organisations in Bolivia. For women, organising around *saya* has had a dual meaning: it offered them the opportunity to operate outside the private sphere, while also promoting community values and ethnic belonging. As Afro-Bolivians were usually seen solely through slavery and oppression, and many expected them always to be submissive and docile, women used *saya* to gain leadership and active agency, as well as to promote a more cheerful image of the Afro-Bolivians (interview in Santa Cruz, 3 February 2024).

During the 1990s, the United Nations launched both the decade for Indigenous peoples and the decade against racism and racial discrimination. Several Afro-Latin American and Afro-Caribbean networks and alliances were established, and consciousness of Afro-affairs and racism in particular, grew substantially in the region (Yañez Inofuentes 2016: 13). In Bolivia, the Afro-Bolivian community started to ally more closely with fellow organisations in peer countries and participated in the UN process for the 2001 Durban Declaration to combat racism. After Durban, Afro-Bolivian leaders began to propose a movement of recognition of Afro-Bolivians as a people, beyond racial differences; it was not just the struggle of Black men and women, but of a people with a common history. According to a young urban Afro-Bolivian female leader in La Paz, that was when the Afro-Bolivian movement became 'politicised'; young people started to gather in capacity-building sessions, to talk about identity and racism. Subsequently, a clear political agenda was formed; 'the Afro-Bolivian peoples start[ed] to have three very central and clear themes: the recognition of the Afro-Bolivian peoples by the Bolivian state, their inclusion in the population and housing censuses, and the law that penalises racism' (interview in La Paz, 23 January 2024).

After the ascendancy of Evo Morales and the MAS to political power in the December 2005 national elections, things started to progress quickly. At the time, social inclusion and racism were widely debated in Bolivian society. The process of the constituent assembly began in 2006 with the lead of an alliance of Indigenous organisations and peasant unions, known as the *Pacto de Unidad* ('Unity Pact'). However, amidst the 200 assembly members, there were no representatives of the Afro-Bolivian community (Zambrana Balladares 2014: 150). This was an important political moment for the Afro-Bolivian community, and two women leaders from the MOCUSABOL started a hunger strike, in which they were joined by members of the persons with disabilities and the

LGBTQIA+ community, who experienced similar forms of exclusion (interview in La Paz, 23 January 2024). Furthermore, the Afro-Bolivian community joined forces with the National Council of Ayllus and Markas of Qullasuyu (Consejo Nacional de los Ayllus y Markas del Qullasuyu, CONAMAQ), which was one of the five leading organisations of the *Pacto de Unidad* and a promoter of Indigenous territorial rights through the notion of *suma qamaña* ('living well') (interview in La Paz, 23 January 2024). According to the senior female leader from Yungas mentioned above, while they did not have their own assembly members, the Afro-Bolivian activists used *saya* drums and dance tactically to enter the assembly meetings and the parliament. As they were seen as performers of Bolivian folklore, they were allowed into the buildings and, instead of starting their performances, they used the opportunity to make their political demands (interview in Santa Cruz, 3 February 2024). Consequently, 'without *saya* we would have achieved nothing,' she concluded (interview in Santa Cruz, 3 February 2024).

In the end, the 2009 constitution recognised the status and rights of the Afro-Bolivians for the first time. Its Article 3 states that Afro-Bolivians, alongside Indigenous peoples, peasants and other Bolivians, comprise the Bolivian people (República de Bolivia 2008: 13). The Article 32 declares that Afro-Bolivians enjoy all the same economic, social, political and cultural rights that the constitution recognises for Indigenous peoples and peasants. These include, among other things, self-determination, territory, recognition of ancestral knowledge, promotion of their own language, rituals and symbols, and prior consultation related to such issues as resource extraction. (República de Bolivia 2008: 22–24.)

In 2011, the first Afro-Bolivian national congress was organised and their own national organisation CONAFRO was established. It meant a distancing from their historically close alliances with the Aymara-led CONAMAQ, where despite having achieved several leadership positions, Afro-Bolivians were not allowed to make similar claims for territories as Indigenous leaders had (Zambrana Balladares 2014: 156–157). In the 2012 census, the Afro-Bolivians were included as a population category for the first time, and the census results made them visible as a population group (Machaca Benito and Ballivián Vásquez 2016). Furthermore, the Ministry of Education approved a specific curriculum related to the Afro-Bolivian people, called 'Currículo regionalizado del pueblo afroboliviano', which was planned in a participatory manner with the CONAFRO (Zambrana Balladares 2014: 158). A major legislative advance was also the approval of Law 045 against racism and all forms of discrimination in 2010, followed by Law 848 concerning the Decade for Bolivian People of African Descent in 2016. With regard to *saya*, some of Bolivia's laws and policy plans, including the Mother Earth and Integral Development for Living Well (Law 300), explicitly refer to dancing as part of maintaining harmonious and spiritual relationships with the Mother Earth and community. In our analysis, however, we do not perceive *saya* as an expression of *vivir bien* policies, but rather as emic to Afro-Bolivians' lives. In everyday lives, many challenges remain in implementation, creating gaps between the rhetoric of *vivir bien* and women's experiences, to which we will turn next.

Persistent challenges: Afro-Bolivian women's experiences of racism and exclusion

Consequently, the Afro-Bolivian people have achieved many of their long-term political, social and cultural demands, including recognition by the plurinational state and legal tools to eliminate racism and discrimination. However, the Afro-Bolivian interlocutors interviewed for this chapter argued that, despite the progress, the national and departmental regulations and institutional arrangements are not yet enforced and Afro-Bolivian issues still remain largely invisible. One of the women commented about the recognition:

> Despite the recognition, one of the great challenges continues to be the invisibilisation of the Afro-Bolivian people. The treatment we receive is as if we were an Indigenous people and not from our particularities as an Afro-Bolivian people. That leads to a series of difficulties. No policy in the country is specifically designed to address the needs of Afro-Bolivians
>
> (interview in La Paz, 23 January 2024).

Due to their history of enslavement, many Afro-Bolivians do not own much property. While some own small parcels of land, particularly in the Yungas, Afro-Bolivians do not enjoy collective rights to land and territories as many minority Indigenous groups do. Among those interviewed, not everyone knew about the *vivir bien* policies. Those women with the highest levels of education or those who were aligned with the MAS party were more aware of them than others. The MAS supporter mentioned earlier explained her criticism:

> Despite having a political affinity with the MAS, I maintain my criticism that none of this has been thought from an Afro-Bolivian perspective. All this has been thought from a very Andean, Aymara, Quechua logic… A capitalist logic, a neoliberal logic, also continues to persist. That's my criticism… All the [Latin American] countries that proposed *vivir bien* have not been able to escape capitalist logic. *Vivir bien* [policies] continue to focus on the Anthropocene, on extractivism, on the development model that goes against the [interests of the] population. In the practice of governments, the logic of *vivir bien* equals capitalist logic… No [government] planned *vivir bien* that was outside the world system … Beyond the discursive and the very nice conceptualisation of what *vivir bien* is, it was never a real thing; it is neither political praxis nor has it ever permeated politics and decision-making in [Latin American] countries
>
> (interview in La Paz, 23 January 2024).

According to her, 'without a doubt, poverty, job insertion, remuneration … and specific policies for Afro-Bolivians are the greatest challenges that the country still faces' (interview in La Paz, 23 January 2024). The need for better educational and income-generating opportunities were often mentioned in the interviews when future goals were discussed. Social exclusion in terms of poverty, difficulty in labour market insertion and lack of education and social services affect both Afro-descendants and Indigenous peoples throughout Latin America (Hooker 2005). In Bolivia, however, the interviewed Afro-Bolivian women felt that the state transformation process during the rule of the MAS had significantly improved Indigenous peoples' political and economic opportunities. Yet, while Indigenous and peasant political inclusion has increased (Htun 2013) and poverty levels have decreased, a fierce criticism has emerged that the peasant rule within the MAS has overshadowed Indigenous concerns, and the accelerated extraction of natural resources has led to severe violations of Indigenous territorial rights (Anthias and López 2023; López Flores and Ranta 2024; Rivera Cusicanqui 2013). Therefore, some Indigenous and peasant peoples may have benefitted; others, not so much.

Regarding discrimination, the interviewed Afro-Bolivian women made two main distinctions: external and internal situations that intersect between each other and at different levels. The internal issues – which we do not discuss in this chapter – relate to family, kin and patrilineality, while external situations relate to the attitudes and actions of public servants, politicians, teachers and other fellow Bolivians, as well as economic and state structures. There are still public instances and social organisations that do not recognise Afro-Bolivian culture and rights, especially when women are concerned, and consequently Afro-Bolivian women still suffer from multiple aspects of vulnerability (Yañez Inofuentes 2016). Intersectional inequalities that Afro-women experience based on their gender, class and race have been widely discussed in the US (Collins 2019; Crenshaw 1991) and throughout Latin America (Roth 2019; Viveros Vigoya and Gregorio Gill 2014; Wade 2009).

Even though Law 045 was considered a clear victory for the Afro-Bolivians by all the interlocutors, its practical implications for everyday life were seen to be minimal. Some of the women interviewed questioned whether the legal penalisation of racism (instead of education and awareness raising) is the best way to go in the first place. Others were more hopeful in trying to use legal means to combat racism and discrimination, even if their efforts had fallen short. One of the female leaders told us about her experiences of Law 045 in a focus group discussion urging for the more effective implementation of the law:

> Everyone mobilised for Law 045 [against racism] but when here in Cochabamba we have seen racist actions, I personally went to complain with a group of brothers, the [police officers] told us 'the law is not yet in force; if it were a public servant, you could do something but as the [racist] person was just a private individual, nothing can be done'. Unfortunately, we had another case with a public servant from the Mayor's Office of Quillacollo

> who offended an Afro-descendant person, and nothing was done either. So, I think that Law 045 should be activated or else, just bury it, right, because it does not work. It may work for a few, but, for me, even dogs have greater justice than us
>
> (focus group in Cochabamba, 30 November 2022).

Thus, while the interlocutor had maintained a certain hope in the law, the focus group excerpt also shows a deep distrust in the government's treatment of Afro-Bolivian community as a whole and also a suspicion that some Afro-Bolivians might be benefitting from the government policies and revenues, while others are not. Another female leader from the same focus group event explained these dynamics:

> Obviously, this government has given us the opportunity to have the first Afro-Bolivian deputy, the first supranational deputy, the first vice minister, assembly member, yes, there has been that. Why? Obviously because when you want to win over the mother-in-law, you must bring her the cake, flowers, gifts for the children, a bone for the dog, I mean, obviously you must do that. But when you have already married her daughter, if you see [the mother-in-law's] dog, you would rather kick it and continue your way, because she is already in your way. So, I consider that we are seen that way by the government
>
> (focus group in Cochabamba, 30 November 2022).

Clearly, she recognised that the Afro-Bolivian community has enjoyed increased inclusion of Afro-Bolivian representatives in national politics during the MAS rule. However, she also implied that the MAS had used the Afro-Bolivian community's support to gain political power, after which their concerns had been largely abandoned. A similar view of the instrumental use of the Afro-Bolivian community by politicians was reflected in Carmen Angola Campos's example at the beginning of the chapter: an MAS-promoting Afro-Bolivian person had been invited to the celebrations of the plurinational state, providing the government a public image of inclusivity and diversity, while the legitimate representative of the CONAFRO was left outside the gates.

In addition to the potential instrumentalisation of Afro-Bolivian concerns, the wider political conflict and polarisation have both deepened political divisions amidst the Afro-Bolivians and increased racism towards them. During the autumn of 2019, Evo Morales' 14-year rule ended in a political conflict that some call a 'coup d'état' and others 'electoral fraud' (Claros and Díaz Cuéllar 2022; Ranta 2024; Zegada et al. 2021). Before that, the MAS regime had merged and co-opted most social movements into its party structures and government (Ranta 2022; Tapia 2017), and the CONAFRO was no different. Autonomous societal organising had become difficult, as one of the women recalled in the focus group meeting: 'If you are not from the MAS, they do not listen to you; you cannot think differently' (focus group in Cochabamba, 30 November 2022). Consequently, when Morales was exiled from the country, it had repercussions for the Afro-Bolivian organising, as one of the women recalled:

> As Afro-Bolivians, we felt helpless, because everything was politicised at that time, everything was a division between the left and the right and, well, our authorities, especially our representatives, were aligned with the ruling party. Then, since the president [Evo Morales] was in trouble, everyone who followed him was also in trouble, so what happened… they disappeared, right? And as Afro-Bolivians, we had no representation, no one said anything and it was like we were abandoned, abandoned like that, it's like they had gone underground. It was incredible, at least that was what I felt and we all asked ourselves, where is our [CONAFRO] president and our executive?
>
> (focus group in Cochabamba, 30 November 2022).

Furthermore, the 2019 conflict also increased racist attacks and racist language, while racism has also become instrumentalised in political fights between the governing regime and the opposition (Zegada and Canedo 2023). While the Afro-Bolivian community faced multiple discrimination in increasingly polarised and racist public spheres and political spaces, they also had an opportunity to rethink their political alliances and autonomous organising, as one of the CONAFRO female leaders reassured us in an interview:

> CONAFRO … is a *de facto* apolitical organisation. So, the idea is to always work with whoever is in the government because what we always ask for are public policies in favour of the Afro-Bolivian people. Whoever is there to give us what really belongs to us by right. We should not have to belong to any political party to receive what is due to us
>
> (focus group in Santa Cruz, 3 February 2024).

To conclude, major discrepancies have emerged between the Afro-Bolivian community and the ruling MAS party. In situations of political crisis and uncertainty, it has been *saya* that has offered the Afro-Bolivian community an autonomous form of organising socially, culturally and politically, while also signifying a community-based way of being, acting and networking within the Afro-Bolivian community. We move to discussing *saya* next.

Afro-Bolivian alternatives: *saya* as space of resistance and alternative visioning

As already discussed earlier, the Afro-Bolivian community's own alternative visioning and organising focuses around the *saya* dance, music and singing assemblage. Historically, as explained above, it provided a collective space in which resistance against slavery and enforced labour was enacted. This historical memory of resistance is still a major part of women's lives and identities, as one of the Afro-Bolivian female leaders explained: 'For me, being of African descent is the most beautiful thing there can be, because in my roots, in my blood, we carry the fight, the determination, and the construction [of the community] from very below' (focus group in Cochabamba, 30 November 2022). Another woman joined in praising the importance of solidarity and community for the Afro-Bolivians:

> I believe that a very important thing is solidarity... Due to distances, being in an urban space, we are separated but when you need to do something we are always there, we always appear. So, I believe that this spirit of solidarity of Afro-Bolivians, in a city that has Quechuas, Aymaras and everything ... To me that moment of encounter – solidarity – is a very important element of Afro-Bolivian culture
>
> (focus group in Cochabamba, 30 November 2022).

One of the women, however, complained that the sense of community has been withering away, now that people live in different cities and municipalities and have more individual lifestyles. She also complained that *saya* has become a 'mere dance', and not an encounter of resistance, solidarity and community. For the rest of the women interviewed, though, *saya* meant so much more than just a dance. For one of them, 'it is not only about the dance, but also about representing culture and the whole trajectory of [Afro-Bolivian] experiences, traditions and customs' (interview in Cochabamba, 26 August 2023). Another woman tied it closely to her identity: 'Since the day they put the *saya* dress on me, until I leave this world, they will have to bury me with the *saya* dress on because that runs through my veins. For me, it is my identity' (focus group in Santa Cruz, 3 February 2024). While many criticised *vivir bien* policies for being very much centred on Indigenous peoples, Ballivian (2012: 271) has suggested that for Afro-Bolivians, *saya* could be perceived as 'living well [*vivir bien*] in joy with the community from our own cosmovision and from our being as Afro-Bolivians'.

In terms of networking and political organising, *saya* has played an important role in the emergence and growth of Afro-Bolivian organisations. It connects the various Afro-organisations, thus bringing people from diverse points of view, political stances and ideologies together. While national politics tend to polarise Afro-Bolivians, *saya* encounters promote articulations between organisations, thus cherishing plurality and differences. Women, in particular, recognise how *saya* as a form of social-political organisation provided them with opportunities that they would not otherwise have had.

> *Saya* has always been, and will be, I think, our guiding star. Thanks to *saya*, we were able to open doors and gain public and political spaces in which we would not have been accepted otherwise
>
> (focus group in Santa Cruz, 3 February 2024).

It has provided Afro-women with spaces for political mobilisation and leadership in Bolivian society, but major changes have also happened in gender relations within *saya* and the Afro-Bolivian community in general. One female leader recalled:

> I was raised by my uncles, and I had never seen a woman playing drums (*tambor*). When I wanted to play with the *jaucaña* (Afro-Bolivian

> drumsticks), the uncles got really angry, and I didn't do it anymore. One of the first things that we gained as a people and as Afro women was that this kind of machismo was left behind; the idea that only the men can play *caja* (drums) was left behind... It is a great achievement to be able to say that we are a people and both women and men are equal and that within our people we can all do the same things.
>
> (focus group in Santa Cruz, 3 February 2024).

Consequently, it is fair to say that *saya* has been instrumental in the political organising and mobilisation of the Afro-Bolivian community. It has provided them an autonomous space for enacting politics from their own perspectives. This space has been particularly relevant for Afro-Bolivian women, whose educational, occupational and political opportunities have traditionally been limited. *Saya* has widened women's agency within Afro-Bolivian families and communities. Furthermore, through *saya* – which could easily be considered as mere folklore – women have widened their spheres of action from homes and communities to constituent assemblies and associations. Another thing is whether the Bolivian society and politicians perceive *saya* as a tool of politics.

> We are mostly seen as either *saya* dancers or foreigners or, in the case of men, football players. In other words, we are only identified with these roles. As a representative of the Afro-Bolivian community here in Cochabamba, when I have had to make a request for a meeting or a hearing with a higher authority such as a governor or a mayor, what happens is that they only see us through culture or sports. I am asking to speak with the mayor because I want to request something, but they direct us directly to the section of culture because they think 'ah! they are from CONAFRO, they want to dance *saya*, they want to do a cultural activity'. We are classified solely as dancers and if they invite us somewhere, it is always that 'we will invite you to this activity if you could then perform *saya*'
>
> (focus group in Cochabamba, 30 November 2022).

While identity politics has been used for ethnic recognition and rights, Afro-Bolivians seem to be reduced to that, or at least their channels of participation are limited to their culture and not to substantive citizenship. Ethnic and racial minorities face such stances in many countries. On the part of politicians and public servants, this tactic of overriding the rights of Afro-Bolivians by folkloricising them is a sign of the continuation of discrimination and racism within the plurinational state, and a hindrance to gaining inclusive citizenship.

Conclusions

This chapter has examined what state-led claims of practising alternatives to 'Western' development have meant in the lives of Afro-Bolivian women, who have – in the course of history – been severely discriminated against and excluded from Bolivian society and state. The *vivir bien* rhetoric in Bolivian legislation and public policies draws on the ideals of Indigenous peoples living a more harmonious and balanced life with their lands, territories, nature and community. To an extent, this locally grounded conceptualisation can be viewed from the perspective of post-development. In terms of the Afro-Bolivian community, and particularly the women who were the focus of this chapter, *saya* – rather than *vivir bien* – has represented an autonomous form of being and living. For women, *saya* has improved their influence and leadership within the Afro-Bolivian community, but also opened arenas for political organising in Bolivian society. *Saya* has functioned as a glue that bonds diverse Afro-Bolivian groups and communities together, providing articulations in a society that is experiencing increasing polarisation and racism.

However, it is important to note here that *saya* complements, and is not an exclusive alternative to, women's wider calls for recognition and inclusive citizenship. While many Afro-Bolivian women find comfort in ecological lifestyles – by choice or necessity – and strongly cherish the value of the Afro-Bolivian community, many of their desires for better futures focus on fair legislation and equitable public services, as well as the abolition of discrimination and racism. Instead of mere recognition and invocation of their culture and folklore, they are demanding better accountability, better public services and equal treatment by the plurinational state. Thus, if development is viewed from the perspective of equal opportunities, better public services and state accountability to its citizens, the women's views did not reflect a post-development stance. One of the women interviewed tied the issue more to criticism of capitalism as a world system, and her perceptions were nearer to the post-development perceptions than those of the others. In general, however, women's perceptions of desirable development were claims of citizens who have experienced multiple forms of discrimination and racism, as well as structural violence, from the state in various stages of history. However, they were not seeking an exemption from the state, but rather an opportunity to combine autonomous forms of organising (often in the name of *saya*) with a more responsive, responsible, and truly plurinational state.

Notes

1 The video is from the Facebook page of the Afro-Bolivian news personality Omar Torrez. He shared the video on 22 April 2024 to his nearly 7,000 Facebook followers.

2 Indigenous and native peoples imply pre-colonial cultural heritage, and the term peasant peoples was introduced during the Agrarian Reform in 1953. The entire (Indigenous) rural population began to be called peasants. The race-based term *Indio* (Indian) was abolished as pejorative, and the proclamation of Bolivia as the *Mestizo* nation (Mixed-Race nation) relied on the idea of there being only one race (Spedding 2013: 144). Although many peasants descend from Aymaras or Quechuas, their self-identification is not based on ethnicity or indigeneity, but rather on small-scale farming, household-based land ownership, and trade union organising. Those who are called Indigenous peoples in Bolivia are minority Indigenous groups residing mostly in the Amazonian region in Indigenous territories (more than 30 groups). Native peoples are usually those Aymaras and Quechuas residing in the mountain areas who maintain and

revitalise collective landownership and territorial self-governance structures and self-identify through ethnic and Indigenous identity rather than peasant union organising. The conjunction of the three terms – *indígena originario campesino* – was employed for the first time in the National Development Plan 2006–2011 and it has gained popularity through its enactment in the constitution.

3 The chapter is part of the research project Social Justice and Raciality in Post-Utopian Latin America (2021–2026), financed by the Research Council of Finland (project number: 346411).

4 In a few Latin American countries (Brazil, Colombia, Ecuador, Guatemala, Honduras, and Nicaragua), Afro-descendants have been able to gain territorial rights, but only in Honduras, Guatemala, and Nicaragua do they have the exact same territorial rights as Indigenous peoples (Hooker 2005: 286). They have gained these rights when they have portrayed themselves as a distinct ethnic group akin to Indigenous groups, instead of mobilising on the basis of racial difference and racism (Hooker 2005: 286).

References

Alonso González, P. and Macías Vázquez, A. (2015). 'An Ontological Turn in the Debate on buen vivir – sumak kawsay in Ecuador: ideology, knowledge, and the common', *Latin American and Caribbean Ethnic Studies*, 10 (3), pp. 315–334.

Angola Maconde, J. (2010). 'Las raíces africanas en la historia de Bolivia'. In *Conocimiento desde adentro: los afrosudamericanos hablan de sus pueblos y sus historias*, edited by Walker, S. La Paz: Fundación PIEB, pp. 145–222.

Anthias, P. and López, P. (2023). *Neoextractivism and territorial disputes in Latin America: social-ecological conflict and resistance on the front lines.* Abington: Routledge.

Ballivian, M. M. (2012). *La saya boliviana: un espacio comunitario afrocéntrico e intercultural de enseñanza y aprendizaje / conociendo "desde casa adentro y casa afuera"* nuestra historiografía y saberes ancestrales. MA Dissertation. Universidad Mayor de Sán Simon. Unpublished.

Bridikhina, E. (1997). 'Coca, dinero o jornales: la situación económica social de los ex-esclavos negros en Nor-Yungas, segunda mitad del siglo XIX'. In *El siglo XIX: Bolivia y América Latina*, edited by Barragán, R., Cajías, D. and Qayum, S. La Paz: Muela del Diablo Editores, pp. 463–474.

Burman, A. (2017). 'La ontología política del vivir bien'. In *Ecología y reciprocidad: (con) vivir bien, desde contextos andinos*, edited by de Munter, K., Michaux, J. and Pauwels, G. La Paz: Plural editores, pp. 155–176.

Busdiecker, S. (2009). 'The emergence and evolving character of contemporary Afro-Bolivian mobilization: from the performative to the political'. In *New social movements in the African Diaspora: challenging global apartheid*, edited by Mullings, L.New York: Palgrave Macmillan, pp. 121–137.

Busdiecker, S. (2019). 'The promises and limits of Bolivia's antiracism law for Afro-Bolivians: tundiqui, the National Afro-Bolivian Council, and the battle against blackface', *Latin American and Caribbean Ethnic Studies*, 14 (3), pp. 334–347. Available at: Doi: doi:10.1080/17442222.2019.1664722.

Caicedo Sarralde, D. (2023). 'Colombia's New Way Towards "Living Well"', *Versus*, 20 February. Available at: https://www.versuslehti.fi/tiededebatti/colombias-new-way-towards-living-well/.

Choque Mamani, T. (2014). *Estado plurinacional aparente.* La Paz: Autodeterminación.

Claros, L. and Díaz Cuéllar, V. (eds.). (2022). *Crisis política en Bolivia 2019–2020.* La Paz: Rosa Luxemburg Stiftung and Plural Editores.

Collins, P. H. (2019). *Intersectionality as Critical Social Theory*. Durham: Duke University Press.

Crenshaw, K. (1991). 'Mapping the margins: intersectionality, identity politics, and violence against women of color', *Stanford Law Review*, 43 (6), pp. 1241–1299. Available at: Doi:doi:10.2307/1229039.

Crespo, A. (1995). *Esclavos negros en Bolivia*. La Paz: Libreria Editorial 'Juventud'.

Cubillo-Guevara, A. P. and Hidalgo-Capitán, A. L. (2015). 'El sumak kawsay genuino como fenómeno social amazónico ecuatoriano', *OBETS: Revista de Ciencias Sociales*, 10 (2), pp. 301–333. Available at: https://doi.org/10.14198/OBETS2015.10.2.02.

Farah, I. and Vasapollo, L. (eds.). (2011). *Vivir Bien: ¿paradigma no capitalista?* La Paz: CIDES–UMSA.

Gudynas, E. (2011). 'Buen Vivir: today's tomorrow', *Development*, 54 (4), pp. 441–447.

Hooker, J. (2005). 'Indigenous inclusion/black exclusion: race, ethnicity and multicultural citizenship in Latin America', *Journal of Latin American Studies*, 37 (2), pp. 285–310.

Htun, M. (2013). *Inclusion without representation in Latin America: gender quotas and ethnic reservations*. Cambridge: Cambridge University Press.

Huanacuni Mamani, F. (2012). '*Cosmovisión andina*', in *Conjunto de visiones sobre post modernidad* (Ciclo de conferencias). La Paz: Publicaciones Casa de la Libertad, pp. 23–35.

Instituto Nacional de Estadísticas (INE). (2015). *Censo de población y vivienda 2012*. Características de la población. La Paz.

Klein, H. S. (2003). *A Concise History of Bolivia*. Cambridge: Cambridge University Press.

Komadina, J. and Regalsky, P. (2016). *La política de la saya: el movimiento afroboliviano*. La Paz: Plural Editores.

Kunstek Salinas, L. C. (2021). *Buscando el sentido: una mirada comunicacional de la construcción del estado Plurinacional de Bolivia*. Cochabamba: Editorial Verbo Divino Bolivia.

Lalander, R. (2014). 'The Ecuadorian resource dilemma: sumak kawsay or development?', *Critical Sociology*, 42(4–5), pp. 623–642. Available at: https://doi.org/10.1177/0896920514557959.

Lang, M. (2019). 'Plurinationality as a strategy: transforming local state institutions toward buen vivir'. In *Postdevelopment in Practice: Alternatives, Economies, Ontologies*, edited by Klein, E. and Morreo, C. E.London: Routledge, pp. 176–189.

Loayza Bueno, R. (2014). *Halajtayata: racismo y etnicidad en Bolivia*. La Paz: Fundación Konrad Adenauer.

López Flores, P. and Ranta, E. (2024). 'Post-extractivist horizons in Latin America: between utopias and struggles for re-existence against neo-extractivism', *Sociological Research Online*. Available at: https://doi.org/10.1177/13607804241275293.

Machaca Benito, G. C. and Ballivián Vásquez, J. C. (2016). *El pueblo afrodescendiente en Bolivia: de la clandestinidad a la visibilidad protagónica*. Cochabamba: FUNPROEIB Andes.

Macusaya Cruz, C. (2022). *En Bolivia no hay racismo, indios de mierda*. La Paz: Jichha.

Mamo, D. (2022). *Indigenous world 2022*. Copenhagen: IWGIA.

Nuñez del Prado, J. (2015). *Utopía indígena truncada: proyectos y praxis de poder indígena en Bolivia plurinacional*. La Paz: CIDES/UMSA.

Ponce Vargas, M. I., Ballivian, J. C. and Ballivian, M. M. (2014). 'Sociedad y cultura'. In *El pueblo afroboliviano: historia, cultura y economía*, edited by Zambrana, A. Cochabamba: FUNPROEIB Andes, pp. 169–225.

Postero, N. (2017). *The Indigenous state: race*, politics, and performance in plurinational Bolivia. Oakland, CA: University of California Press.

Radcliffe, S. A. (2012). 'Development for a postneoliberal era? Sumak kawsay, living well and the limits to decolonisation in Ecuador', *Geoforum*, 43 (2), pp. 240–249.

Radhuber, I. M. (2012). 'Indigenous struggles for a plurinational state: an analysis of Indigenous rights and competences in Bolivia', *Journal of Latin American Geography*, 11 (2), pp. 167–193. Available at: http://www.jstor.org/stable/24394817.

Ranta, E. M. (2016a). 'Towards a decolonial alternative to development? The emergence and shortcomings of vivir bien as state policy in Bolivia in the era of globalization', *Globalizations*, 13 (4), pp. 425–439. Available at: Doi:doi:10.1080/14747731.2016.1141596.

Ranta, E. M. (2016b). 'La compleja construcción histórica del buen vivir en Bolivia: de resistencias indígenas a política del Estado'. In *Perspectivas sobre el buen vivir: el buen vivir como paradigma societal alternativo*, edited by García-Quero, F. and Guardiola, J. Madrid: Economistas sin Fronteras, 22(23), pp.18–21. Available at: http://base.socioeco.org/docs/dossieres-esf-23.pdf.

Ranta, E. (2022). 'Ethnography of the state in plurinational Bolivia: indigenous knowledge, clientelism and decolonizing bureaucracy'. In *State and statehood in the Global South: theoretical approaches and empirical studies*, edited by Fahimi, M., Flatschart, E. and Schaffar, W. Cham: Springer, pp. 221–237.

Ranta, E. (2023). 'Nascent activism in times of disillusionment: struggles between Indigenous self-determination and state co-optation in plurinational Bolivia', *AlterNative: An International Journal of Indigenous Peoples*, 19 (4), pp. 841–851. Available at: https://doi.org/10.1177/11771801231196637.

Ranta, E. (2024). 'Narratives of authoritarianism in times of crisis: democracy and limitations of progressive politics in plurinational Bolivia', *Journal of Latin American Studies*, 56 (1), pp. 91–114. Available at: https://doi.org/10.1017/S0022216X23000950.

República de Bolivia. (2008). *Nueva constitución política del estado*. Versión oficial aprobada por la Asamblea Constituyente 2007 y compatibilizada en el Honorable Congreso Nacional.

Rey Gutiérrez, M. (1998). *La Saya como medio de comunicación y expresión cultural en la comunidad Afroboliviana*. Tesis de licenciatura. Universidad Mayor de San Andrés. Bolivia.

Rivera Cusicanqui, S. (2013). *Mito y desarrollo en Bolivia: el giro colonial del gobierno del MAS*. La Paz: Piedra Rota and Plural.

Roth, J. (2019). 'Intersectionality'. In *The Routledge handbook to the history and society of the Americas*, edited by Kaltmeier, O., Raab, J., Foley, M., Nash, A., Rinke, S. and Rufer, M.London: Routledge, pp. 330–338. Available at: https://doi.org/10.4324/9781351138703.

Schavelzon, S. (2015). *Plurinacionalidad y Vivir Bien/Buen Vivir: dos conceptos leídos desde Bolivia y Ecuador post-constituyentes*. Quito: CLACSO, pp. 75–285.

Sessarego, S. (2009). 'On the evolution of Afro-Bolivian Spanish subject verb agreement: variation and change', *Sintagma: Revista de Linguistica*, 22, pp. 107–120.

Spedding, A. (2008). 'Los Yungas y el norte de La Paz: cocaleros, colonisadores y afrobolivianos'. In *¿Indígenas o obreros? La construcción política de identidades en el Altiplano Boliviano*, edited by Arnold, D. Y. La Paz: Fundación Unir, pp. 429–470.

Spedding, A. (2013). 'La racionalidad del racismo: Reflexiones sobre la ausencia de un debate', *Temas Sociales*, (33), pp. 109–153.

Tapia, L. (2017). 'Análisis de Bolivia'. In *América Latina, entre movilización y derechización: cuatro análisis de país*, edited by Svampa, M., Tapia, L., Atanassova, D. and Lander, E. Quito: Fundación Rosa Luxemburg, pp. 29–40.

Tejerina Vargas, V. S. (2014). 'Los afrobolivianos y su historia colonial y republicana'. In *El pueblo afroboliviano: historia, cultura y economía*, edited by Zambrana, A. Cochabamba: FUNPROEIB Andes, pp. 33–84.

Viveros Vigoya, M. and Gregorio Gil, C. (2014). 'Sexualidades e interseccionalidad en América Latina, el Caribe y su diáspora', *Revista de Estudios Sociales*, 49, p. 9–16. Available at: http://hdl.handle.net/10481/32440.

Wade, P. (2009). *Race and Sex in Latin America*. London: Pluto Press.

Wade, P. (2010). *Race and Ethnicity in Latin America*. London: Pluto Press.

Yampara, S. (2001). *El ayllu y la territorialidad en los Andes: una aproximación a chambi grande*. La Paz: UPEA/Inti-Andino/CADA.

Yañez Inofuentes, P. (2016). 'Cartografías y discursos del movimiento afroboliviano'. In *La política de la saya: el movimiento afroboliviano*, edited by Komadina, J. and Regalsky, P. La Paz: Plural Editores, pp. 11–16.

Zambrana Balladares, A. (2014). 'El pueblo afro y su historia contemporánea'. In *El pueblo afroboliviano: historia, cultura y economía*, edited by Zambrana, A. Cochabamba: FUNPROEIB Andes, pp. 85–168.

Zegada, C. T. and Canedo, V. G. (2023). *Mi delito es ser indio: política y racismo en Bolivia (2006–2021)*. La Paz: CERES/Plural.

Zegada, M. T., Brockmann, E., Guzmán, D. and Ojeda, A. (2021). *Disonancias en la representación política: partidos aparantes y sociedad en acción (1982–2020)*. La Paz: CERES and Plural Editores.

7 Revisiting the Indigeneity–modernity relationship

Vivir bien in the Bolivian Highlands

María Fernanda Córdova Suxo

Introduction

Vivir bien (living well) in the post-development discourse represents an alternative to conventional development paradigms that prioritise economic growth and Western-centric notions of progress. For post-development thinkers, *vivir bien* offers a framework that emphasises holistic wellbeing, environmental sustainability and harmony with nature. It rejects the idea of development as mere economic growth and instead promotes a more balanced and culturally sensitive approach to human and environment relationships. The key actor in the pursuit of this alternative was positioned as the Indigenous subject (Medina 2001; Gudynas 2011; Acosta 2017).

In the Bolivian context, the concept of *vivir bien* has diverged from the qualities generally associated with it in post-development discourse. Although the Bolivian constitution and national development plans present *vivir bien* as a civilisational horizon that rejects capitalist progress and offers a viable alternative for development (Constitution of the Plurinational State of Bolivia 2009; Ministerio de Planificación del Desarrollo 2006), its practical implementation reveals a different reality. In practice, this narrative has been used to justify projects involving natural resource exploitation (Coaquira Siñani 2010; Blanco et al. 2017), displacement of Indigenous populations (Achtenberg 2017), and limited state intervention in regulating employment and private entrepreneurship (Wanderley 2009; Chambi Mayta 2017). Nonetheless, these activities have been framed within the context of positive economic growth, poverty reduction, and expanded basic service coverage (Wanderley 2018, UDAPE 2021). Thus, *vivir bien* has served as the rhetorical backdrop for a developmental and modernisation agenda pursued by a government that leverages an Indigenous narrative for its positioning.

Amid this scenario, contradictions and paradoxes emerge that challenge the principles of post-development and its main advocates. For instance, the use of ancestral Indigenous rhetoric alongside a sense of modern development appears contradictory, challenging conventional ideas about indigeneity and development. This paradox, which integrates ancestral rhetoric with a developmentalist approach, presents an important juncture for exploration. It underscores the

DOI: 10.4324/9781003477921-9

necessity to reassess the analytical frameworks applied to understanding what might be seen as an 'opposition,' or more accurately, a complex encounter.

This article employs three analytical frameworks – hybridity, coloniality, and the division of labour – to examine narratives derived from material collected during a collaborative doctoral research project conducted between 2021 and 2024. The analysis includes statements from Indigenous leaders of social movements (such as the Confederación Sindical Única de Trabajadores Campesinos de Bolivia, CSUTCB; and the Bartolina Sisa National Federation, Bartolinas), authorities, intellectuals, and local academics, as well as official documents (laws, development reports, and speeches). The aim of reviewing these frameworks is to understand how indigeneity is positioned alongside the narrative of *vivir bien* within the context of practical experiences in Bolivia. The analysis entails multiple apparent paradoxes and ambiguities: there is not only a perceived discrepancy between development policy and the rhetoric of *vivir bien*, but also in the conceptualisation of the Indigenous subject and the aspiration for modernity.

While hybridity approaches provide an explanation of how two contradictory elements merge into a third hybrid, coloniality is the condition for indigeneity to emerge (Escobar 1995; De la Cadena 2010). Coloniality also refers to the persistence of colonial legacies in structures of power in spite of the shifting of stakeholders (González Casanova 2006; Rivera Cusicanqui 2010). The third analytical approach, which foregrounds the division of labour and the market through economic and class considerations, suggests a reframing of the Indigenous subject towards the most accurate readings that emphasise the material aspects in which it unfolds and therefore its challenges (Macusaya 2022; Tassi 2023). The experience of Indigenous communities and political organisations – as key subjects of post-development – in the Bolivian Andes, in relation to the *vivir bien* proposal, suggests interesting practical evolutions to date, inviting us to revisit the limits and possibilities of analytical frameworks that describe and interpret such paradoxes, and ultimately provide evidence for development theories.

The chapter begins with the introduction of theoretical considerations on the conceptualisation of the Indigenous subject from the post-development perspective and the relationship of this subject with modernity. It continues by presenting the evolution of the Bolivian scenario in its social and political experience with *vivir bien*. Based on this context, the approaches of hybridity and coloniality are explored as frameworks for analysing the intersections between indigeneity and modernity. This analysis is supported by testimonies and contributions from local actors and scholars. Lastly, the division of labour and market approach is introduced, which highlights economic factors often overlooked by the previous two approaches. The overall analysis, providing evidence to advocate for a cohesive articulation of needs, calls for re-engagement with local challenges within a global framework.

Theoretical considerations

The Indigenous subject in post-development

The post-development critique of the development discourse highlights the ambiguity and vagueness of the concept and argues that development perpetuates social polarisation and inequality within countries (Sachs 1992; Escobar 1995). Development, according to the post-development critique, has failed to achieve transformation from poverty to modernity, disrupted social structures and created a feeling of alienation and cultural displacement among individuals and communities (Sachs 1992). This critique, emerging from a strong post-structuralist perspective, highlights the structural machinery – which involves conceptual frameworks, institutions and global power dynamics – that have enabled the narrative of underdevelopment to prevail, thereby characterising the subjects of that underdeveloped setting.

These subjects shaped by systems of representations within the development framework are analysed by Escobar (1995). He describes these systems of representation 'as places of encounter where identities are constructed and also where violence is originated, symbolised, and managed' (Escobar 1995: 10). Escobar (1995: 155) analyses the discursive practices of the World Bank, where subjectivities – such as peasants or women – are defined through a process of 'enframing'. This process refers to the objectification of subjects, who then internalise and adopt the label of 'new client categories', transforming themselves into spectacles (Escobar 1995: 155). By spectacles it is meant that they become representations that serve specific interests and power structures.

This theoretical framework defines what is referred to in this article as subjects of development, whether beneficiaries, aid recipients or other roles analysed by Escobar (1995) when addressing 'peasants' or 'women'. The Indigenous subject, consequently and perhaps unintentionally, was thus placed as a spectacle of post-development by being depicted as the central figure in the alternative approach to the contested development. Proposals of post-development rely on enframing whereby characteristics and practices are attributed to Indigenous peoples: characteristics, such as the holding of alternative worldviews or resistance against extractive practices (Kothari et al. 2019: 14), embodying cultural resilience and autonomy and solidarity (Kothari et al. 2019: 1), and being a steward of the environment (Kothari et al. 2019: 3). By portraying Indigenous peoples as central to alternative development narratives, the essentialisation of their identities becomes unavoidable and the complexity of their realities and the persistence of their marginalisation are overlooked (Kiely 1999).

The Indigenous subject, as a key figure in post-development, emerges gradually. In its early stages, it is shaped by local, traditional and ecological discourses (see Shiva 1988; Rahnema 1992; Escobar 1995). Critics argue that by reducing subjectivities to discourse, post-development theory fails to capture their diversity, stripping the subject of agency and rendering them passive recipients of external influences (see Kiely 1999). This critique warns against romanticising

Indigenous subjects within post-development discourse. Asher and Wainwright (2019) emphasise the danger of oversimplified portrayals that reduce Indigenous peoples to symbols of resistance against capitalism and guardians of nature, overlooking their agency and diverse experiences their role in the international division of labour. Despite such warnings, the radical approach persists, grounded in the notion of a singular, articulated indigeneity, disregarding the diversity, dissidence, and varied experiences of organised subjects. The introduction to the book *Pluriverse: A Post-Development Dictionary* (Kothari et al. 2019) reaffirms Indigenous peoples as central actors challenging dominant paradigms and promoting alternative ways of life. The recognition of their capacity for mobilisation and resistance remains confined to opposing the dominant colonial capitalist patriarchal world system and advocating for the rights of nature (Kothari et al. 2019: 14). These characteristics encounter limitations in the practical case of Indigenous organisations in Bolivia. Furthermore, as will be shown below, even more divergence is evident in their understanding and application of *vivir bien*, as a purported alternative to conventional development.

New indigeneities

There are approaches that explain the emergence of indigeneity in the light of a colonial order that defines it, encapsulated by the notion that: 'for every settler, there is a native' (Mamdani 2004: 11). However, the complexity of the Indigenous subject transcends the boundaries of colonial determination. The articulation of the international Indigenous rights movement incorporates transnational actors such as governmental and non-governmental organisations, financial and legal institutions, and activists (Niezen 2013), thus modifying and broadening what constitutes the Indigenous subject. This movement has expanded to include other marginalised groups beyond those traditionally considered 'Indigenous' due to settler colonialism. The Indigenous movement became a strategy of resistance against forms of domination and exploitation in their own contexts, such as authoritarian regimes (see Yeh 2007). Over time, indigeneity is also expressed in a way that is detached from its originally constitutive elements – land, self-determination and sovereignty – as evidenced by diasporas (see Schein 2007). It also assumes positions of power, such as can be seen in the case of the Indigenous government in Bolivia, and establishes itself as a narrative in academia and knowledge, thereby enabling its dissemination as a discourse of empowerment and recognition worldwide.

Within the context of globalisation and an ongoing ideal of modernity, new means of expression and spaces of action come to light. To approach modernity as a constitutive element of Indigenous peoples is considered an incompatible statement, especially in the case of the Indigenous subject of post-development that promotes the Indigenous subject as a way to rescue untouched practices and knowledge. But in light of the aforementioned new forms of indigeneity, modernity is very much present in its unfolding. While modernity is often understood as being characterised by the rise of industrialisation, urbanisation and the emphasis on rationality and scientific progress, authors such as Comaroff and Comaroff (1993) contest this by observing that in different contexts the term connotes a sense of belonging to the present, while being aware of the past, allowing individuals to both connect and distance themselves from historical continuities. Modernity is positioned as a metaphor for emerging materialities and cultural expressions in the present. Chatterjee (1997) and Chakrabarty (2000) refer to multiple or alternative modernities, arguing that different cultural contexts can give rise to different forms of modernity, acknowledging the agency of non-Western societies in shaping their own modern experiences. The Latin American experience of modernity is characterised by Echeverría (2002) as a tension between the imposition of Western rationality and the persistence of Indigenous, *Mestizo*, or non-European cultural elements. He formulates the concept of baroque modernity, emphasising the coexistence of seemingly contradictory elements within the modernisation of societies (Echeverría 2002). The baroque, in this sense, represents a form of expression that embraces hybridity, ambiguity and cultural diversity.

The hybrid characteristic is notable for attributing inherent traits to both the coloniser and colonised, the Indigenous and non-Indigenous, and the modern and traditional. This means that hybridity involves the blending of these diverse and often opposing elements. Hybridity can only manifest when these contrasting characteristics are well-defined and meet in a hybrid expression (Escobar 1995). In the context of modernity, the emergence of new features in Indigenous identities adds such dynamism that it becomes challenging to determine their defining traits for developmental purposes. While the agency of the Indigenous subject is more visible in the discourse of multiple or alternative modernities, a cultural focus often predominates in categorising the subject, disregarding the political and economic forces that also shape its constitution. Hybridity approaches allow for categorising and labelling the convergence of apparent contrasting elements, yet this may not address the roots of coloniality and other forms of violence that emanate from current power structures. As we will explore further in the case of the Bolivian Andes, even in situations of apparent hybridity where indigeneity is emphasised, coloniality, exploitation and appropriation persist, perpetrated by various actors in different contexts.

The political relevance of *vivir bien* in Bolivia

The concept of *vivir bien,* known as *suma qamaña* in Aymara, embodies an anti-capitalist development paradigm. This paradigm was officially incorporated into Bolivia's Development Policy Plan in the year 2006 (Ministerio de Planificación del Desarrollo) and is enshrined in the country's political constitution as an ethical principle for a plural society (Constitution of the Plurinational State of Bolivia Art 8 2009: para I). According to this paradigm, the discourse of *vivir bien* aims to recover the wisdom and knowledge of ancestral Indigenous peoples as a mechanism to combat contemporary challenges such as food, climate economic and energy crises (Morales Ayma 2011).

Although *vivir bien* is presented as an ancestral concept, its articulation has only emerged in the past 50 years. Its institutional political positioning traces back to discourses within the circles of peasant syndicates, particularly the Confederación Sindical Única de Trabajadores Campesinos de Bolivia (CSUTCB), during the 1980s. This period witnessed the organised re-articulation of peasant-worker alliances as a form of resistance against authoritarian regimes and the ensuing economic crises (Ávila Rojas 2018). The neoliberal crisis, characterised by the privatisation of natural resources and relocation of rural populations, was the scenario for social articulation, consolidating the proposal of the Political Instrument for the Sovereignty of the Peoples MAS-IPSP (Zuazo 2009). This proposal positioned Indigenous peasants as the protagonists and promoters of their own development, taking up the narrative of *vivir bien* to conduct their aspirations.

While *vivir bien* is often associated with Indigenous knowledge, or is considered a concept of Indigenous peoples, its integration into development plans and academic discourse reflects a broader collaborative effort. Researchers, academic institutions, international organisations and NGOs collaborated to establish *vivir bien* as an alternative to conventional development. This shift gained traction through publications like Medina's (2001) and investment in development programs promoting *vivir bien*. From 2006 to 2019, the Bolivian government facilitated discussions among post- and decolonial thinkers to conceptualise this new paradigm in Bolivia. Key figures like Gayatri Spivak contributed to these dialogues (Vicepresidencia del Estado Plurinacional 2011). In Bolivia, debates persist regarding the ancestral origins of the term (see Ávila Rojas 2018; Macusaya 2022). Nevertheless, its significance lies in its portrayal of the brief yet impactful opportunity as a unique development initiative supported by Indigenous, peasant and native communities in Bolivia.

Vivir bien derailing from the post-development discourse

Under the leadership of Evo Morales, renowned as the first Indigenous president, and the MAS-IPSP, Bolivia transitioned into the Plurinational State in 2009. During this period, *vivir bien* emerged as a prominent slogan within official discourse, extending from being a component of authorities' rhetoric during national celebrations to featuring in various forms of public advertising, including infrastructure projects such as roads, sewerage systems, and industrial ventures like hydrocarbon and lithium extraction. However, the assertion in official documents and speeches that prioritised a harmonious and balanced relationship with nature and the utilisation of local and traditional knowledge was questioned during the conflict regarding the Isiboro Sécure National Park and Indigenous Territory (TIPNIS). In the IX March for the Dignity of Territory and Life in 2012, Indigenous peoples from the Amazon region united to oppose the government's plan to construct an inter-oceanic highway cutting through their territory. This protest garnered support from social movements in the highlands, who were key players in the political movement of the then Indigenous government. This mobilisation marked the emergence of a counter-hegemonic Indigenous movement (Burman 2014), which positioned itself against the policies of the Indigenous government.

Bolivia's exploitative economic base has not been altered with a new development discourse, nor has *vivir bien* provided an alternative framework to Bolivia's dependence on and extraction of natural resources. On the contrary, the social turnaround with respect to fiscal policy on natural resources allowed for positive economic growth (see Ministerio de Economía y Finanzas Públicas 2015, 2018, 2022), and was finally institutionalised through the Mother Earth Framework Law (2015). In this law, the rights of human beings are not subordinated to those of Mother Earth, but are on the same level, thus giving rise to the conduct of extractive policies in the name of social welfare (Postero 2017). Villanueva Rance et al. (2022: 96) state: 'economic growth and social integration policies seem to have led to a rapid process of capitalist modernisation in Bolivia and a corresponding expansion of the demands of its citizens'. The current *vivir bien* discourse is configured in this contrasting way, referring to an idea of ancestry and preservation of the environment, but also used as a political banner related to economic growth and social stability based on conventional development measures, such as the exploitation of natural resources.

The case of Bolivia illustrates the tension between rhetoric and reality, between the idealised notion of *vivir bien* and the actual policies and practices on the ground. Despite being promoted as a transformative alternative to conventional development paradigms, *vivir bien* has not fundamentally altered Bolivia's exploitative economic base or dependency on natural resource extraction. Rather, it has been co-opted into a discourse that simultaneously invokes notions of ancestral wisdom and environmental preservation while serving as a political tool to justify economic growth through resource exploitation. This stark contrast is evident in the trajectory of Bolivia's economic policies, which, while fostering positive growth, have also accelerated capitalist modernisation and widened societal demands. Indigenous peoples, representing diverse perspectives and experiences, have assumed different positions with varying degrees of resistance and compliance (see also the chapter by Ranta and Zenteno in this volume). While some have found avenues for self-determination and access to basic services within the political framework, others continue to face marginalisation and displacement due to extractive projects.

The Bolivian highlands, a hybrid scenario?

The Bolivian highlands are located in the western part of the country at approximately 3,600 metres above sea level, encompassing two of Bolivia's largest cities, La Paz and El Alto. Additionally, this region has the highest numbers of people identifying as Quechua and Aymara, the two largest Indigenous groups in Bolivia. Together, these groups make up about 60% of the Indigenous population in Bolivia (Centro de Documentación e Información Bolivia [CEDIB] 2013).

When referring to hybridity in this context, it is commonly associated with cultural notions, addressing the encounter of two opposites, merging Indigenous, native elements with modern or external ones. Scholars such as Escobar (1995) and de la Cadena (2010) offer insights into this formation, making reference to processes of cultural hybridisation. Escobar (1995), building on the work of García Canclini (1990), understands hybridity as involving negotiated realities and contexts shaped by traditions, capitalism and modernity. However, he also sees hybridity as dialectical images produced in ongoing contexts of conquest and domination (Escobar 1995: 220). Hybridity, viewed as a form of resistance, can be seen as ironic. This is because, as even Escobar acknowledges, resisting modernisation entirely is unrealistic. Hybrid expressions, which blend traditional and modern elements, depend on the continued presence of modern influences to exist. In other words, to resist modernisation, one must engage with modern elements, creating a sort of paradox where resistance relies on the very thing it opposes.

Recognising the presence of hybrid manifestations would imply that the meeting of contrasting elements creates a certain form of conflict. Such conflicts can provide insight into the underlying structure that allows them to manifest in this manner. In this regard, Rivera Cusicanqui (2010) states that, prior to the postcolonial and decolonial wave, local authors were already interpreting reality and analysing it through the conflicts generated by the encounters of antagonistic elements. Approaches such as the *sociedad abigarrada* (variegated or motley society) (Zavaleta Mercado 1986), *bovarista* (Tamayo 1910), or the counter discourse of the *indio* identity (Reinaga 1970), characterise the Andean society in its inherent conflict, diversity and dialogue with modernity. Currently, approaches such as the *chix'i* (Rivera Cusicanqui 2020) emerge from the aforementioned, as a continuity to those contributions. The *chix'i* approach is postulated as an exercise of the sociological imagination, driven by the intention to 'problematise the reality of the here and now' (Rivera Cusicanqui 2020: 13), proposing an embracing of these contrasts, but also a reconciliation between both poles.

Hybridity in Bolivia was notably expressed through the 1952 nation-building and development project of *mestizaje*, through inclusive reforms in education, voting rights, and land distribution. However, this project faced challenges from marginalised populations who protested their exclusion and invisibility under the homogenising effects of *mestizaje*. The 2006 establishment of the Plurinational State, alongside the concept of *vivir bien*, raised hopes for moving beyond the traditional liberal nation-state framework. In this political context, hybrid expressions increased, making Indigenous practices and customs more visible in areas traditionally confined to state functions, office work, and bureaucracy.

De la Cadena (2010) explores the concept of cosmopolitics among Indigenous peoples from the Andes. These cosmopolitics recognise the coexistence of various socio-natural worlds. De la Cadena acknowledges that the integration of other-than-human cultural or ritual elements into politics stems from historical-social practices that often oppose neoliberalism. Furthermore, she suggests that Indigenous politicians, who navigate multiple socio-natural worlds, inevitably become hybrid figures, often embracing this hybridity openly. But additionally, this hybridisation is made tangible by invoking other-than-human representations within the political arena where they operate. According to de la Cadena (2010), those other-than-human elements include rituals – like the *ch'alla,* a gratitude ritual, and the environment, such as the mountains or rivers – which are brought to daily practices and speeches, among other forms of representations, manifesting hybridity. The transfer of rituals into spaces of political engagement by Indigenous subjects also brings about a re-signification. For instance, the ritual will not only perform gratitude to Mother Earth at the beginning of the harvest (as done in August and September in the highlands), but its performance in public spheres will also convey an identity message and a sense of presence and representation in spaces that were previously unavailable to these subjects.

Tito Flores, a community authority in Caluyo who has repeatedly assumed leadership roles in the CSUTCB, shares his experience of incorporating the use of the poncho as a symbol of his authority in the community. He explains that the adoption of this garment as a distinctive feature of communal authority began in the 1990s. He felt particularly empowered wearing this garment, not only in positions of power in Bolivia but also abroad, as he feels, 'you arrive with your identity, with your clothing' (own translation, Flores 2021). Practices such as these are considered to be an exercise of resistance, along the lines that Escobar (1995) would describe. They can offer guidelines for a process of encounter between cultural elements in spaces of political representation, which have traditionally been attributed to be more homogenous and aligned with dominant narratives. However, once the characteristics change, then the space and the subjects are also subject to change, thus the hybrid characteristic is temporal and aims to break away from fixed ideals of one thing or another.

In addition to rituals and Indigenous practices localised in political and discursive spaces, elements configured in a dialogue of modernity and tradition are present in architectural representations, organisational structures and intellectual and artistic expressions of the Aymara population in the Andes (see Thorne 2019). Guido Alejo (2024) refers to them as popular expressions, emphasising the absence of state regulation in their emancipation, in a manner that aligns with modernisation and economic development, facilitated by capital accumulation and the establishment of market networks (see below in the section entitled 'The division of labour and the role of the market'). Given this background, Alejo's description of the current scenario in El Alto could be interpreted as a hybrid expression that merges modern market practices with cultural elements.

However, Alejo's interpretation of this scenario has a deeper undertone of necessity and potential which implies inevitably a form of modernity: 'what people make of modernity is what should be understood by it, but somehow giving it more substance and a better horizon. I'm not talking about creating a *chix'i* world, I'm not talking about *vivir bien*' (own translation, Alejo 2021). As *vivir bien* has turned out to be a demagogic party instrument, Alejo (2021) suggests that the development horizon of this population should reflect its 'more complex and more attuned content to people's daily lives, aimed at the ultimate goal of ensuring that people live well, with dignity'. He notes that many approaches to addressing current challenges necessarily involve finding 'post-modern terms, more oriented towards certain feminisms, certain environmentalism, decolonialisms' but he points out the limits of these thoughts. He announces that rethinking the *alteño* society, with all 'these apparent hybrid social elements, apparent mixtures, is what makes them unique and what they need to express about their current necessities'. He adds that while 'intellectuals are immersed in their struggles over ancestry,' attributing this to academic debates that aim to position Indigenous customs or narratives as ancestral, 'people's daily lives are disregarded' (Alejo 2021).

In Alejo's (2021) understanding, hybridity may characterise encounters between modernity and tradition, and it diverges from *vivir bien* to provide guidelines for an alternative to development. The emphasis is on the need to embrace a form of modernity and traditional development, distanced from the ancestral narrative and more focused on the current needs, issues and other expressions of Andean society.

However, societal complexities can be profound, as within the framework of the hybrid notion, there are also approaches that appeal to biological and racial aspects in subjectivity formation. For example, by referencing *mestizaje*, which refers to the blending of European and Indigenous cultures in Latin America, and *cholaje*, which emphasises Indigenous identity and culture over European influence. Many aspects could make a subject hybrid or not; hybridity is not simply a manifestation of traditional encounters with the modern. In his article on the dynamic interplay between *kataristas* and evangelical Protestantism in Bolivia, Canessa (2000) argues that what may seem like hybrid cultural expressions in the Andes actually challenges the concept of cultural hybridity. Instead, these expressions advocate for essentialist identities and emphasise the importance of preserving historical and cultural continuity over the fluidity of modern cultural expressions. Consequently, hybridity loses explanatory power. Moreover, Lazreg (2002) points out that processes of cultural hybridisation are not exclusive to colonised societies. She states, 'all cultures (including those of industrial nations) are hybrids in one sense or another: they have borrowed from one another and continue to do so' (Lazreg 2002: 139).

According to De la Cadena and Escobar's approaches, hybrid expressions between indigeneity and modernity are a form of resistance, though ironic, as they rely on modern elements for their existence. While these approaches might describe the current configuration of *vivir bie*n as hybrid – blending ancestral knowledge with liberal state actions – the view of 'Indigenous' actors of the Bolivian Andes differs: Hybrid expressions can arise when these subjects gain access to spaces previously closed to them. But this inclusion comes along with a reaffirmation of essentialist cultural identities. Here, modernity is not a defining feature but the dominant framework in which these manifestations take place. Moreover, as a concept it is intended to be appropriated and reinterpreted with the purpose of achieving self-reaffirmation in a globalized context. Consequently, *vivir bien* has shifted to a different plane, representing the current government's rhetoric, and failing to capture the dynamic nature of the subjects it represents.

This continuous bifurcation of apparent opposites highlights numerous explanatory limits. Advocates of the hybridity approach not only rely on a persistent inclination towards essentialism but also on a strong focus on cultural and ontological terms that tend to rigidify characteristics on one side or the other, ultimately negating themselves.

Examining the Indigenous-modernity nexus through coloniality

In post-development discourse, Indigenous people are often depicted as being in a subordinate position due to colonial influences. This narrative suggests that development perpetuates this subordination by undervaluing their knowledge and practices. Therefore, reclaiming and acknowledging their suppressed knowledge is viewed as a form of resistance against coloniality. In Bolivia, Indigenous people, primarily from the Andes, have embarked on a process of inclusion in political, organisational, and economic spheres. Despite this apparent empowerment, they still face inequalities and exclusion. While colonial legacies may explain this ongoing marginalisation, is coloniality also responsible for their aspirations towards modernity? What insights does coloniality provide into the meeting of indigeneity and modernity, and how is it perceived by various Indigenous social actors?

Internal colonialism

The so-called colonial continuities (as specific instances of coloniality) indicate that, despite processes of independence, the configurations of dependence of the Global South on the Global North persist by not breaking away from the order that determines global power dynamics. But coloniality doesn't just flow from outside; it also becomes entrenched within the institutional framework of local organisations. Authors such as González Casanova (2006) and Rivera Cusicanqui (2010) have referred to this situation as internal colonialism. These authors argue that colonialism does not end with the culmination of a process of independence, but is perpetuated by new actors, in many cases by the same ones who were the protagonists of an independence process. In the new configurations of republics or independent states, forms of domination are reproduced, not necessarily by the previous perpetrators, but by the former victims. This implies that even if there is a turnover of subjects within a particular system, the system itself will remain unchanged, because the underlying factors that constitute it are rooted elsewhere. Rivera Cusicanqui (2010) identifies this rootedness in forms of 'internal' colonialism, which operates in contemporary Bolivia as an underlying mode of domination sustained by a long-term colonial horizon. Recent cycles of liberalism and populism have been articulated within this colonial framework without fully overcoming or completely altering the system of oppression (Rivera Cusicanqui 2010: 45). These recent developments have merely adapted long-standing colonial structures, transforming them into modalities of internal colonialism that remain crucial in explaining Bolivia's internal social stratification, social contradictions and specific mechanisms of exclusion-segregation. These mechanisms underlie the deepest and most latent forms of structural violence.

Contemporary urban areas of the Bolivian Altiplano have been shaped as a result of this expulsion-segregation of different political administrative reforms during the neoliberal period. Certain areas were identified as marginal or peripheral by settling at the edges of modernity (Albó 1991; Espósito Guevara 2008). In the Bolivian Andes, the city of El Alto stands as representative of this phenomenon. Today, the economic significance achieved on these margins places them in a new dimension that has an important bearing on the market. Although the aspects of marginalisation related to economic incorporation have been overcome, marginalities manifested mainly through social stratification and the absence of state regulation persist.

Colonisation of the mind

Related to the idea of internal colonialism is the idea of the colonisation of the mind as an explanation for the embracing of Western, alien, modern models of life by local people, or by societies in transition. Paulo Freire (1972) proposes a model that explains how individuals respond to a supra-structural order from different ascending scales. The categories of 'sense of self, awareness, and agency of subjects' will constitute this model of consciousness. The lowest level will be defined as a level of acceptance and belief that circumstances are determined by forces beyond the subject's control (fate, luck), and the highest level of consciousness refers to a critical consciousness, when individuals can engage in critical reflection on the social, political and economic structures (Freire 1972: 57–71).

Rahnema (1992: 125) highlights Freire's contribution in understanding 'the colonised mind'. He argues that societies in a transitional phase lack critical consciousness and instead exhibit a semi-transitive, naive transitive or popular consciousness. This condition leads people to internalise the values of dominant groups and to have a distorted perception of their own condition. The argument is that development as a discourse has also colonised people's minds, hence, an aspiration for Western modernity stems from these circumstances.

The embrace of modernity is often categorised as colonialism of the mind, overlooking that this embracing could be understood as being a struggle for access to public goods, basic services and integration into development. Matthews (2017) questions the idea of mental colonisation by post-development thinkers in order to account for the apparent desire for modernity on the part of subaltern populations. She points out that this idea ignores the agency of the people being talked about and gives insufficient attention to the positionality of the authors who present this explanation. In addition, she emphasises that advocates of mental decolonisation ended up dictating to marginalised people how they should proceed while such a prescriptive approach reproduces what was so much criticised in relation to conventional development. Calling for mental decolonisation then proves to be a very restricted framework in terms of the agency of development subjects.

Colonialism and colonisation from the experience of social actors in the Bolivian Andes

The narrative of activism and political organisation of CSUTCB and Bartolinas and Indianistas is rooted in the revolutionary struggles of 1790, considered the first Indigenous uprising, led by Tupac Katari and his companion Bartolina Sisa, against the Spanish colony. In the narrative of these organisations, there is a strong denunciation of colonialism, which has deprived them of their self-determination and is why they continue to fight to this day. While there have been processes of liberation and inclusion throughout history, discrimination and marginalisation of Indigenous populations still persist. However, these forms of marginalisation are not necessarily framed within the context of colonialism or colonisation of the mind. During my fieldwork, I observed that while colonialism provides an explanatory framework particularly among Indigenous intellectuals, social movement actors argue that the primary issue driving inequalities is the state's failure to meet their demands. Colonialism, therefore, is confined to occupying a discursive space alongside indigeneity and the concept of *vivir bien*.

During an interview with David Choquehuanca (an Aymara intellectual, currently the Vice President of the Plurinational State of Bolivia), he stated, 'since before the founding of the republic, we have never ceased to fight against internal colonialism and external colonialism. Why do we say before the founding? Because we have not been part of that foundation. We have always resisted' (own translation, Choquehuanca 2021: Pos. 98). Additionally, Choquehuanca (2021: Pos. 99) complements this notion with that of a development horizon:

> We have defined the horizon. It says: 'we seek *vivir bien*'. And it says that the Plurinational State must build a Bolivia that is increasingly democratic, increasingly participatory, increasingly inclusive and increasingly transparent. And it says it must be grounded in decolonisation.

In contrast, the social movement actors with whom I conducted collaborative work, attributed the shortcomings and problems they faced to an absence of the state – whether managed by Indigenous or non-Indigenous representatives – rather than referring to the need for a decolonial struggle. Pedro Portugal, an intellectual and *Indianista* activist, asserts that once the discourse of indigeneity and decoloniality is entrenched in power, it takes on a language that correlates 'a political condition to enter the state' (own translation, Portugal 2021), as 'the state has never sought to empower the Indigenous, the Indigenous empowers themselves, clandestinely, and sends out that discourse' (Portugal 2021). Thus, there is a continual negotiation between the subject brought into power and the dominant narrative, which may not necessarily align with their needs and the grassroots horizon, as the latter is constantly shaped by the context.

During a workshop conducted with authorities from the CSUTCB and Bartolinas of the Viacha community, focusing on how international cooperation works in Bolivia, participants indicated that their understanding of *vivir bien* as a development horizon was 'to have stable funding to cover health, education and food needs, with zero corruption in the process' (focus group in workshop on how external cooperation works in Bolivia 2023). This suggests that, there is an evident capacity for responsiveness and negotiation of concepts, resulting in the emergence of new projects through engaging with hegemonic development narratives. This responsiveness underscores the agency of development subjects who can carve out their own spaces to challenge authority and assert power (Arce and Long 2010). As Alejo (2024) argues, the popular or marginal evolves alongside the accumulation of capital and engages in dialogue with modernity. Therefore, the incorporation of 'modern' elements into the daily practices of the Andean population should not be seen as a surrender to ongoing colonial domination, but rather as an expression of their desire to communicate and connect with the world.

The division of labour and the role of the market

It has been argued that *vivir bien* has grown out of the responsiveness of the subjects – Indigenous people, organisations of the Bolivian highlands and government – who call for it, and that these subjects bring seemingly paradoxical elements together in their articulation of *vivir bien*. The approaches of hybridity and coloniality highlight interesting characteristics of the encounter between indigeneity and modernity, but fail to make visible the needs and aspirations of grassroots movements, as well as forms of violence that are underlying the development narrative of *vivir bien*.

The ongoing Bolivian Development Plan emphasises employment as a fundamental pillar for economic stability. Therefore, employment must be formalised and inclusive, particularly in terms of gender (Plan de Desarrollo Económico y Social [PDES] 2023). The history and material conditions surrounding the social movements in question highlight an economic dynamic based on capital accumulation, leading towards a unique form of modernity, as defined by Alejo (2021). This unique characteristic, as previously discussed, is shaped by the cultural elements it exhibits and the lack of state attention to their demands. Although this context has achieved economic incorporation, marginalities continue to be reproduced or emerge.

The following section describes the background of this economic incorporation, aiming to explain why this material dimension challenges interpretations of the interaction between modernity and indigeneity based on hybridity or coloniality. Approaches rooted in hybridity or coloniality tend to rely on rhetoric and focus on resistance and culture. The division of labour and the role of the market provide a more historical and economic perspective of social actors. This dimension also explains the background of social actors in the Bolivian highlands yearning for modernity and distancing themselves from the narrative of the Indigenous subject with ancestral knowledge resilient and resistant to coloniality.

As previously discussed, Bolivia has experienced recent economic growth primarily driven by market activities of the burgeoning middle class, which comprises Indigenous peoples historically integrated into the economy, through their struggles and the surplus generated by the country's extractive policies. This economic expansion occurred particularly under an Indigenous government that introduced a development plan within the framework of *vivir bien*. In the following sections, I present two contributions that explain how the population of the Bolivian Andes, collectively as articulate subjects, succeeded in incorporating themselves into this middle class through their economic activity, engaging in practices of capital accumulation, thereby navigating the intersection of indigeneity and modernity (Macusaya 2022). An additional contribution highlights how market networks were formed as a reaction to existing inequalities (Tassi 2023). While there have been positive advancements, it is crucial to recognise that patterns of exploitation and structural violence persist and continue to be perpetuated.

Macusaya (2022) proposes an analytical framework on racism in Bolivia, explaining why racism persists against Indigenous people despite structural changes in the economy and power dynamics. The author relies on analytical categories related to the division of labour, arguing that the racialisation in the division of labour has conditioned the exploitation of certain population groups. The process of racialisation that classifies and conditions subjects not only normalises exploitation but allows its expression in the most acute way (Macusaya 2022: 57). The colonial order dictated that heavy labour should be carried out by Indigenous people and enslaved Africans, particularly in the Andean region – as a centre of mining activity – leading to their exploitation. This fact has transcended the historical colonial situation, and this condition remains naturalised to this day. The extraction of natural resources continues to be the main source of income for the national economy. Although the labour force has turned to corporate labour, the result of this dynamic is the emergence of other nuclei of exploitation.

The modernisation of the state and its integration into the global market have led to resistance from Indigenous communities, who feel disconnected from the idea of a unified Bolivian national identity (see Reinaga 1970; Macusaya 2019). This has strained existing racial hierarchies, prompting privileged groups to defend their positions of power. In societies where labour divisions are based on race, different groups' identities are shaped by the racialisation of their physical and sociocultural characteristics. These attributes are seen as markers of their social status or category (Macusaya 2022). According to Macusaya (2022), traits such as 'brute force', poverty, and more recently, labels like 'peasants' and 'wise natives', have been historically associated with Indigenous peoples as labour providers.

As we delve into the characteristics mentioned above, we find that these practices predominantly unfold in spaces where capital is generated, such as markets.

Market activities and entrenched practices not only reflect the revitalisation of longstanding regional circuits, but also permeate various organisational spaces, including grassroots assemblies, trade fairs and cultural events such as festivals (Rivera Cusicanqui 2020: 67). A market logic intertwines with the fabric of small-scale guilds, unions and entire communities, all of which persist in their reproductive practices (Rivera Cusicanqui 2020). Moreover, the market serves as a driving force behind the expansion of the middle class (Villanueva et al. 2022), thereby amplifying the visibility of emerging indigeneities. But how is it that the market-Indigenous subject relationship has come about in this way?

Studies of the economic and commercial circuits of the Aymara population describe trade and commerce as a reconfiguration of marginality into a possibility of social and economic affirmation (Tassi 2023: 57). It has been noted above that the settlement of these populations on the margins of urban centres emerged as a result of the displacement of rural populations during the incursion of neoliberal policies on the privatisation of mines. Aymara people relocated to the margins of the cities and began to engage in commercial activities. Tassi (2023) states that in the 1990s, these popular and Indigenous economies were seen as alternatives to the market economy, challenging the traditional capital-labour dynamics. This perspective however, corresponded to the narrative that led to Indigenous practices being depicted as folkloric or decorative, regardless of their background of displacement.

The gradual emergence of small businesses gained ground through rotating loan systems (Tassi 2003) in addition to the expansion of micro-financial lending institutions (Muller 2007). Initially small businesses became 'informal' enterprises, as growth was only possible outside of state regulations on taxes and on the importation of goods. The emerging economic activities involved trade with international merchandise as well as forms of social regulation, in order to cover absences of the state in matters of infrastructure, such as fixing streets or providing basic services (Tassi 2023: 61). But more than that, these networks sustained in market logics have intertwined neighbourhood councils with unions, kinship and neighbourhood relations. These networks have also installed practices for conflict management, limiting the access of government institutions – often considered a burden – to these spaces (Tassi 2023: 62).

This scenario configures a subject who, although anchored in sectoral and territorial organisations, establishes links with producers, traders, transporters and consumers, also affecting those various spaces. These characteristics have been criticised on the one hand, for deviating from formal economic guidelines dictated by the state, while on the other hand for not aligning with an anti-capitalist logic and being in harmony with the environment. The racialised system in which this Indigenous subject has established itself in its dialogue with modernity evidences the permanence of exclusions, as it is beyond the control and attention of the state, yet it also evidences strong characteristics of self-determination. The predominant feature is that despite this economic success and visibility, it is still a marginal subject. Part of this can be explained by the prevailing colonial social stratification in society (see the section examining the Indigenous-modernity nexus through coloniality), but it also calls into question the division of labour that dominates the scope of these subjects within the framework of a global economic system that relies on extractive and exploitative dynamics to exist, and therefore on subjects that remain in this inconclusive integration.

At this point, looking at the historical context, we can see that the involvement and aim of organised Indigenous groups in trade, market activities and the development of once marginalised cities like El Alto is less a meeting of contrasting, paradoxical, or hybrid elements; instead, it is a result of their longstanding political, economic and social roles. The experience of social actors organised within Indigenous social movements shows that their goal of achieving modernity is explained by a historical correlation and the integration into an economic circuit, based on their labour roles. These dynamics distance themself from ancestral practices and knowledge, as understood in post-development discourse. In this context, a narrative of *vivir bien* as an anti-capitalist alternative and respect for Mother Earth, is entirely absent. Moreover, this experience reinforces that concepts of indigeneity, *vivir bien* and also coloniality, are mostly linked to specific spaces of knowledge production that do not necessarily correlate with the experience of grassroots actors. These concepts are not fixed but appear to be in constant negotiation, expanding and being challenged, based on the experiences and needs of its main actors. This highlights how Indigenous communities, based on historical experiences and also on economic necessities, actively shape their own narratives and contribute to broader socio-economic changes.

Final remarks

The analysis of the meeting of indigeneity and modernity has been explored through three approaches that explain this encounter, with its strengths and limitations. *Vivir bien* and its application in the Bolivian Andes as a context of analysis, has offered valuable information, especially by showing a paradox between narratives presenting *vivir bien* as an alternative to conventional development and the practice in which *vivir bien* is being realised, which includes natural resource exploitation and extraction projects, towards the consolidation of a modern capitalist state.

Its historical setting in Bolivia tells us that although the Indigenous subject is considered the bearer of this approach, the way in which the concept of *vivir bien* is positioned in development plans, academic references and other official documents alludes more to a concept that results from the articulation of different agents, hence the influence of different sources of power. Although the characteristics attributed to the Indigenous in post-development writing align with certain aspects of local discourses, post-development thinking has failed to capture the complexity in which it is constructed. It was seen, further, that interesting practical transformations of the empirical implementation of *vivir bien* challenge the frameworks in which an alternative to development is sustained. This is a topic that can be explored more deeply through an analysis of Indigenous subjectivities within the framework of the *vivir bien* discourse.

The academic production and insights from social movements, intellectuals and collectivities from the Bolivian Andes suggest that hybrid manifestations representing the convergence of contrasting elements resulting in conflict, align with a longstanding theoretical tradition characterising Andean society's inherent conflict, diversity and engagement with modernity. However, certain aspects of this approach are limiting and essentialising, as they depend heavily on cultural factors in configuring the subject. Additionally, it has been observed that the discourse of coloniality often parallels the narrative of *vivir bien* but is primarily confined to academic and governmental institutions. This differs from the understanding expressed by grassroots movements when referencing *vivir bien.* It has been observed that the rhetoric of coloniality is highly present in governmental spaces, yet notably absent in the narratives of grassroots movements. Within social movements, criticism and demands are more directed towards the government and its inability to address their concerns.

The incorporation of economic categories is useful for providing the historical and material context of the current position of these social actors. Although social movements use the narrative of *vivir bien*, they use it to contextualise their demands, such as the provision of basic services and a rejection of corruption. The persistence of these shortcomings, despite an Indigenous government that has generally achieved economic incorporation for a marginalised sector of society, finds more correlation with the historical and economic development of this sector. Within this context, an understanding of the marginalisation of indigenous actors makes it possible to see that the co-existence of claims of indigeneity and their interaction with modernity are not a paradox, but rather a consequence of this marginalisation.

While there are colonial structures that remain even after independence processes, forms of structural and symbolic violence also prevail. Marginalisation generated by the capitalist order and sustained by racialised local structures is perpetuated. These are determining factors in the perpetuation of Bolivia's economic matrix based on the exploitation of natural resources and the development of market networks on the margins of formality. These market networks, instead of offering an alternative or serving as a form of resistance to the existing order, manifest the very marginalisation experienced by their participants.

Paying attention to the division of labour helps to illuminate the forces at play beyond that are not captured by dominant narratives of alternatives to development, such as *vivir bien,* where accumulation practices are seen as counterproductive. Thus, the landscape becomes larger and more complex when attempting to interpret or advocate for an alternative to development. The apparent contradiction between indigeneity and modernity merely underscores that both poles of the contradiction are more complex, which complicates the idea of desiring or rejecting an alternative. Priorities and needs are embedded within structural inequalities that perpetuate forms of exploitation and will be continually denounced by the affected social actors in their forms of organisation and protest.

The experience of organised social actors within Indigenous social movements indicates that their longing for inclusion in modernity can be explained by a historical correlation with the integration into an economic circuit, a process that distances itself from ancestral practices and knowledge as understood in post-development approaches. In this context, a narrative of *vivir bien*, as an anti-capitalist alternative that respects Mother Earth, is entirely absent. At the same time, the subject of development, being more dynamic and ever-changing, requires different lenses of analysis to be understood in its entirety and complexity, thereby informing development horizons.

References

Achtenberg, E. (2017) 'The Growing Resistance to Megadams in Bolivia', *Rebel Currents. Nacla*, 14 February. Available at: https://nacla.org/blog/2017/02/20/growing-resistance-megadams-bolivia.

Acosta, A. (2017). 'Living Well: ideas for reinventing the future', *Third World Quarterly*, 38 (12), pp. 2600–2616.

Albó, X. (1991). 'El retorno del indio', *Revista de Estudios Sociales*, (1), pp. 299–366. Available at: Doi:doi:10.7440/res1.1998.19.

Alejo, G. (2021). *Interview with Maria Fernanda Cordova Suxo*, 26 November.

Alejo, G. (2024). 'Interpreting Modernity: Exploring El Alto, Bolivia's Perspective', *EADI Blog. Debating Development Research*. Available at: http://www.developmentresearch.eu/?p=1733.

Arce, A. and Long, N. (2010). 'Reconfiguring modernity and development from an anthropological perspective', in *Anthropology, Development and Modernities*, chapter_1, pp. 15–44. Available at: Doi:doi:10.4324/9780203450895.

Asher, K. and Wainwright, J. (2019) 'After Post-Development: On Capitalism, Difference, and Representation', *Antipode*, 0(0), pp. 1–20.

Ávila Rojas, O. (2018). *Indianismo vs. Vivir Bien. La disputa vigente del indio en Bolivia.* Popayán, Colombia: U. del Cauca.

Blanco, J.F.P.U., Amaya Panche, J. and Diaz Aguirre, C.F. (2017) 'La teoría y la realidad del discurso de protección ambiental y las políticas extractivas en Bolivia', *Revista Internacional de Cooperación y Desarrollo*, 4(1), pp. 137–155. Avaiable at: Doi: doi:10.21500/23825014.3121.

Burman, A. (2014). '"Now we are Indígenas": Hegemony and Indigeneity in the Bolivian Andes', *Latin American and Caribbean Ethnic Studies*, 9(3), pp. 247–271. Available at: DOI:doi:10.1080/17442222.2014.959775.

Canessa, A. (2000) 'Contesting hybridity: Evangelistas and kataristas in highland Bolivia', *Journal of Latin American Studies*, 32 (1), pp. 115–144. DOI:doi:10.1017/S0022216X99005489.

Centro de Documentación e Información Bolivia [CEDIB]. (2013). Indígenas: Quién gana, quién pierde DATOS COMPARATIVOS DE LA POBLACION INDÍGENA CENSOS DE POBLACIÓN, 2001 Y 2012. Available at: https://www.cedib.org/biblioteca/indigenas_quien_gana_quien_pierde/.

Chakrabarty, D. (2000). *Provincializing Europe: Postcolonial Thought and Historical Difference.* Princeton: Princeton University Press.

Chambi Mayta, R. D. (2017) 'Vivir Bien, child labor, and indigenous rights in Bolivia', *Latin American and Caribbean Ethnic Studies*, 12 (2), pp. 95–112. DOI:doi:10.1080/17442222.2017.1318542.
Chatterjee, P. (1997). *Our Modernity.* Rotterdam/Dakar: South-South Exchange Programme for Research on the History of Development (SEPHIS) and the Council for the Development of Social Science Research in Africa (CODESRIA).
Choquehuanca, D. (2021). *Interview with Maria Fernanda Cordova Suxo*, 28 June.
Coaquira Siñani, T. (2010) 'Análisis ambiental de la política energética boliviana', *Investigaciones de la plataforma energética.* La Paz: Centro de Estudios para el Desarrollo Laboral y Agrario CEDLA. Available at: https://biblioteca-repositorio.clacso.edu.ar/bitstream/CLACSO/1327/1/AMBIENTAL.pdf.pdf.
Comaroff, J. and Comaroff, J. L. (1993). *Modernity and its Malcontents: Ritual and Power in Post-Colonial Africa.* Chicago: University of Chicago Press.
Comunidad de Viacha. (2023). *Focus Group conducted byMaria Fernanda Cordova Suxo*, 23 March.
Constitution of the Plurinational State of Bolivia. (2009). Art 8. 'Political Constitution of the Plurinational State of Bolivia'. Available at: https://www.constituteproject.org/constitution/Bolivia_2009.
De la Cadena, M. (2010). 'Indigenous cosmopolitics in the Andes: Conceptual reflections beyond "politics"', *Cultural Anthropology*, pp. 334–370. Available at: DOI: doi:10.1111/j.1548-1360.2010.01061.x.
Echeverría, B. (2002). 'La clave barroca en América Latina', in *Exposición en el Lateinamerika Institut de la Freie Universität Berlin. Berlin.* Available at: https://bolivare.unam.mx/ensayos/la_clave_barroca_en_america_latina.
Escobar, A. (1995). *Encountering development: The making and unmaking of the third world.* Princeton University Press. Available at: doi:10.2307/3034652.
Espósito Guevara, C. A. (2008). 'Exclusión política, des-ciudadanización y profundización de la pobreza urbana en Bolivia'. In *Procesos de urbanización de la pobreza y nuevas formas de exclusión social: Los retos de las políticas sociales de las ciudades latinoamericanas del siglo XXI*, edited by Siglo del Hombre and CLACSO. Bogotá, pp. 295–317.
Flores, T. (2021). *Interview with Maria Fernanda Cordova Suxo*, 27 October.
Freire, P. (1972). *Cultural Action for Freedom.* Harmondsworth, Middlesex, England: Penguin Books.
García Canclini, N. (1990). *Culturas Híbridas: Estrategias Para Entrar y Salir de la Modernidad.* Grijalbo.
González Casanova, P. (2006). 'El colonialismo interno', in *Sociología de la Explotación.* Instituto Nacional de Estadística Bolivia [INE] (2024). Bolivia: Líneas de Pobreza Extrema, según área 2005–2018, Encuesta de hogares, pp. 185–205.
Gudynas, E. (2011). 'Buen Vivir: Today's tomorrow', *Development*, 54 (4), pp. 441–447.
Kiely, R. (1999). 'The Last Refuge of the Noble Savage? A Critical Assessment of Post-Development Theory', *European Journal of Development Research*, 11 (1), pp. 30–55.
Kothari, A., Salleh, A., Escobar, A., Demaria, R. and Acosta, A. (2019). *Pluriverse: A Post-Development Dictionary.* New Delhi: Tulika Books.
Lazreg, M. (2002). 'Development: Feminist Theory's Cul-de-sac'. In *Feminist Postdevelopment Thought. Rethinking Modernity, Post-Colonialism and Representation*, edited by Saunders, K.New York: Zed Books Ltd.
Macusaya, C. (2019). *Batallas por la identidad. Indianismo, Katarismo y descolonización en la Bolivia contemporánea.* (1st ed.). Edited by Coronel, D. Lima, Perú: Nanuk E.I.R.L.

Macusaya, C. (2022). *En Bolivia no hay racismo, indios de mierda. Apuntes de un problema negado.* La Paz: Jichha.

Mamdani, M. (2004) 'Race and Ethnicity as Political Identities in the African Context', in Hack, R. D. (ed.) *Key Words Identity.* France: Alliance of Independent Publishers, pp. 1–24.

Matthews, S. J. (2017). 'Colonised minds? Post-development theory and the desirability of development in Africa', *Third World Quarterly*, 38 (12), pp. 2650–2663. Available at: Doi: https://doi.org/10.1080/01436597.2017.1279540.

Medina, J. (2001). 'Suma Qamaña. La comprensión indígena de la Vida Buena', La Paz: programa de Apoyo a la Gestión Pública Descentralizada y Lucha contra la Pobreza de la Cooperación Técnica Alemana (PADEP/GTZ).

Ministerio de Economía y Finanzas Públicas (2022) 'Memoria de la economía Boliviana 2021', pp. 338. Available at: https://www.economiayfinanzas.gob.bo/memorias-economia-boliviana.

Ministerio de Economía y Finanzas Públicas (2018) 'Memoria de la economía boliviana 2017', pp. 350. Available at: https://www.economiayfinanzas.gob.bo/memorias-economia-boliviana.

Ministerio de Economía y Finanzas Públicas (2015) 'Memoria de la economía boliviana 2014', pp. 284 Available at: https://www.economiayfinanzas.gob.bo/memorias-economia-boliviana.

Ministerio de Planificación del Desarrollo. (2006). 'Plan nacional de desarrollo: Bolivia digna, soberana, productiva y democrática para Vivir Bien'. *Estado Plurinacional de Bolivia.* Available at: https://www.bivica.org/files/plan-nacional-desarrollo.pdf.

Morales Ayma, E. (2011). 'Prólogo', in Farah, I. and Vasapollo, L. (eds), in *Vivir bien: ¿Paradigma no capitalista?* Plural Editores, pp. 7–10.

Muller, H. (2007). 'Las microfinanzas reguladas en Bolivia', *Tinkazos* [online], 10(22), pp. 71–82. Available at: http://www.scielo.org.bo/scielo.php?script=sci_arttext&pid=S1990- 74512007000100005&lng=es&nrm=iso.

Niezen, R. (2003). 'The Origins of the International Movement of Indigenous Peoples', *The Origins of Indigenism*, pp. 29–52.

Plan de Desarrollo Económico y Social [PDES]. (2023). PDES – 2021–2025.

Portugal, P. (2021). *Interview with Maria Fernanda Cordova Suxo*, 26 November.

Postero, N. (2017) *The Indigenous State.* Oakland, California: University of California Press.

Rahnema, M. (1992). 'Participation', in *The development dictionary.* London: Zed Books Ltd., pp. 116–131.

Reinaga, F. (1970). *La revolución India.* (4th ed.). La Paz: MINKA. Available at: https://enriquedussel.com/txt/Textos_200_Obras/Giro_descolonisador/Revolucion_india-Fausto_Reinaga.pdf.

Rivera Cusicanqui, S. (2010). *Violencias (re) encubiertas en Bolivia.* La Paz: WA-GUI T.

Rivera Cusicanqui, S. (2020). *Un mundo Ch'ixi es posible.* (2nd ed.). La Paz: Piedra Rota y Tinta Limón.

Sachs, W. (1992). *The Development Dictionary. A Guide to Knowledge as Power.* Edited by Sachs, W. London: Zed Books Ltd.

Schein, L. (2007). 'Diasporic Media and Hmong/Miao Formulations of Nativeness and Displacement', in *Indigenous Experience Today.* Berg Publishers, pp. 225–245.

Shiva, V. (1988). 'Development, Ecology and Women', in *Staying Alive: Women, Ecology and Survival in India.* New Delhi: Zed Books Ltd., pp. 1–13.

Tamayo, F. (1910). *Creación de la pedagogía nacional.* (2nd ed.). La Paz: Universidad Catolica Boliviana San Pablo.

Tassi, N. (2023). 'La emergencia de la economía popular en Bolivia', in *Economías populares. Una cartografía crítica latinoamericana.* Buenos Aires: CLACSO Consejo Latinoamericano de Ciencias Sociales, pp. 11–54.

Thorne, M. (2019) 'Cuando el subalterno construye: Freddy Mamani y la emergencia del cholo power boliviano', *Lógoi*, 0(35), pp. 75–86. Available at: http://dle.rae.es/?id=8xj3EL8.

Unidad de Análisis de Políticas Sociales y Económicas de Bolivia [UDAPE] (2021) 'Informe nacional voluntario'. La Paz: UDAPE. Vicepresidencia del Estado Plurinacional. (2010). *Pensando el mundo desde Bolivia.* Instituto Internacional de Integración del Convenio Andrés Bello.

Villanueva Rance, A., Paz Gonzales, E. and Rance, S. (2022). 'The Middle Classes in Bolivia: "Not a Good Idea"?', in Villanueva Rance, A., Paz Conzales, E. and Ranse, S. (eds.) *Middle Class Identities and Social Crisis.* London: Routledge.

Yeh, E. (2007). 'Tibetan Indigeneity: Translations, Resemblances, and Uptake', in *Indigenous Experience Today*, pp. 69–98.

Wanderley, F. (2018) *Los avances sociales y laborales en el periodo de boom económico y los Desafíos con el fin de la bonanza*, Documento de Trabajo. 02/18. La Paz. Available at: https://www.ptonline.com/articles/how-to-get-better-mfi-results.

Wanderley, F. (2009) Crecimiento, empleo y bienestar social ¿Por qué Bolivia es tan desigual? *Umbrales. Revista del Postgrado Multidisciplinario en Ciencias del Desarrollo.* 1st. Edited by CIDES-UMSA. La Paz: Plural Editores.

Zavaleta Mercado, R. (1986). *Lo nacional-popular en Bolivia.* (1st ed.). Edited by Soler, M. Mexico: Siglo XXI Editores.

Zuazo, M. (2009). *¿Cómo nació el MAS-IPSP? La ruralización de la política en Bolivia.* La Paz: Friedrich Ebert Stiftung-Bolivia (FES).

8 'Money is a universal need'

Exploring Indigenous peoples' engagement with externally-led development in the Peruvian Amazon

Léna Prouchet, Vanessa Alessandra Azañedo Gamarra, Jane Wills, Stefano Pascucci and Greg Molecke

Introduction

A strand of post-development theory contends that 'development' is a concept emerging from the West, which sustains a colonial system and considers lifestyles and practices from the Global South as inferior (Escobar 1995; Rapley 2004). From this perspective, development initiatives led by external parties, including Non-Governmental Organisations (NGOs), international organisations (e.g. the World Bank, United Nations) or even those led by the local state, are deemed to pose direct threats to the cultural integrity and wellbeing of these communities. Consequently, some post-development scholars and activists advocate for the outright rejection of the development paradigm (Escobar 1995; Garcia-Arias and Schöneberg 2021), promoting a shift towards alternatives to development, as encapsulated in the Latin American concept of *buen vivir* (or *vivir bien*) that can be translated as 'good life' (Gudynas 2011).

While *buen vivir* has become a popular concept across diverse fields, recent years have witnessed a growing debate about the degree to which Indigenous peoples and local communities are endorsing these perspectives (Recasens 2014; Ranta 2016; Domínguez et al. 2017). One argument posits that *buen vivir*, especially when framed as an alternative to development approach, often diverges from the empirical realities experienced by Indigenous peoples and local communities in the Global South (Domínguez et al. 2017). Moreover, the *buen vivir* perspective has tended to overlook some communities' desire to embrace development rather than reject it, even though their visions of development may not (completely) match the ones promoted by international development agencies (Wilson 2017). Overcoming these paradigmatic clashes and supporting marginalised communities in realising aspirations aligned with their values and needs requires attention to local experiences of 'development' and efforts to put local people at the forefront of intellectual reflection (Matthews 2017). Our research seeks to develop an approach which offers a more comprehensive understanding

DOI: 10.4324/9781003477921-10

of the intricate dynamics between development interventions and community members' responses.

Our fieldwork was conducted within an Awajún Indigenous community located in the Peruvian Amazon. Through two phases of fieldwork and qualitative data collection, we identified that community bonds were critical to Awajún people's life, manifesting through communal activities such as sports and collective work. Nevertheless, shifting life conditions, marked by the commodification of labour and a younger generation's inclination towards education and waged labour over traditional agricultural work, indicate rapid transformations. Monetary considerations emerged as central to ensuring a tranquil life in the community, with cacao cultivation – strongly supported by external organisations – identified as a key avenue for obtaining cash. Noteworthy, however, is the high degree of heterogeneity among Awajún people concerning their visions of development and their reactions to projects.

Our work contributes to post-development debates in three ways. First, we present a context-based understanding of the concept of a 'good life'. Second, we highlight the importance of accounting for community heterogeneity when researching development interventions and working with local communities. Thirdly, we contend that replacing one hegemonic development framework with another (such as replacing mainstream development with a post-development alternative) is insufficient and can have detrimental consequences for marginalised communities. Instead, future research should recognise the diversity of reactions to external support both between and within groups, avoiding predefined ideas regarding communities' lifestyles and aspirations that reflect externally imposed values and choices.

Buen vivir as an alternative to mainstream economic development

While there have been many critics of the development paradigm, post-development remains to this day 'the most popular critical approach to development' (Asher and Wainwright 2019: 25). Among the several criticisms mobilised by post-development thinkers, a key one is that 'development' emerges from a Western ideology that preserves a colonial system and considers lifestyles and practices in the Global South inferior: it implies that 'developing countries' should aspire to become 'developed' countries.

Some authors argue for a model of endogenous development opposed to exogenous visions of development which are pursued through development programmes led by external entities (Giovannini 2012). Indeed, what distinguishes post-development from other critiques of development is the central argument that the development paradigm cannot be improved through notions such as sustainable development because these newer versions still perpetuate the idea that inhabitants of developing countries should aim to achieve a Western model of development (Rapley 2004). Additionally, some authors contend that the combined projects of globalisation and development create the opposite effects to those intended by furthering the social and economic disadvantages suffered by most of the world's people (Peredo 2019). Instead, authors such as Escobar (1995), propose that the entire paradigm of development should be rejected. This 'full abandonment of "development" as a discourse, vision and as a practice' (Garcia-Arias and Schöneberg 2021: 866) is considered a necessary step to allow the flourishing of alternatives already embedded in local and Indigenous knowledge communities.

One of the most discussed alternatives in Latin America revolves around the concept of *buen vivir*, which can be translated as 'Good Life' (Gudynas 2011). *Buen vivir* has been described as originating in 'the ancestral culture of the Andean-Amazonian Indigenous peoples' (Cubillo-Guevara and Hidalgo-Capitán 2015: 302) and it embodies a diverse array of Indigenous concepts and practices that have developed and evolved over time in various geographic contexts. These concepts and practices have been articulated differently, with reference to *sumac kawsay* in Quechua (which means 'life in plenitude') or *tajimat pujut* in Awajún (which translates as 'life in abundance'), (Kantner and Peixoto 2023: 473). Despite such variations, however, all versions of *buen vivir* emphasise a community-based conception of wellbeing, centred on exchanges and reciprocity between peers, but also with the natural environment (Giovannini 2012). A related characteristic of *buen vivir* is a close link between identity and place, including a strong connection with land and the elements and beings sharing that space (Monni and Pallottino 2015). Beyond serving as an alternative, the endeavour to achieve *buen vivir* has been viewed as a direct resistance to top-down 'development aggression' – a term coined to encapsulate the encroachment upon Indigenous individuals and collectives, and the associated denigration of existing ways of life (Tauli-Corpuz 2010).

Criticism of *buen vivir*

While *buen vivir* has gained traction in diverse fields, including finding support among non-Indigenous intellectuals who perceive it as a reachable utopia for a post or de-colonial lifestyle (Domínguez et al. 2017), the past two decades have seen a growing debate about the extent to which Indigenous peoples and local communities endorse these alternative paradigms (Recasens 2014; Ranta 2016; Matthews 2017, see also the chapters by Ranta & Zenteno and by Cordova Suxo in this volume). One criticism sets out that *buen vivir*, especially defined as an alternative approach to development, is not always in line with the empirical reality of Indigenous peoples and local communities in the Global South. An issue of concern in the *buen vivir* literature is its tendency to homogenise Indigenous communities and their values, across and within countries, thereby ignoring their plurality and heterogeneity (Hope 2017; Beling et al. 2021). Furthermore, critics suggest that there cannot be a clear dichotomy and opposition between 'Western' and Indigenous knowledge, as Indigenous peoples have engaged for centuries with modern epistemologies (Mendoza 2018). Another concern pertains to how arguments for *buen vivir* present Indigenous peoples as living a lifestyle akin to that of their ancestors while in many instances, such ways of living do not exist anymore and cannot be recovered (Matthews 2017). This runs the risk of romanticising Indigenous peoples' lifestyles and their relationship to the environment. In his book about development projects in the Amazon, Gasché Suess (2004: 107) shared his impressions that the anthropological description and interpretations of Amazonian societies had a certain degree of 'professional esoterism' and tended to describe such groups in ways that give non-specialists the chance to read about extraordinary and exotic particularities, which do not correspond with the empirical reality. Adopting such framing can also overlook situations where Indigenous communities have engaged in environmentally and socially damaging practices, such as mining and related exploitation (Hope 2017). Besides, this perspective on Indigenous peoples and local communities' lifestyles and, more generally, post-development theory, has failed to engage with some communities' desire to embrace rather than reject development (Matthews 2017). This is especially true because some post-development thinkers consider that poverty is a relative concept emerging from the mainstream development discourse (Rahnema 2010). They claim that it is exposure to the idea of development, for instance through the presence of development organisations or programmes, that leads people to perceive themselves as poor (Escobar 1995; Shrestha 1995). It thus follows that communities targeted by development projects should opt to reject them and instead embrace their existing lifestyles rather than coming to see themselves as poor and in need of development. In contrast, other authors have illustrated the willingness of marginalised communities to benefit from development projects especially to address their basic needs such as providing access to food, sanitation, and electricity, without necessarily fully embracing the agenda of external development organisations, that may include the promotion of privatisation, for instance (Shahraki and Keikha 2022). In turn, some post-development thinkers have responded to this apparent appeal with the argument that the minds of the latter have been colonised (Nandy 1997), and what is needed is a 'decolonization of the imagination' (Sachs 2010: ix). However, questioning the validity of this argument becomes possible when we avoid automatically linking the fundamental rights of dignity and equality solely to people living in the Global North (Matthews 2017: 2651).

Understanding Indigenous peoples' experiences of development

The ongoing debate about contrasting development paradigms has been summarised by Farahani and Esfahani (2020: 245) as an opposition between a project of globalisation and modernisation led by international development agencies and 'dominant powers underpinning mainstream economic thinking' and the post-development counter-narrative focusing on endogenous development and the rejection of external interventions. To overcome the clash between paradigms and support marginalised communities to achieve a future genuinely in line with their aspirations, it is essential to put 'development' subjects' experiences at the centre of intellectual reflection (Matthews 2017). Such an endeavour has been at the centre of geographer Cindy Katz's research. Notably, Katz advocates for an approach that challenges academic 'voyeurism', understood as the propensity for scholars to adopt *a priori* conceptions of what they want to find in the field (Hughes et al. 2022). In the context of her work on responses to economic 'development' policies in Sudan, Katz (2004) stresses that researchers tend to predefine the ways that people are going to resist development practices, which leads to a self-fulfilling process whereby researchers confirm their ideas. This approach to the *a priori* identification of the 'right kind' of resistance represents an example of 'major theory', that 'encompasses the theory or theories that are dominant in a particular geography under a specific set of conditions' (Katz 1996: 490). In contrast, Katz proposes that researchers should focus on 'minor theory', which is 'not a coherent or unified theory, but rather describes an approach to knowledge production that is never comfortable' or fixed (Katz 1996; Hughes et al. 2022: 2). She argues that researchers should arrive in the field with an open mind rather than seeking to apply *a priori* ideas and concepts regarding how marginalised communities respond to development efforts, and instead, build theory from their observations in the field.

Following this intellectual approach, Katz (1996) posits that the reaction of local populations to development projects incorporates a complexity and nuance that cannot be captured within a single analytical category such as 'resistance'. Such oversimplification risks emptying the word of its meaning, as well as conveying a romanticised vision of local communities' approaches to development (Hughes et al. 2022). As an example, previous work focusing on mining projects that involved local communities in the Global South has shown that, contrary to the prevailing view in academic literature, which often simplifies the issue into a binary opposition between organised grassroots resistance movements and multinational mining companies, most community members do not directly oppose such projects. However, there is not full support either; instead, some contend that participating in the projects can bring them certain benefits, indicating that individuals who do not resist are not 'docile subordinates or uncritical devotes' (Hughes et al. 2022: 4) as depicted by some authors (e.g. Machado Aráoz 2014), but rather prefer to engage on their own terms as circumstances allow (Scott 1985). Similar studies have yielded comparable findings, including in the Peruvian Amazon region where our fieldwork was conducted (Alvarado Jesús et al. 2015).

The focus of our research is on development projects fostering entrepreneurship within Indigenous contexts. Such a focus is of relevance because the promotion of entrepreneurship to combat poverty and marginalisation has emerged as a central element of the international development agenda in recent decades (Lee 2023). In this context, the promoted vision of entrepreneurship is 'influenced by world cultural norms of empowered individualism and agency' and 'becomes perceived as something that any individual can engage in as long as they have the motivation, drive, and vision to do so' (Lee 2023: 2). This idea has faced substantial criticism by some scholars who have called for a 'rejection of the entire notion of EDA [entrepreneurship as a development apparatus]' (Smit and Pretorius 2020: 62). Going beyond this Manichean approach, we explore 'the broad range of messy and contradictory responses of those disenfranchised by global globalism', providing thereby an under-researched and 'much-needed perspective' (Hughes et al. 2022: 4).

Research context

Our fieldwork took place in an Awajún native community (***comunidad nativa*** [1]) located in the district of Nieva, which belongs to the province of Condorcanqui in the northwest of Amazonas. It lies next to the Marañón river basin and is connected to a road that provides Nieva commercial access to the larger city of Bagua. Condorcanqui has a large Indigenous majority: 81.7 percent of the population self-identifies as Indigenous and 9.7 percent as *Mestizo* (mixed race). Condorcanqui is the seventh poorest province in Peru, out of a total of 196. According to the last census, 90.4 percent of the Condorcanqui population live in rural areas (Instituto Nacional de Estadística e Informática (INEI), 2018a; 2018b; 2018c in Ramos-Cortez and MacNeill 2022: 37), (see Figure 8.1).

While Awajún people's colonial history dates from the 16th century (Inoach Shawit 2021), since the 1940s processes of integration into the rest of the Peruvian society have accelerated, including settlements led by religious missions and domestic settlers (*colonos*). The establishment of schools and health posts also had an impact on both the social and spatial organisation of the Indigenous communities (Barclay Rey de Castro et al. 1991). Integration also happened through the construction of roads to connect these areas with consolidated urban centres, as well as a legal framework that facilitated economic development and population growth. From the 1980s, the integration of the

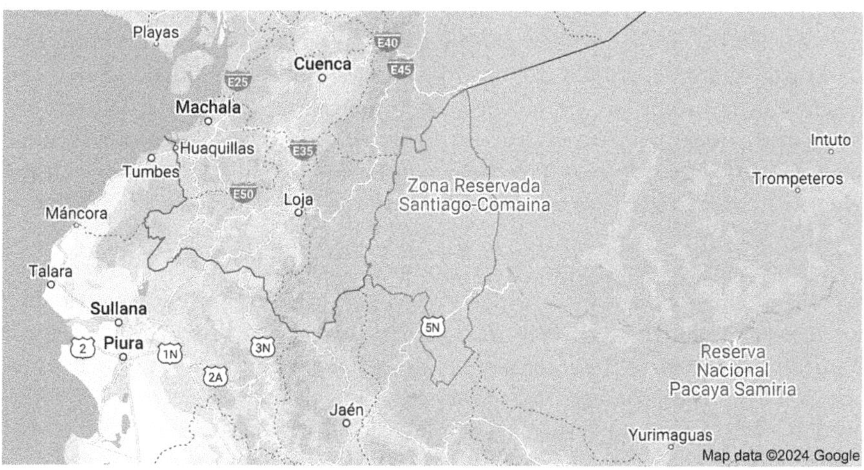

Figure 8.1 Map of the study location, Condorcanqui, in Peru (Google Maps, 19 January 2024)

Amazon into wider society allowed the exploitation of its resources to reach unprecedented levels. This led to the development of sectoral policies for the Amazonian region through Special Projects[2]. The Jaén-San Ignacio-Bagua Special Project, though geographically distant, had a strong presence in the area, fostering the cultivation of cacao crops. In the following years, local and international organisations and NGOs also started working in the area, promoting cash crop cultivation to support economic development. For instance, in 1993, the Jesuit Church established the *Servicio Agropecuario para la Investigación y Promoción Económica* (Agricultural Research and Economic Promotion Service – SAIPE), a local NGO, following a request from the Awajún and Wampis communities. The organisation prioritises the valorisation of the Amazonian culture. Its primary objective is to address the necessities of Awajún and Wampis communities through the development of productive activities within the population (Ramos-Cortez and MacNeill 2022).

However, the relationship between the Awajún people and some external entities, particularly the national state, has at times escalated into direct conflict. Notably, the year 2009 marked the occurrence of the *Baguazo*, an event characterised by the violent repression of Indigenous protesters by the police during the national Amazonian strikes, organised to oppose neoliberal reforms enabling the division and sale of Indigenous land (Ramos-Cortez and MacNeill 2022). The Indigenous communities vehemently opposed extractive projects encroaching upon their territories, specifically targeting oil exploration and exploitation in Lot 116 and gold mining in the *Cordillera del Cóndor* (Garra 2012; Manacés Valverde and Gonzáles Calleja 2013). This conflict resulted in a total of 23 police fatalities and ten civilian deaths among the Awajún and Wampis communities. Nowadays, Indigenous communities in the Condorcanqui province remain the focus of several – frequently juxtaposed – development projects and programmes led by NGOs and the public sector.

Methodological approach

Our research process entailed immersing ourselves in the community and engaging with a diverse range of local actors. In this way, we gained a comprehensive understanding of the social, economic, and cultural aspects surrounding cacao production projects in the community and how this related to Awajún people's vision of development.

When fieldwork started in February 2022, the first author contracted two additional collaborators to support the data collection and interpretation: the second author of this chapter, a Peruvian anthropologist; and a member of the Awajún community, Loyda Paukai Wasum, who was recruited to act as a language and cultural interpreter to ensure that our analysis was not based on misunderstandings of local phenomena. The first phase of fieldwork lasted for about ten weeks and followed an ethnographic approach. The two first authors were hosted in the house of the partner NGO in an Awajún Indigenous community. During the early days, we observed and participated in daily activities in the community. We also followed the NGO staff in their different activities, especially the ones concerning cacao farming. In the next phase of data collection, we started interviewing community members, including the participants of NGO programmes and community members who worked for the NGO, to understand their lifestyles and their perspectives on the idea of development. We also travelled to Nieva, the capital of the district, to interview staff implementing similar projects to the one we initially focused on in the region. The second phase of the project took place from October 2022 for four weeks. Our team wanted to understand more about the diversity of needs and aspirations, and engagement in projects among participants. Interviews were scheduled with Loyda's support, and she also recommended appropriate compensation for peoples' time. To gain a deeper understanding of the community dynamics, we also consulted with community authorities, who provided us with valuable perspectives on the local history and the changes the community were experiencing.

Results

In the following section, we use the term 'peaceful life' instead of *buen vivir* or *tajimat pujut*, which refers to Awajun people's conceptualisation of a 'good life'. This is because as we asked our research participants questions regarding their perception of *buen vivir* or *tajimat pujut*, we soon realised that the interviewees' tone was shifting and that they seemed to echo more of an external perspective rather than genuinely answering. After some conversation with our community facilitator, we decided to use a term which was not linked to concepts used in academic, activist, and political spheres, such as *buen vivir* or *tajimat pujut*, but instead ask about what they considered they needed to live a 'peaceful life' (*vida tranquila*) in the community.

Community ties constituted a central element of Awajún life. Throughout our fieldwork, we observed a variety of events that shed light on communal activities and social dynamics. For instance, we had the opportunity to witness and participate in sports events, which appeared to facilitate social bonding. In line with Abizaid et al. (2018: 99) who wrote that 'soccer is an exceptionally popular sport and an important pillar of rural life in Amazonia', we found that sports activities were at the centre of community life. In the Indigenous community where we lived, the most popular activity was volleyball, followed by soccer. Volleyball was played by both men and women, and tournaments were organised every weekend (see Figure 8.2).

Such games were an opportunity for people to come together and discuss different issues. Another noteworthy event we observed was the cooperative labour known as *minga*, where community members came together to work collaboratively on farming tasks or other community endeavours. This practice is widely spread across various communities in Latin America including among Indigenous communities in the Ecuadorian Amazon (Coral-Guerrero et al. 2021). The chief

Figure 8.2 A volleyball game taking place in an Awajún Indigenous community (22 March 2022) (Vanessa Alessandra Azañedo Gamarra)

of an Awajún community explained to us how *mingas* comprised an important part of community wellbeing:

> For the Indigenous world, doing *minga* is a way of working, and being united as a family ... You have to show that you are generous, that you take care of people so that other families will take care of you. It is a social fabric for *buen vivir* ... Because yes, the Awajún has managed to maintain cooperation and solidarity.

Nevertheless, an evident shift towards the commodification of labour is underway. The hiring of *peones* (agricultural labourers) to work on the farms is becoming more frequent among producers whose productive capacity exceeds the labour force available in the family. The same leader explained later in the interview:

> *Minga* .... is practised, but very little... And the way of sharing, customs have also changed. For example, in the Nivea sector, they invite people for *minga* and say, 'there is going to be food', but people don't go ... When they come, they don't do a good job.

Another Awajún, formerly chief of the same Indigenous community, told us: 'It used to be like that, we would quickly organise a *minga*. But now everyone wants them to pay, before it was with *masato* [3] and game they had hunted but now it's all about money'.

Such reliance on paid agricultural workers increases in the case of families whose children have left the community to work or study. Access to education appeared as a growing priority for Awajún people. The manager of a cacao cultivation project we interviewed explained:

> The young people go to Lima to study careers that do not allow them to return to the community, such as electronic engineering. The parents say 'Study! If you don't, I'll send you to the farm'. In other words, going to the farm is a punishment. So, we have to look at this generational issue.

This idea of becoming 'professional', which does not include agricultural labouring was regularly mentioned by Awajún people, especially young generations. This especially became evident during a workshop we organised with young cacao farmers (under 30 years old) to understand their aspirations for the future. Tasked with representing the life they envisioned for their children when they would reach their age, one of the participants wrote: 'When my children are my age, I would like them to be something in life and to have a job that they can live on' (see Figure 8.3). They also represented in this picture a road, buildings, and a football field, symbolising the attachment to social events alongside the willingness for the construction of new infrastructure.

Figure 8.3 Drawing from a workshop participant

To obtain cash, community members have become increasingly reliant on cash crops, as forest resources do not provide cash, but become scarce due to population growth and the change from dispersed spatial distribution patterns towards settlement. For those who do not have sufficient material resources to expand their production by opening new farms, performing salaried work cleaning, harvesting, and transporting produce for other members of the community's parcels is a more viable and less risky alternative. Additionally, occupations in temporary jobs such as cleaning, security and construction works were popular, especially among young people. Indigenous authorities shared the idea of a transition of lifestyle through agriculture:

> Historically the Awajún people have not been producers of specific crops for the market. Rather, all produce has been for self-sufficiency for family and personal consumption. That implies that as we are a culture of progression we are in a transitional level, of how to continue to improve the system of life.

This increasing need for cash and a general increase in needs among Awajún people was a recurring theme during our fieldwork. The leader of an Indigenous community of the low Marañón complained: 'Many people here talk about *buen vivir*, but how can you talk about that with all the needs that people have?'. He explained to us the increasing economic needs of Indigenous communities, especially the ones that were less connected to the road and therefore had fewer chances to sell goods.

Subsequently, we conducted interviews with 91 cacao farmers and sought insights into their conception of a peaceful life. The predominant answer we received when asking what was required for a peaceful life was 'money'. Participants explained further: 'money is a universal need, to have money here you can grow cacao or sell handcraft'. Money, according to community members, permeated every aspect of their lives, and was intricately linked to happiness. As one participant expressed:

> If you don't have money, how do you live? When you get sick, money; to dress, money; to buy food, money. I'm going to increase my income, raise guinea pigs or chickens to sell. That's what I need to be happier.

Several interviewees formulated their desire to expand their cacao cultivation to increase their income, but indicated that they lacked the financial capital to do so. An Awajún man working with an NGO to support local cacao culture told us: 'As there is a lack of money here, we can't have more farms, we can't open new *chacras*'.[4] The intensification of the use of land, as well as the development of other sources of income depends on various factors, such as kinship networks, community status, capital availability, age or past migration experiences.

Despite some consensus regarding what is needed to live a peaceful life, we also uncovered some nuances in participant responses. For instance, among our 91 interviewees, five Awajún people mentioned the importance of community life and collaboration. Two farmers addressed the environmental dimension and talked about a life 'without pollution and with good quality food'. This heterogeneity of perspectives became even more apparent during discussions about transitioning to a *centro poblado* or remaining a *comunidad nativa*. While the first status facilitates the economic development of the area by allowing the opening of business by external stakeholders, the second prevents external stakeholders from buying land in the area but also limits the ability to open services such as banks or state services. Opinions were highly divided among community members: a first group considered *centro poblado* to equate to the loss of their land and rights:

> With *centro poblado*, Spanish speakers are coming. Spanish speakers take loans and come to the jungle to do business. With them we are fighting, with them we are making war. With their relatives, others also come, they give them a piece of land. Then another person comes, and they give him a piece. This is how they take the land from the Indigenous people.

Instead, *comunidad nativa* allowed them to preserve their culture: 'We cannot forget our community and our customs'. However, an opposing group of Awajún inhabitants promoted *centro poblado* as a means to accelerate market integration and facilitate economic development:

> *Centro poblado* is better because we will not always live as we do now. The population is growing. Eventually, this community will be a district, there can be banks, events, and more movement.

Some partisans of *centro poblado* directly referred to market logics: 'I want to live in a *centro poblado* because more merchants will mean more competition and the prices will go down'. The opinion of people was partly related to geographical location: people who lived further away from the road and had less market access were more in favour of *comunidad nativa* and those who lived closer to the road were more in favour of the *centro poblado*.

The diverse perspectives among Awajún people regarding the goals and future of the community could be observed through the different reactions to development projects that Indigenous peoples displayed. During our fieldwork, we discovered that most Awajún were cultivating cacao in their fields. This is mainly because cacao is currently one of the only options for Awajún to generate some cash for community members who do not have a diploma and are therefore not *profesionales*. *Profesionales* is a term used by community members to refer to people who have had access to higher education and now have a working contract, for instance as a nurse or a teacher, and opposed to informal work, such as construction workers or farmers. When discussing the consultation process between Indigenous communities and NGOs, the director of a local NGO told us:

> The demands [Awajún people] make of us are 'productive projects, productive projects …'. They recognise this as the first strategy to confront illegal mining or the coca trade. Because there are no other alternatives.

Cacao farmers usually work on small areas and with rudimentary tools. The support of external organisations is considered a means to access better tools to cultivate and harvest cacao as well as to receive help in the *chacra*. The project allowed farmers to increase the quantity and sometimes the area of cacao produced, which resulted in an increased income. Our interviewees regularly mentioned they were grateful for the presence of NGOs in the region, as they were sometimes the only institutions providing support. The chief of a remote Awajún Indigenous community we visited told us:

> They [NGO] are the only ones who are arriving here, the other institutions, including the state do not! We need to keep working with them!

When we asked participants what they liked about the cacao programme of the NGO we initially focused on compared to others, they often mentioned the fact that this programme was permanently (*'permanente'*) in the community. This referred to two aspects of the programme: the constant presence of NGO staff in the community and their monthly visit to participants' *chacras*, which differed from other projects where staff would only occasionally visit the community and rarely individual participants. The absence of a termination date for the programme contrasted with other initiatives that lasted on average three years. Therefore, people appeared to be favouring a more intensive and lasting presence of NGOs. Interestingly, we uncovered an instance where a state organisation in charge of forest-protected areas had had to shift their budgets from forest monitoring to productive projects following demands from the Indigenous communities living in the targeted territories. The programme manager explained:

> We should be talking about conservation, but we don't like to go to the community and just talk to them about conservation and not giving them anything.

Consequently, although the organisation employed staff specialised in conservation issues, they all had to become cacao experts: 'our team, our park rangers, our specialists, and our people, including myself, support all the [cacao production] processes'. This example illustrates the way in which some people in the Indigenous community leverage any available resources to engage in productive activities and therefore generate an income. In sum, it appears that Indigenous farmers adhere to projects to cope with the several crises they are faced with and turn to the only option available, due to the lack of alternatives.

While most individuals we spoke with were in favour of such initiatives and were taking part in (or had taken part in) such initiatives, they did not wholeheartedly and comprehensively embrace the approach proposed by external organisations and managed to rework several aspects of the projects. Such behaviours could be observed throughout and after the project. During the project, participants adopted a 'pick-and-choose' approach, where they would refuse to apply advice or take part in events that did not align with their needs and lifestyle. A community member declared:

> People here don't work much in the *chacra*. They work around three hours a day normally, but they work more when they need more money: if their children are sick and if they have to pay for things for school, for example.

Throughout our participant observation phase, we understood that the rest of the day was dedicated to other activities, including attending community events. Notwithstanding the repeated efforts of organisations to modify the working patterns of the community, and to recommend that farmers spend more time in their field (around eight hours was advised) to produce more cacao and therefore receive more money, most farmers maintained their usual working schedule. Non-governmental organisation staff also mentioned several instances when they had proposed that Awajún people work extra time to support an event, for example, and despite offering double pay no one had accepted the offer because 'there is a football game in the community at the same time'. Besides this issue of time, another striking example of project reworking was the lack of willingness to be involved in community cacao cooperatives created by external organisations. Such cooperatives represented a key element of the sustainability goals of cacao projects. All organisations shared the same rationale for promoting cooperatives: when selling cacao individually, farmers are not able to obtain a good price from local buyers because they have low bargaining power. They also cannot sell to bigger cooperatives which require a certain quantity of cacao to be delivered periodically as agreed by contract. Several community members agreed with these claims, which reassured organisations to follow this path. However, this strategy did not consider that most farmers seemed to consider cacao as a savings account that they could access in case of need or emergency, and not as a long-term investment. Therefore, they were not willing to wait for a certain date to harvest their cacao and sell it to the cooperative, as they often needed the money within a few hours or days. As a participant of our workshop explained, 'When I need to buy medicine, I harvest a few kilograms of cacao and I sell them in the village'. Similarly, when people could choose between selling to the cooperative or to the local merchant who increased their buying prices just above the price offered by the cooperatives, farmers also preferred to sell to the highest bidder. Consequently, even though participants agreed to be members of the cooperative, they often broke its rules. Although these responses do not directly question the theory of change of external organisations, they represent a pragmatic response to the mismatch between programme goals and participants' aspirations.

We did find some instances where Indigenous peoples opposed external organisations' interventions. Such attitudes could be observed both at community and individual levels. During our fieldwork, community members often mentioned the case of another community nearby that had refused to renew their partnership agreement with an NGO. When we asked the reasons for this refusal, some people mentioned that they wanted to receive direct cash to buy goods instead of the NGOs providing the goods to them. Another man mentioned that the community wanted to plant bananas in what was currently virgin land, and since this was forbidden by this agreement, they decided to not sign it. Overall, it appeared that the Indigenous community had wanted to take back control to use resources based on their own will and not an externally imposed agenda. We also met several individuals, who despite living in areas that had signed agreements with the NGO, were strongly opposed to their work: 'When they come to ask me how my cacao is and if I want support, I tell them that my field is abandoned. Here is it free market, and I sell to whoever I want!' What also appeared to cause the rejection of the NGO presence by some Awajún people was the constraints they imposed as well as their working styles:

> There are people who don't want to work with the NGOs because they require that people are constantly on the farm [and] many people don't want that! I don't like the farm; it is a lot of work, and you get bitten by mosquitoes!

Such strong stances against the projects brought by NGOs reflect the resistance that NGOs faced among some Indigenous communities and individual Awajún in the community.

At the opposite end of the spectrum to opposition, some farmers were highly engaged in the projects proposed by the NGO and responsive to their strategies, which they considered as an opportunity to 'move forward' (*salir adelante*). We first identified this type of attitude while looking at a Facebook post of an Awajún who had sent us a 'request to become 'friends' a few days after our arrival. The post included the following picture showing Peruvian currency bills attached to mature cacao fruits and the following caption: 'Let's work together with the cacao factory that will give us money' (see Figure 8.4).

The factory that the farmer is referring to was part of an NGO programme that aimed to build cacao processing facilities in the community. Unlike infrastructures built by other organisations, the goal was also to equip it with machines allowing the production of chocolate, which adds a significant economic value to the product. While the NGO's strategy was to engage all its

Figure 8.4 Picture published on Facebook showing bank notes attached to cacao fruits (Facebook post, 7 March 2022)

participants in the process of chocolate creation, only a minority of cacao farmers seemed interested. As our investigation unfolded, we aimed to understand the profile of these highly committed participants. They displayed several common traits. First, they had studied and/ or worked in business-related sectors outside of the community. When a farmer shared with us some business ideas, he was planning to implement we asked:

> Where did you get all these business ideas?
>
> I study administration in Nieva, on Saturdays and Sundays. They teach us how to create our business, how to plan, how to ask ourselves: 'what is missing in your community?'

Such experiences reinforced an entrepreneurial attitude. The NGO projects represented an opportunity to discover new business ideas and expand the existing ones: 'Before the projects, the community was blind', commented one cacao farmer hired by the NGO to work in the plant. Whereas other participants mostly focused on cacao production, this group wanted to find new outlets/openings for their cacao thanks to this external support, and increase their economic profit: 'cacao jam, chocolate, this brings money!' A central element to elaborate their business strategy relied on experimentation:

> I thank the NGO for giving us ideas. In this little house in front, I am going to make my shop here and I'm going to sell chocolate, with ice cream. I want to experiment.

In another instance, a farmer explained how he had calculated the best return for investment for his cacao:

> Believe me, miss, that selling cacao fresh or dry, is a complete loss. I experienced it. For instance, I get two kilograms of cacao paste from the cacao mill. And from one kilogram of paste, I get 50 soles worth of chocolate. Each bar costs five soles. So, selling it dry, for 7 soles per kilogram, is a great loss.

They sought to maximise benefits by consecutively or simultaneously joining several projects. Some of these farmers had also been hired to support the further implementation of projects which also strengthened their skills and knowledge of cacao culture:

> I also worked with a programme from the agricultural ministry a few years ago. We planted 20,000 cacao trees in the area. The majority of people here who have cacao now, it is thanks to my work at that time. During the project, I carried out special project training in Jaen, for cocoa and nursery management.

Lastly, this group differentiated themselves from the rest of the community by putting forward the importance of effort and hard work to achieve one's goals. They regularly emphasised that other community members should work as much as they did, for the community to have a better future:

> I tell them 'do you think I'm going to work for you on your farm?' because I already know the people who work and the ones who don't. We have to tell them to their face, so that they will do the work.

In conclusion, this group of participants was highly responsive to NGO values and endeavours. They constituted a critical form of support for NGO work, and strongly questioned and even criticised the attitudes of less engaged villagers and cacao farmers.

Discussion and conclusions

We suggest that the principles of 'the good life' have been mainly used in the academic literature to refer to practices that seem to correspond to an ideal system of traditional Indigenous economy. However, we find that the Indigenous community members considered *buen vivir* or *tajimat pujut* as part of an external discourse rather than representing their needs and aspirations. Additionally, it appears there is no rigid dichotomy between 'modern' and 'Indigenous' or 'traditional' systems. In the current transition towards market integration, community links appear to weaken, although they are still present. Previous research has concluded that 'available studies on Indigenous peoples show no evidence of *buen vivir* as social practice of communities' (Domínguez et al. 2017: 143). In this chapter, we do not go as far as negating the existence of *buen vivir*. Instead, we advocate for researchers to pay greater attention to understanding and analysing the concept critically, as failing to do so can construct a vision of 'unspoiled and authentic "natives" requiring protection' which silences 'complex engagements with ideas of development' (Wilson 2017: 2684). In the context we studied, a peaceful life is related, at least for some people some of the time, to access to money, which in turn, is associated with economic development. Money provides access to services and goods, and quality of life. Ramos-Cortez and MacNeill (2022) presented similar findings from their research in Condorcanqui and reported that one interviewee explained that the Awajún 'good life' was now defined by 'money, enough land, products, canoes, a motorcycle taxi, a car'.

Our research uncovered a high degree of heterogeneity among community members regarding conceptions of a peaceful life, involvement in entrepreneurship for development projects and aspirations for the future. Notably, the perspectives shared by some of our participants have been considered as 'wrong' by organisations and high-level Indigenous representatives of the Permanent Council of the Awajún and Wampis Peoples & Agricultural Service for Research and Economic Promotion and SAIPE (2021), translated by the authors (2024):

> Currently, some indigenous organisations and native communities mistakenly relate good living to the economic income that has to be generated by exploiting natural resources for good living …
>
> (Ermeto Tuesta Cerrón, 15 September 2020).

Our findings contrast with the literature that often simplistically uses the term 'community' as if it were a 'homogeneous and harmonious' entity (Hoang et al. 2006: 515). This simplification is especially problematic as it runs the risk of defining concepts and designing policies to support Indigenous communities based on a perspective which is not shared across the group and can have contrasting effects or even reinforce inequalities through processes of elite capture, for instance (Saito-Jensen et al. 2010).

Our analysis of the reaction of individuals to projects contributes to the work questioning the unambiguous opposition of local communities to externally led projects on their territories (Wanvik and Caine 2017). Our chapter shows that community members develop ambiguous and nuanced relationships with development projects. The scope of our work did not allow us to fully grasp the personalised relationships between ideas of 'peaceful lives' and attitudes towards programmes. This gap could be addressed by future research. Besides, it is crucial to mention that the attitudes we described can change rapidly. As illustrated by events such as *Baguazo,* the occurrence of certain events in Awajún territory can cause a strong movement of resistance, especially when the expectations of the local population are not fulfilled.

Furthermore, our proposal converges with the work of Faharani and Esfahani (2020), which underlines the importance of not falling into the trap of atemporal and acontextual development models. As explained by Matthews (2017: 2657) 'for those in the West to dismiss any apparent desire for development … entails assuming they know what is best for non-Western "others" and prescribing, once again, to such "others" how they ought to live'. Future research should refrain from anticipating what principles should constitute a 'good life' in Indigenous contexts and how it should be pursued. It should acknowledge the different reactions to external support between and within groups. Meanings of development should be defined pragmatically as an idea that 'is useful and enables the participants to accomplish their targeted goals and makes possible a social agreement' (Faharani and Esfahani 2020: 247).

Our work has implications for practice. The arguments formulated by post-development theorists and the attention to concepts of *buen vivir* have been useful in questioning the mainstream, top-down development paradigm and programmes (Matthews 2017). However, this approach should not constitute a framework to guide the action of external organisations, as they are likely to be disconnected from empirical realities. A context-based approach that respects the aspirations of Indigenous peoples and local communities should be developed because this is more likely to work for the people, rather than respond to a predefined ideal. This should include a deep engagement with local knowledge and practices, meaningful participation and approaches that reflect local needs and desires.

Notes

1 Native communities *(comunidades nativas)* have their origins in the 'tribal' groups (*grupos tribales*) of the jungle and are made up of groups of families linked by the following main elements: language or dialect; cultural and social characteristics; and common and permanent tenure and use of the same territory with nucleated or dispersed settlement (Decree – Law 22175), (Ministerio de Cultura de Perú 2024).
2 State programs which have administrative autonomy; hence, are not subordinated to Ministries' budget.
3 Traditional drink prepared with fermented manioc.
4 A term used to designate a small farm or plot of land used for subsistence farming in Peru, and more generally in Latin America.

References

Abizaid, C., Coomes, O. T., Takasaki, Y. and Arroyo-Mora, J. P. (2018). 'Rural Social Networks along Amazonian Rivers: Seeds, Labor and Soccer among Communities on the Napo River, Peru', *Geographical Review*, 108 (1), pp. 92–19. Available at: https://doi.org/10.1111/gere.12244.

Alvarado Jesús, J., Druschke, M. and Pajares G. E. (2015). *Estudio sobre los pueblos indígenas de la amazonía peruana en la región de integración fronteriza del Perú con el Ecuador*. Lima: Plan Binacional de Desarrollo de la Región Fronteriza Perú – Ecuador.

Asher, K. and Wainwright, J. (2019). 'After Post-development: On Capitalism, Difference, and Representation', *Antipode*, 51 (1), pp. 25–44. Available at: https://doi.org/10.1111/anti.12430.

Barclay Rey de Castro, F., Rodríguez Achung, M. and Valcárcel Carnero, M. (1991). *Amazonía 1940–1990: el extravío de una ilusión*. Lima: Terra Nuova.

Beling, A. E., Cubillo-Guevara, A. P., Vanhulst, J. and Hidalgo-Capitán, A. L. (2021). 'Buen vivir (Good Living): A "Glocal" Genealogy of a Latin American Utopia for the World', *Latin American Perspectives*, 48(3), pp. 17–14. Available at: https://doi.org/10.1177/0094582X211009242.

Coral-Guerrero, C. A., García-Quero, F. and Guardiola, J. (2021). 'What is *Sumak Kawsay*? A Qualitative Study in the Ecuadorian Amazon', *Latin American Perspectives*, 48 (3), pp. 35–50. Available at: https://doi.org/10.1177/0094582X211004913.

Cubillo-Guevara, A. P. and Hidalgo-Capitán, A. L. (2015). 'El sumak kawsay genuino como fenómeno social amazónico ecuatoriano', *OBETS. Revista de Ciencias Sociales*, 10 (2), pp. 301–333. Available at: https://doi.org/10.14198/OBETS2015.10.2.02.

Domínguez, R., Caria, S. and León, M. (2017). 'Buen Vivir: Praise, instrumentalization, and reproductive pathways of good living in Ecuador', *Latin American and Caribbean Ethnic Studies*, 12(2), pp. 133–154. Available at: https://doi.org/10.1080/17442222.2017.1325099.

Escobar, A. (1995). *Encountering Development. The Making and Unmaking of the Third World*. Princeton University Press.

Farahani, A. F. and Esfahani, A. H. (2020). 'Exploring possibilities for a pragmatic orientation in development studies', *The power of pragmatism*. Manchester University Press. Available at: https://doi.org/10.7765/9781526134950.00022.

Garcia-Arias, J. and Schöneberg, J. (2021). 'Urgencies and imperatives for revolutionary (environmental) transitions: from degrowth and postdevelopment towards the pluriverse?', *Environmental Politics*, 30 (5), pp. 865–871. Available at: https://doi.org/10.1080/09644016.2021.1911443.

Garra, S. (2012). 'El despertar de Kumpanam: historia y mito en el marco de un conflicto socioambiental en la Amazonía', *Anthropologica*, 30 (30), pp. 5–28. Available at: https://doi.org/10.18800/anthropologica.201201.001.

Gasché Suess, J. (2004). *Crítica de proyectos y proyectos críticos de desarrollo. Una reflexión latinoamericana con énfasis en la Amazonia*. Instituto de Investigaciones de la Amazonía Peruana.

Giovannini, M. (2012). 'Social enterprises for development as *buen vivir*', *Journal of Enterprising Communities: People and Places in the Global Economy*, 6 (3), pp. 284–299. Available at: https://doi.org/10.1108/17506201211258432.

Gudynas, E. (2011). 'Buen Vivir: Germinando alternativas al desarrollo', *América Latina en Movimiento*, pp. 1–20.

Hoang, L. A., Castella, J. C. and Novosad, P. (2006). 'Social networks and information access: Implications for agricultural extension in a rice farming community in northern Vietnam', *Agriculture and Human Values*, 23 (4), pp. 513–527. Available at: https://doi.org/10.1007/s10460-006-9013-5.

Hope, J. (2017). 'The constraints of an "ironic scholar": Negotiating critical engagement with indigeneity and nature conservation', *Geoforum*, 78, pp. 74- 1. Available at: https://doi.org/10.1016/j.geoforum.2016.11.008.

Hughes, S. M., Murrey, A., Krishnan, S., van Teijlingen, K., Daley, P. O., Nowicki, M., Fannin, M. and MacLeavy, J. (2022). 'Interventions in the political geographies of resistance: The contributions of Cindi Katz, 15 years on', *Political Geography*, 97, p. 102666. Available at: https://doi.org/10.1016/j.polgeo.2022.102666.

Inoach Shawit, G. (2021). *Entre la Dependencia y la Libertad: Siempre Awajún*. Fundación Nia Tero, Equidad y IWGIA.

Instituto Nacional de Estadística e Informática (INEI). (2018a). Población Indígena u Originaria de la Amazonía. In *La Autoidentificación Étnica: Población Indígena y Afro-peruana*, https://www.inei.gob.pe/media/MenuRecursivo/publicaciones_digitales/Est/Lib1642/.

Instituto Nacional de Estadística e Informática (INEI). (2018b). Amazonas: Resultados Definitivos. Vol. V., https://www.inei.gob.pe/media/MenuRecursivo/publicaciones_digitales/Est/Lib1567/.

Instituto Nacional de Estadística e Informática (INEI). (2018c). Departamento de Amazonas Alberga a 379,384 Habitantes, https: // censo2017 inei.gob.pe/departamento–de- amazonas–alberga-a–379–384–abitantes/#:~:text=El%20departamento%20de%20Amazonas%20se,el%20%C3%A1rea%20urbana%20157%20560.

Kantner, B. and Peixoto, R. (2023). 'Thinking with *Bem Vivir* across rural and urban Amazonia: Indigenous and Black spaces of resistance', *Journal of Political Ecology*, 30 (1), pp. 471–496. Available at: https://doi.org/10.2458/jpe.5462.

Katz, C. (1996). 'Towards Minor Theory', *Environment and Planning D: Society and Space*, 14 (4), pp. 487–499. Available at: https://doi.org/10.1068/d140487.

Lee, S. S. (2023). 'Entrepreneurship for all? The rise of a global "entrepreneurship for development" agenda, 1950–2021', *World Development*, 166, 106226. Available at: https://doi.org/10.1016/j.worlddev.2023.106226.

Machado Aráoz, H.A. (2014) 'Territorios y cuerpos en disputa. Extractivismo minero y ecología política de las emociones', *Intersticios: Revista Sociológica de Pensamiento Crítico* [Preprint].

Manacés Valverde, J.M. and Gonzáles Calleja, C.G. (2013). *Informe en Minoría de la Comisión Especial para Investigar y Analizar los Sucesos de Bagua*. Lima: Comisión de Derechos Humanos (COMISEDH).

Matthews, S. (2017). 'Colonised minds? Post- development theory and the desirability of development in Africa', *Third World Quarterly*, 38 (12), pp. 2650–2663. Available at: https://doi.org/10.1080/01436597.2017.1279540.

Mendoza, B. (2018). 'Can the subaltern save us?', *Tapuya: Latin American Science, Technology and Society*, 1 (1), pp. 109 – 122. Available at: https://doi.org/10.1080/25729861.2018.1551462.

Ministerio de Cultura de Perú. (2024). 'Glosario – Base de Datos de Pueblos Indígenas u Originarios'. [Preprint]. Available at: https://bdpi.cultura.gob.pe/glosario.

Monni, S. and Pallattino, M. (2015). 'Beyond growth and development: buen vivir as an alternative to current paradigms', *International Journal of Environmental Policy and Decision Making*, 1 (3), pp. 184–204. Available at https://doi.org/10.1504/IJEPDM.2015.074300.

Nandy, A. (1997). 'Colonization of the Mind.' In *The Post-Development Reader*, edited by Rahnema, M. and Bawtree, V.London and New Jersey: Zed Books, pp. 168–178.

Peredo, A. M. (2019). 'El buen vivir'. In *Routledge Handbook of Indigenous Wellbeing*. Abingdon, Oxon; New York, NY: Routledge. Series: Routledge international handbooks: Routledge, pp. 156–169. Available at: https://doi.org/10.4324/9781351051262-14.

Rahnema, M. (2010). 'Poverty'. In *The Development Dictionary: a guide to knowledge as power*, (2nd ed.), edited by Sachs, W.London and New York: Zed Books, pp. 174–194.

Ramos-Cortez, C. and MacNeill, T. (2022). 'Situating in Place Indigenous Engagements in Capitalist Market Relations', *Journal of Latin American Geography*, 21 (1), pp. 32–60. Available at: https://doi.org/10.1353/lag.2022.0001.

Ranta, E. M. (2016). 'Toward a Decolonial Alternative to Development? The Emergence and Shortcomings of *vivir bien* as State Policy in Bolivia in the Era of Globalization', *Globalizations*, 13 (4), pp. 425–439. Available at: https: //doi.org/ 10. 1080/ 14747731.2016.1141596.

Rapley, J. (2004). 'Development studies and the post-development critique', *Progress in Development Studies*, 4 (4), pp. 350- 54. Available at: https://doi.org/10.1191/1464993404ps095pr.

Recasens, A. V. (2014). 'Discursos "pachamamistas" versus políticas desarrollistas: el debate sobre el sumak kawsay en los Andes', *Íconos – Revista de Ciencias Sociales*, (48), pp. 55–72. Available at: https://doi.org/10.17141/iconos.48.2014.1209.

Sachs, W. (2010). *The Development Dictionary: A Guide to Knowledge as Power*. (2nd ed.). London and New York: Zed Books.

SAIPE and Consejo Permanente de los Pueblos Awajún y Wampis & Servicio Agropecuario para la Investigación y Promoción Económica. (2021). *Programa de Formación Intercultural: Escuela de Líderes y Lideresas de los Pueblos Awajún y Wampis*. Santa Maria de Nieva, Condorcanqui: SAIPE and Consejo Permanente de los Pueblos Awajún y Wampis & Servicio Agropecuario para la Investigación y Promoción Económica.

Saito-Jensen, M., Nathan, I. and Treue, T. (2010). 'Beyond elite capture? Community-based natural resource management and power in Mohammed Nagar village, Andhra Pradesh, India', *Environmental Conservation*, 37 (3), pp. 327–335. Available at: https://doi.org/10.1017/S0376892910000664.

Scott, J. C. (1985). *Weapons of the Weak: Everyday Forms of Peasant Resistance*. New Haven, CT: Yale University Press.

Shahraki, H. and Keikha, A. (2022). 'How the entrepreneurship can set aside the rural development process: a historical and discursive reflection on rural entrepreneurship and development policies in Iran', *Journal of Global Entrepreneurship Research*, 12 (1), pp. 219–235. Available at: https://doi.org/10.1007/s40497-022-00323-3.

Shrestha, N. (1995). 'Becoming a Development Category '. In *Power of Development*. (1st ed.). Routledge, pp. 259–270.

Smit, M. and Pretorius, M. (2020). '"Un"trepreneurship Undoing the Myth of Entrepreneurship as a Development Apparatus', *African Journal of Business Ethics*, 14(1), pp. 62–81. Available at: https://doi.org/10.15249/14-1-273.

Tauli- Corpuz, V. (2010). 'Human development framework and indigenous peoples' self-determined development', *Towards an alternative development paradigm. Indigenous people's self-determined development*. Baguio City, Philippines: Tebtebba Foundation, pp. 117–161.

Wanvik, T. I. and Caine, K. (2017). 'Understanding indigenous strategic pragmatism: Métis engagement with extractive industry developments in the Canadian North', *The Extractive Industries and Society*, 4 (3), pp. 595- 605. Available at: https://doi.org/10.1016/j.exis.2017.04.002.

Wilson, K. (2017). 'Worlds beyond the political? Post-development approaches in practices of transnational solidarity activism', *Third World Quarterly*, 38 (12), pp. 2684- 2702. Available at: https://doi.org/10.1080/01436597.2017.1354694.

Part III

Alternatives?

This section brings together reflections on attempts to build alternatives to development revealing some of the difficulties and hesitations, but also the possibilities, that arise in relation to attempts to build alternatives to development.

DOI: 10.4324/9781003477921-11

9 Economies of solidarity in Tehran

New commons and diverse economies on the margins?

Reihaneh Saremi, Hadi Darvishi, Somayeh Momeni and Aram Ziai

Introduction

Post-development claims to find economies of solidarity on the margins of capitalism which could be seedbeds of a new society, while its critics reject this as a romanticisation of survival strategies. On the basis of fieldwork in marginalised communities in Tehran, Iran, this chapter will analyse the economic practices of four different minority groups: Mazandari Ghorbats, Afghan Hazara refugees, Azeri migrants and drug addicts. Building on the theories of Esteva (1992) and Gibson-Graham (2006; 2010), the text analyses to what extent these practices differ from the capitalist logic of 'economic man' and in how far they can be seen as manifestations of 'new commons' and a 'diverse economy'. It argues that these survival strategies often employ non-capitalist logics which are, however, not free from exclusions. In this chapter, we will investigate the post-development claims that those marginalised by capitalism and the 'development project' create new, alternative economic practices based on a logic of solidarity. Our empirical focus is marginalised communities in Tehran. Our chapter starts with the theoretical background: the claims by prominent post-development writer Esteva (1992) and the counterclaims by his critics. The next section will deal with our methods, our analytical tool – the diverse economy model by Gibson-Graham (2006; 2010) – and the context of Tehran. The following section presents the case studies of the Mazandaran Ghorbats of Darvaze Ghar, the Hazara Afghan refugees in Shams Abad kiln, the Azeri community in Akbar Abad and the drug addict community behind the Kazemi stadium. The analysis of these cases will allow us to formulate some conclusions.

Theoretical background: post-development and its critics

We will start with the claims of post-development scholar Gustavo Esteva (1992). He argues that the post-war project of 'development' continued the 'violent transformation' of societies (first performed in and then exported from Europe through colonialism). Through this project, the economic sphere is excised from society and culture as an autonomous sphere and installed 'at the centre of politics and ethics', subjecting them to the imperative of maximising production and

DOI: 10.4324/9781003477921-12

productivity and disvaluing allegedly unproductive activities (Esteva 1992: 14–15). This new project no longer relied on domination by Europeans and was compatible with anti-colonialism. At the individual level, it implied the transformation of humans into economic beings as a 'precondition for the emergence of economic society' predicated on the assumption of chronic scarcity (Esteva 1992: 15). A new society geared to endless accumulation was based on the idea of human beings possessing infinite needs for material goods, acting as rational maximisers of utility pursuing this goal. However, this assumption of *homo economicus* acting according to this logic is 'untenable when confronted with what we know about ancient societies and cultures and even with what we can still see in some parts of the world', says Esteva (1992: 17). He argues that after realising that the project of 'development' (in the sense of the universalisation of Western models of society, the economy and politics in the regions designated as 'underdeveloped') failed to deliver the good life that was promised, people on the margins resisted the 'economic invasion of their lives' by 'disengaging from the economic logic'. They created 'new commons' through 'strengthening forms of interaction embedded in the social fabric and by breaking the economic principle of the exchange of equivalents' (Esteva 1992: 19). Esteva (1992: 20) asserts that through these alternatives to 'development', 'common men' and women manage to re-embed the economic sphere within social relations (Esteva 1992: 14), engaging in practices of reciprocity and solidarity.

Esteva's (1992) claims have been disputed by critics, accusing post-development of romanticising poverty (Corbridge 1998) and mistakenly identifying practices arising out of practical necessity as resistance to Western models. 'When those excluded unite in groups and forge ties of solidarity', so Schuurman (1993: 28) seconds the criticism, 'this must be seen not as an embryonic form of a new society, but rather as a survival strategy.'

Against the backdrop of this academic debate on the question of whether or not practices arising out of practical necessity or survival needs can be considered as resistance or at least alternatives to Western models, we ask: can we find alternative economic practices of reciprocity and solidarity on the margins of Iranian society? Or do people on the margins conform to the model of the 'economic man', the utility-maximising individual?

Context, methods, analytical tools

Context: Iran's development approach and marginalisation in Tehran

The contemporary history of Iran presents a complex case in its approach to development and capitalism. The 1979 revolution, which followed decades of political activism by left-wing parties alongside religious groups, was rooted in critiques of capitalism and Westernisation advocating for an alternative system (see Abrahamian 1982). However, within a few years of the establishment of the Islamic Republic, leftist parties were overshadowed by Islamist groups, which then consolidated power (see Bayat 1997). Crucially, the Islamic Republic of Iran

(IRI) upheld the belief that Islam, as the traditional culture and internal ideology of Iranians, could serve as a principal framework for alternative development. In the early years of the revolution, numerous efforts were made to reconcile Islam with modern issues. Theories sought to posit Islam as a solution or reference point for these problems. Although the pursuit began before the 1979 revolution, many theories gained prominence after the rise of the Islamic Republic. Notable among these were the republishing of Baqir al-Sadr's *Our Economics* and Abolhassan Banisadr's *Monotheistic Economics*, both of which were referenced as foundations for an Islamic approach to economics. Even in the field of science, books such as Mehdi Bazargan's *Love and Worship or Man's Thermodynamics* were trending, offering an Islamic foundation of scientific concepts.

Despite the rivalry and low tolerance between leftist and Islamist parties, the discourse of 'supporting the impoverished' was prevalent among all factions during the first decade of the revolution (Bayat 1997: 20). A new wave of volunteers was deployed to impoverished villages to provide electricity, gas, piped water and renovated housing for those in need. The objective was to offer facilities to the so-called poor, who were perceived as having been oppressed under the Pahlavi monarchy. Numerous welfare organisations were also established (Harris 2017: 40). Concurrently, anti-Western critiques of development remained widespread.

A decade after the revolution, following the eight year Iran-Iraq war, new development policies were implemented, aligning with global trends. Structural adjustment plans under the International Monetary Fund (IMF) were introduced in the 1990s and numerous international economic initiatives were undertaken. Nevertheless, critiques of development persisted among academics. Relevant books were translated and the government supported these writings, viewing them as anti-imperialistic and anti-Western. In 2012, the Specialised Council for the Development and Promotion of Human Sciences was established to expand an Islam-based human science academy and provide academic and theoretical foundations for an alternative 'progress path', leading to the establishment of new departments within human science faculties.

Overall, while various administrations of the Islamic Republic showed minimal deviation from mainstream development and economic plans (see Maljoo 2017; Momeni 2015), the state's anti-Western stance, focusing on Islam as the core of its alternative ideology, remained central. Over time, this alternative approach evolved into primarily a cultural project rather than an economic one, resulting in the government aligning with international economic norms while resisting ideological and cultural aspects.

In addition to the state's approach to development, international relations have significantly impacted the economic behaviour of the IRI. A notable factor is the sanctions imposed on Iran's economy, aimed at limiting government revenues from oil exports and restricting the country's trade with the outside world. Although these sanctions aim to challenge Iran's alignment with international economic relations, its economic trajectory has largely shifted towards militarisation (see Bajoghli et al. 2024). This shift reflects a military rather than a socio-economic alternative. Furthermore, the reduction in oil revenue has weakened the IRI's cash transfer programmes, leading to a significant drop in consumption across the spectrum (see Salehi-Isfahani 2020). Consequently, there has been an increase in privatisation and outsourcing programmes, even within welfare organisations.

In the greater metropolitan area of Tehran, the capital and largest city of Iran, live 16 million people. There has been a massive influx of rural migrants in recent decades. This could be understood as a result of the social transformation processes described by Esteva, which we discussed in the theory section above. The advent, spread and intensification of capitalist practices and the imperative of competition and ever-increasing productivity have led to the destruction of traditional rural livelihoods. Rural people then attempt to find new livelihoods in the modern, urban sectors of the economy. However, the promises of 'development' have not materialised for the majority of migrants. In Tehran, marginalised communities are characterised by insecure employment or unemployment; lack of access (or extremely difficult access) to social security, public facilities, hospitals and universities; low literacy, few years of schooling; and insufficient transport infrastructure. Our geographical focus was Tehran and its suburbs and we chose four different marginalised communities with different degrees of marginalisation:

1 the Mazandaran Ghorbats of Darvaze Ghar;
2 the Afghan (Hazara) refugees in Shams Abad kiln;
3 the Azeri community in Akbar Abad; and
4 the drug addict community behind the stadium of Shahid Kazemi.

Methods

Case Study 1 draws on data collected during field research conducted from September 2019 to June 2020 in Tehran and Sari, with a follow-up field research phase from January to March 2024 in Tehran. The research employed a combination of participant and non-participant observations, as well as semi-structured interviews. Access to the Ghorbat community was facilitated through the intermediary support of an NGO actively involved in Darvaze Ghar since 2010. Interviewees were selected using a snowball sampling method, with trust established through participatory observations in some instances, eventually leading to interviews. Additional interviews were conducted with NGO members and schoolmasters working with Ghorbats, facilitated by providing a university introduction letter. Again, interviewees were selected through a snowball sampling method. Data was also provided by community members themselves on the basis of (oral) informed consent. Since both members of the research team and the interviewees spoke Persian, the use of translators was deemed unnecessary. Interviewees did not participate in the research design, and the research process encountered no conflicts or challenges.

Case studies 2–4 are based on data collected during field research from January to May 2020 in Tehran (and have already been presented in Schöneberg et al.

2022). The research methods included participant observation and interviews which were backed up by a literature review. We gained access to the communities through family ties (one of the authors originally comes from the Azeri community in Nasimshahr/Akbar Abad) and intermediaries who have worked with the Afghan refugees and the drug addict community in District 19 for several years, building up relations of trust. Data was also provided by community members themselves on the basis of (oral) informed consent. Translators were not necessary. The interviewees did not take part in the research design. There were no conflicts or challenges during the research process, apart from one intermediary being called upon to 'first take care of his own people' (Iranians) before worrying about Afghan immigrants. Research results will be presented only informally and orally to community members.

Analytical tool

To examine the economic practices of the marginalised communities, we utilised the diverse economy model of post-development theorist Gibson-Graham (2010).

Gibson-Graham (2006) rejects the idea that progressive politics is faced with a coherent, omnipresent and almost totalitarian global capitalism based on capitalist enterprises, wage labour, private property and the market. He argues that 'economists have rendered non-capitalist economic activity non-credible or non-existent' and that 'most of the world is sustained by diverse economic relations, many of which cannot be framed as capitalist' (Gibson-Graham 2010: 227–228). Some of these economic practices correspond to Esteva's (1992) idea of 'new commons'. In the following, we will categorise the economic practices encountered in marginalised communities in Tehran according to the typology of Gibson-Graham (2010) and thus use it as an analytical tool to map economic space and to differentiate between different types of enterprises, labour, property, transactions and finance.

Mazandarani Ghorbats of Darvaze Ghar

The ethnic minority of Ghorbats in Iran has historically been a small subset of the larger ethnic group commonly referred to as Kowli in Persian, known for their nomadic mode of life. Some contend that they belong to the same ethnic group as European Romas (Djuric et al. 1996). The prevailing narrative in Iran suggests that Ghorbats, originally from the lower castes of India, were brought to Iran for entertainment during the reign of Bahram (5th century AD). However, a decade after Bahram lost his crown, they were dispersed to the deserts, where they experienced severe social and economic exclusion (Zoka 1956). Over the course of centuries, the Iranian Kowlis were traditionally engaged in vending small handicrafts, including items like baskets and other iron-made products (Sykes 2013). However, the advent of industrialisation marked a shift in their economic engagement; as their traditional products witnessed a decline in demand, they

Table 9.1 Gibson-Graham's (2010) diverse economy model

Enterprise:	*Labour:*	*Property:*	*Market:*	*Finance:*
Capitalist	*Wage*	*Private*	*Market*	*Market*
Alternative capitalist • state-owned • environmentally responsible • socially responsible • non-profit	Alternative paid • self-employed • reciprocal labour • in-kind • work for welfare	Alternative private • State-managed assets • customary (clan) land • community land trusts • Indigenous knowledge (intellectual property)	Alternative market • fair trade • alternative currencies • underground market • barter	Alternative market • cooperative banks • credit unions • community-based financial institutions • micro-finance
Non-capitalist • worker co-operations • sole proprietorships • community enterprise • feudal • slave	Unpaid • housework • volunteer • self-provisioning • slave labour	Open access • atmosphere • international waters • open source IP • outer space	Non-market • household sharing • gift giving • hunting, fishing, gathering • theft, piracy, poaching	Non-market • sweat equity • family lending • donations • interest-free loans

Source: (Gibson-Graham 2010: 228)

were largely excluded from the formal labour market or chose not to partake in it. Instead, they adhered to their distinctive approach to earning a livelihood through trade or, in some instances, begging (Safikhani et al. 2016).

They were traditionally associated with a nomadic lifestyle, residing in tents, often situated beyond the confines of urban areas. Nevertheless, with the establishment of the nation-state and policies against nomadic lifestyles, they largely abandoned their tents and adopted a more sedentary existence (Amanolahi and Norbeck 1975). This section will specifically concentrate on the community of Ghorbats situated in a marginalised area of Tehran, Darvaze Ghar, originating from Mazandaran province, particularly from the cities of Babol and Sari in northern Iran.

Most of the Ghorbats' residences in Darvaze Ghar are collective houses, featuring a shared yard and typically a shared bathroom and kitchen (if available). Each family occupies a room with a maximum area of 20 m^2, and it is common for relatives to reside together in a shared house. Given that the traditional preference is for short-term or unofficial marriages, the nuclear family structure is an uncommon arrangement among them.

The Ghorbat community's existence is notably characterised by informality. A notable portion of this community lacks formal identity documents and official marriage statements and resides in informal settlements. Their employment is predominantly within the informal sector. A clear indication of their marginalisation is the covert manner in which they conceal their ethnic identity and avoid identifying as Ghorbats, coupled with their practice of communal living to safeguard against discrimination.

Those residing in Darvaze Ghar generally engage in street peddling or, on occasion, begging at intersections in Tehran. Specific areas have been designated for particular groups for an extended period, and newcomers are typically prohibited from peddling without permission. Typically, within Ghorbat communities, the male figure assumes the responsibility of safeguarding the territory from law enforcement, municipal patrols and competing groups seeking to generate income in a similar manner. The actual work, however, is undertaken by females or predominantly children. While each individual is accountable for their own earnings, it is common for the male figure in charge to collect the accumulated money at the conclusion of each day.

The nomadic lifestyle, not entirely eradicated from the lives of Ghorbats, has resulted in a situation where the majority consider Tehran as their workplace and Mazandaran as their homeland. They aim to accumulate savings in Tehran and spend them in Mazandaran. Some invest in building houses, and many own cars. Typically, they spend several months on vacation before returning to work in Tehran. This dynamic creates significant conflicts between schools and Ghorbat families, as they often show minimal attention towards their children's education and allow them to miss numerous sessions during these breaks. While some families align with school programmes, the majority adhere to their established schedules.

An additional crucial aspect that warrants consideration is the initiatives aimed at compelling families to enter the labour market, not necessarily the formal sector. As mentioned earlier, the entire Ghorbat lifestyle hinges on their labour relations, but due to criminalisation and societal perceptions of impropriety, their work is both undervalued and prohibited. For adults, panhandling has been criminalised, while for children, many NGOs and schools have been inclined to guide them towards profitable 'skilled' jobs. Numerous Ghorbats resist this transition, asserting that they 'already have a job', rendering it exceedingly challenging for social workers to impose a lucrative role on Ghorbat families. The criticism is not only their lack of profitability, but also the notion that the social lives of Ghorbats pose a threat to society. One primary reason is the Ghorbats' resistance to assimilation. Additionally, it is widely said that some Ghorbats are involved in activities such as robbery, drug dealing and gambling, which contribute to their perception as a menace to society.

The extent to which the Ghorbat engage in sharing is complicated. Ownership is often overlooked within extended families. Regarding property, it is common to witness siblings dedicating years and pooling their funds to assist each other in constructing a house. Family members give loans to one another for extended periods, sometimes exceeding 20 years. While the properties may be officially registered in one member's name, they are collectively utilised. In many instances, fully constructed houses are not purchased outright. Instead, members of the community acquire land and gradually build houses on it. Often, the construction process involves collaborative work: members residing in Mazandaran carry out the construction while those working in Tehran finance the project. This cooperative effort reflects the strong ties and mutual support within the community. The collaboration extends beyond land properties; families often pool their resources to purchase a car and use it collectively.

Ownership is not considered a contentious issue within these familial arrangements, as claimed by the members. Within extended families, children are also observed to be under the support and care of all members, not necessarily only the parents. Additionally, a customary practice involves providing substantial monetary gifts to newlyweds to aid them in establishing their lives, despite the financial challenges faced by families. During challenging times, Ghorbats typically seek assistance from their families.

As mentioned previously, each Ghorbat belongs to a trade group led by male individuals. These trade groups are primarily composed of members of an extended family. Members within these groups share their working domain and trade commodities and, therefore, pool their income and collaborate on their sales. In many cases, the money earned is added together and given to one member who is responsible for managing and allocating the funds. This one member is also in charge of collecting charity goods and distributing them among group members.

Another complexity of the concept of ownership among the Ghorbats is their desire to make their belongings as glamorous as possible. For instance, in neighbourhoods known for being marginalised and impoverished, some Ghorbats use luxurious facades or doors to make their houses look more elegant. Although this is not very common, as many cannot afford to complete their houses and they even live in half-built structures, those who earn more money often choose to remain in their neighbourhoods while making their small, impoverished houses appear more glamorous and fancy. This behaviour can be attributed to the Ghorbats' uncommon practice of saving and accumulating money. It is often said among the Ghorbats that what is saved during their work in Tehran is spent during their free time in Mazandaran. However, nowadays, the difficult economic situation in Iran makes it challenging for Ghorbats to earn more than their basic needs. Even the small amounts of money saved are often spent on cosmetic procedures for women or on gaming clubs and fitness studios for men. This spending behaviour has been a concern for many social workers, leading them to emphasise 'financial literacy' as a key subject to teach the Ghorbats.

However, Ghorbats do adhere to the idea of ownership outside of their extended family, particularly in the context of claiming a traffic intersection as their designated working territory. This hierarchy has led to economic disparities within their community, with some belonging to the wealthier class and others to the lower class. Those with a higher economic standing possess more lucrative intersections, enabling them to engage in transactions involving higher-priced commodities (such as flowers), resulting in increased earnings. Additionally, they tend to reside in different neighbourhoods within their home city. For instance, in the city of Sari, the middle-wage or lower-wage groups of Ghorbats inhabit the Ghaffari neighbourhood, a marginalised and less affluent area, while the wealthier groups live in a neighbourhood that, despite its marginalised status, is closer to the sea and therefore more expensive.

The concept of neighbourhood is crucial for the Ghorbats, who feel a strong sense of belonging to their neighbourhood and its residents. This attachment is so significant that even across generations, few Ghorbats change their neighbourhood despite having the financial means to do so. Whether they belong to an extended family or not, all Ghorbats within a neighbourhood support one another. However, despite living in the same neighbourhood and operating in the same market, Ghorbats object strongly to Afghan refugees. They claim that Afghans receive aid intended for Iranians and believe they are encroaching on their job opportunities. This rivalry is so pronounced that Ghorbats and Afghans even resist attending the same school. A schoolmaster laments, 'It's not a day that we don't have our students fighting with each other, calling each other 'Nasty Ghorbat' and 'Miserable Afghans', or words like that'.

Afghan refugees in Shams Abad kiln

In various regions of Iran, Afghan refugees have established distinct communities. Residing in proximity to their extended families and relatives, they typically seek to congregate. New refugees entering their familial network are readily embraced by the community, and this is often the mechanism through which the entire network grows. The Afghan refugees inhabiting the brick kilns of Shams Abad share a similar circumstance. They constitute a group of refugees who have migrated to Iran over the course of three decades.

In Tehran's District 19, live approximately 450 Afghan families with 80 of them residing in brick kilns in this district. The area consists of more than ten kilns, but only a few are operational. The houses adjacent to each kiln are predominantly rented, with a significant number being occupied by Afghan families. The specific kiln examined in this research accommodated 30 Afghan families.

The majority of these Afghans were born in Iran, specifically in the cities of Mashhad and Tehran, yet they are not recognised as Iranian citizens. Their ancestral roots trace back to the cities of Daikundi and Bamyan in Afghanistan, and they identify as Shiites and Hazaras. Having faced persecution in their homeland, particularly during the Taliban era, they lack capital or assets in

Afghanistan. Their migration to Iran is driven by the pursuit of work and a better life, and they hold refugee cards issued by the UN.

Within these families, girls pursue education until they attain diplomas, while boys typically conclude their studies at middle school level due to the necessity of entering the workforce in their early teens. While many were previously employed in the kilns, which are now closed, they have transitioned to working in the nearby Kholazir Bazaar, primarily engaging in roles such as porters or blacksmiths.

In contrast to Ghorbats, the Afghan refugees generally aspire to establish a stable life and actively strive for inclusion in society. Kiln residents face challenges in sending their children to school due to the distance, but despite the high costs, families pool their resources to secure daily taxi services for their children. Afghan workers are often recognised for their strong work ethic; however, due to their informal status, their employment exists in the black market, resulting in lower wages compared to Iranian workers.

Their dwellings consist of 18-metre rooms without kitchens or bathrooms. Constructed from bricks, most lack windows and exhibit signs of ageing and wear. Residents rely on the electricity and gas provided by the brick kiln, while water is sourced from wells. Every four or five families share a small backyard, where communal kitchens and two or three shared bathrooms are situated. Within these families, there are households led by widowed women, who often face challenges in finding a secure neighbourhood. However, this community enables them to live peacefully. Our survey revealed that in 90% of cases, new marriages also occur among members of the community.

The Hazara Afghans are excluded from public services such as education, healthcare, financial aid, property rights, and, in some cases, the right to work. Confined to refugee status or substandard housing, they have formed a close-knit community of friends and families. In the face of financial difficulties, community members primarily support each other by lending money, while during sickness, neighbours offer the main support. Additionally, when someone requires assistance with repairing their houses or equipment, fellow community members provide free services. Living without government support has compelled these families to rely on each other for survival, fostering the formation of a resilient community.

Moreover, when an individual secures a job opportunity, they make an effort to facilitate employment for other unemployed members within the same vicinity. This practice is a key reason why community members predominantly work in the same workshop or employment area. In some instances, Afghans prioritise other members of their community over themselves when seeking employment, particularly in the case of those seeking daily work. They also encourage each other to enhance their working skills. They express contentment with their status, viewing themselves as refugees who should be grateful for having a roof over their heads, meals to eat, and job opportunities provided by Iranians.

This occurs while official social support policies deny any form of inclusion for Afghans and other foreign nationals. Afghan cases are not accepted by support organisations such as Komite-Emdad and the Ministry of Welfare, which handle issues such as poverty and malnutrition (Alaedini and Emami 2005: 275; see also Nasr Esfahani 2018). Before 2013, Afghan children were also denied access to education. However, a supreme order in 2014 mandated the inclusion of all Afghan children in public schools. Despite this mandate, Afghan children's registration is often delayed until the final weeks, resulting in many being left out of school under the pretext of limited capacity in public schools (Haghighattalab et al. 2022: 9–13). For example, when addressing child labour, the state welfare organisation responsible for supporting street children only offers aid to Iranian children, while initiating deportation processes for Afghan children (The Regulation for Supporting Street Children, 2020). Nonetheless, Afghans do receive some assistance. NGOs provide support to Afghans, and charitable activities such as food distribution in urban poor areas are directed at all residents, regardless of identity. Fourteen out of 31 provinces in the country prohibit the entry and presence of Afghan migrants.

Beyond governmental policies, parts of Iranian society are also unwelcoming toward Afghan migrants. A head of an NGO that primarily offers education to Afghan children states that they do not reveal giving education services to Afghan children in their social media, 'otherwise, many of our funders will withdraw their aid'. In 2023, a social media movement emerged criticising the 'open door' policy for Afghan migrants, with the hashtag 'deporting Afghans, a national demand' trending. Although no survey has quantified the prevalence of these sentiments, many Afghans have experienced exclusion.

In terms of behavioural norms, Afghan refugees interviewed demonstrate a stronger motivation for inclusion compared to the Ghorbats. Although they do not conceal their identities, they do not assert it strongly either. For instance, they avoid wearing their traditional dress in public. An important aspect in this regard is that the Afghan Hazara tradition does not significantly differ from Iranian culture. They are Farsi (Dari)-speaking Shiites who celebrate Nowrooz and share other holidays with Iranians. It can be argued that due to overlapping traditions or a desire for inclusion, Afghans exhibit little behavioural resistance. Regardless of their exclusion from official social support and experience of not being welcome in many societies, Afghan Hazaras still try to maintain close relations with society and express a willingness to be included. An elderly lady in the kiln, watching over her grandson playing in the yard, remarked, 'We see ourselves as Iranians. Our children have never been to Afghanistan, and for them, Iran is their country. We have been living in Iran for about 40 years; how can I think any other way?' The pursuit of inclusion is evident as many pay an annual fee to obtain a refugee card and apply for immigration cards.

Nevertheless, there have been instances where Afghan refugees have protested against Iranian policies, such as the blocking of their bank accounts or restrictions on their children attending schools. However, the frequency and intensity of these protests have been relatively low, and the community we surveyed did not participate in any of these protests or engage in political collective action.

Regarding the notion of sharing, the absence of nuclear family structures and their cohabitation with shared facilities can result in a form of communal living among extended families. This may even include sending money to family members in Afghanistan. In this context, the concept of ownership does not quite fit with its modern interpretation as private and individual.

Azeri Community of Hasan Kandi Roud in Akbar Abad

The largest minority ethnic group in Iran is the Azeris or Azerbaijanis. They are primarily of Iranian descent and were originally Indigenous to the northwest region of Iran (Arakelova 2015). However, due to migration waves from rural to urban areas and from smaller cities to the capital or larger cities, many Azeris have left their homelands in search of better work and improved living conditions.

The inhabitants of the Azeri village Hasan Kandi Roud, in the north-western region of Iran, situated within the West Azerbaijan province, faced recurrent droughts during the 1990s. Engaging in seasonal work as construction labourers in autumn and winter and agricultural activities in spring and summer, they decided to relocate to Tehran when confronted with the persistent drought conditions. The decision to migrate was not solely influenced by drought; the transition from extended families to nuclear families resulted in a diminishing amount of inherited land for the male heads of households over time, rendering it economically unviable to cover expenses. These factors prompted the residents of Hasan Kandi Roud to migrate in groups to Tehran or Booshehr (where some had prior work experience). The immigrants in Tehran established their residence in a suburb known as Akbar Abad (later known as Nasimshahr), subsequently accommodating other migrants from their village.

Initially settling in unowned properties, they gradually built houses and infrastructure. Similar to numerous informal settlements in Iran, they gained access to energy by illegally tapping into the main electricity cables and procured water by diverting it from the main pipes.

In the initial phase, only men relocated to Tehran and engaged in periodic work to support their families back home. Subsequently, as the children pursued education in schools and universities, the entire families moved to Tehran. Presently, they predominantly work as building construction workers and operate small supermarkets.

Our interviews revealed that when in need, Hasan Kandis in Akbar Abad turn to their extended families or relatives for assistance before considering taking a loan from the bank. In times of illness, their primary reliance is on their insurance coverage and income, but they also anticipate support from their spouses and children. Given their proficiency in construction work, they willingly offer free services to close relatives for small, multi-day jobs. Although the people interviewed claimed that among all the residences (approximately 550), only ten people in Akbar Abad are highly addicted to drugs and are often considered a disgrace to the family, in times of illness or a decision to quit drugs, they receive support from their families. The ties within the community remain firm and solid.

They engage in their own rituals, collectively constructing a religious building to practise their shared rituals.

Hasan Kandis represent a typical Iranian immigrant group residing in marginalised areas. They exemplify a stable, quiet encroachment into the mainstream, transitioning from being informal and unaccepted to becoming formal and included. They formalise their land by paying fines to the organisation in charge, and the second generation undergoes a steady inclusion process through schooling, and later securing more stable, highly skilled jobs. According to our interviewees, in Akbar Abad, where Hasan Kandi households reside, most of the settlers do own houses, and more than half of them own cars. All, except for a few of the older members of the community, benefit from retirement insurance.

Through interviews and their life experiences, it is evident that they aspire to be fully integrated into modern society, with a strong desire for stability. Many seek permanent job opportunities, such as janitorial positions in organisations. Their plans are long-term, and through a gradual improvement they pursue long-term goals.

Regarding the question of whether they are pursuing 'alternatives to development', we can observe that among Hasan Kandis, there are no apparent signs of resistance against the political (religious state) or economic model (capitalist economy). However, they strongly emphasise their Azeri ethnicity, speaking Turkish within their families and encouraging their children to do the same. Marriages within the community predominantly involve other Azeris.

The drug addict community behind the Kazemi Stadium

There are ten settlements of drug addicts in the 19th District of Tehran, housing approximately 2000 people. Specifically, the settlement behind the Kazemi stadium, which was the focus of our research, is inhabited by about 100 individuals. Of these, 68 are permanent residents, while 32 are temporary. Among the residents, there are ten women. The permanent residents typically remain in the settlement for two to three months. However, there is one resident who has been living there for approximately two years. Many others rent the space for only a night or two.

The community serves as a gathering place for drug addicts, primarily those using crystal meth. The area behind the stadium is an open space where partitions have been created using metal, wood and plastic waste materials. The sole semi-permanent structure is a room constructed from thatch, which serves as the residence of the person in charge. This slum, commonly referred to as a 'hangout' by the residents, is a gathering place for drug addicts who often bring companions who use drugs and spend their time together. The rooms are not privately occupied; instead, allocation depends on the head of the hangout. Payment for access is not monetary but is made instead by means of drugs or, in the case of women, sexual services. The area does not appear to be a private place, yet it remained unclear to the researchers how the head of the place manages to keep it running without police intrusions. Each member has experienced separation from their family for various reasons. None of the interviewees possessed an official ID, often due to loss, sale, or use as collateral. At the time of the research, approximately ten individuals in the hangout were illiterate. One person held a bachelor's degree, 11 had diplomas, and the rest had received primary and secondary education. The settlers generate income through activities such as selling drugs, collecting and selling recyclable waste, begging, and in some cases, engaging in robbery. Additionally, sex work is prevalent among women.

The slum is under the ownership of an individual named Seyed Shapour, who oversees room rentals and determines who is permitted to stay. It is widely acknowledged among the residents that Shapour exploits many of them, requiring certain individuals to provide free sexual services, while others must offer drugs or other services to secure accommodation. The Shapour hangout offers shelter and often, food is provided through charitable means. However, it lacks electricity, with residents resorting to candles and fire for illumination. The hangout also lacks access to gas and water, with only one water pipe located approximately 150 metres away.

The municipality in Tehran provides night shelters for homeless addicts, offering free beds and dinner. While the shelters are used more during winter, many addicts prefer not to use them and explore alternative options. A significant reason is the prohibition of drug use in the shelter, and the fact that the doors close at around 11 pm. The entry process is also cumbersome for some, involving identification checks, changing clothes, taking a shower and then gaining entry. These factors contribute to their preference for staying in a hangout for many addicts.

Drug addicts are subjected to various rehabilitation as well as work-enforcement programmes, and their visible homelessness is also criminalised. Consequently, their preference for informality, akin to many Ghorbats, can be viewed as a resistance to formalisation. Since drug addiction has become criminalised, the government, in collaboration with cooperating NGOs, makes significant efforts to compel addicts to overcome their addiction and receive training in skilled vocations. However, these efforts often encounter resistance. They are labelled as a societal harm and deemed unprofitable members. Many initiatives aim to induce change or, at the very least, render them less visible. A male resident who has been in the hangout for several months states,

> I was caught a few times; they keep us in captivity for a few months to make us get clean, but it's no use. In the beginning, I tried once or twice to quit drugs, but to be honest, now I don't want to quit. It's over for me now.

The residents, originating from diverse backgrounds, are essentially individuals brought together by the common necessity for shelter, which engenders some degree of mutual help (Tohidi et al. 2018: 9). In times of need, mutual support is often lacking: when a woman required hospitalisation, and the nurses sought someone to accompany her to the hospital, no one volunteered. 'It's trouble', remarked one resident. A month later, the woman committed suicide in the hangout. Although the sharing of food and drugs takes place (if they are available), solidarity among the residents is not as apparent as in other communities we studied.

While the community demonstrates minimal assistance and support, often the support provided is predominantly transactional in nature and as mentioned, there are instances of exploitation, exemplified by the actions of Seyed Shapour himself. The hangout essentially comprises individuals who lack a shared origin and history but who are brought together solely by their shared experience of social exclusion and way of life. No inherent ties bind them together except for their current needs. Consequently, any acts of resistance or disobedience are rooted in individual expressions of freedom and survival. The term 'community' may not be entirely suitable in this context.

Analysis and conclusions

Let us now return to our research question. Just as proponents of post-development like Esteva (1992) claim, we do find economic practices of reciprocity and solidarity among the marginalised communities in Tehran, constituting what he has described as 'new commons', a sense of community, cooperation and collective ownership and responsibility (mostly related to religious sites). However, this seemingly positive finding has to be qualified in important respects, pointing to negative dimensions not mentioned by Esteva (1992) or, in general, by the post-development debate.

We agree that these economic practices partly arise as survival strategies, but still argue that they may well be seedbeds of a new commons and embody alternatives to the dominant economic order, so they do not have to be either one or the other. Regarding the economic practices we observed in the case studies, a number of them did not conform to capitalist models of the utility-maximising individual, capitalist enterprise, wage labour, private property and the market. According to Gibson-Graham's (2006; 2010) diverse economy model, we can categorise these practices as follows.

The economic organisation of the Ghorbat community is based on trade groups, which can be seen as capitalist enterprises based on extended families, where practices of sharing are common. Towards other groups, there is a relation of territorial rivalry potentially backed up by force. Petty trading, which provides livelihoods, is self-employed and can be seen as alternative paid labour. However, as the male head of household collects the income of the group members, this can be seen as a feudal appropriation of surplus in a patron-client relationship based on unpaid family labour. Other alternative practices are collective volunteer work within the extended family as well as family lending, i.e. non-market finance. Even property which is registered individually (land or cars) is treated as collective and, therefore, as alternative private property. Care and household duties are gendered but also shared, based on unpaid labour. However, the economic practices of solidarity are usually confined to the in-group of the extended family, while there is rivalry with other groups and even racist discrimination towards Afghans.

The Afghan Hazaras make a living through wage labour or as self-employed traders of goods and services in the bazaar. Alternative economic practices can be found in pooled resources, the shared yards and working areas, and the communal kitchens, which allow us to speak of alternative private property. Lending money on interest-free or concessional terms can be seen as non-market finance. The support given to sick neighbours consists of either volunteer work (unpaid labour) or gift-giving (non-market transactions) and can be interpreted as a precarious and informal version of health insurance.

While the Azeri community seems the least marginalised of the four cases, its roots can be seen in the activities of squatting on unused land and illegally tapping into the state's energy and water infrastructure: what the authorities would call theft is a type of non-market transaction according to our analytical model. Again, the provision of support for sick community members constitutes volunteer work/unpaid labour and gift-giving/non-market transactions. The collective construction and maintenance of religious buildings is another clear case of the economy of solidarity (in the form of unpaid labour) transcending the sphere of the family.

The economy of the drug addicts is based on self-employed and partly criminal activities like drug dealing, robbery and prostitution, which can be classified as alternative paid labour. The housing situation can be described as a feudal system based on private property and market transactions, where the rent is partly demanded or paid through the provision of drugs (barter/alternative market) or sex (in-kind alternative paid labour).

These analyses allow us to answer our research question in the affirmative: yes, on the margins of the Iranian society we can find a number of alternative economic practices which do not conform to the standard capitalist model. In this respect, Esteva's (1992) post-development claims can be confirmed, but with a number of qualifications and limitations. Firstly, the practices of reciprocity and solidarity are sometimes embedded in gendered patron-client relations, which are hierarchical and not based on equality. Among the drug addicts, we find an extreme case of exploitation and dependency, mainly based on unequal access to housing, but entangled with other hierarchies based on gender, ethnicity and citizenship status. Secondly, the practices of reciprocity and solidarity are limited to an in-group and not universal. The group can be primarily the family (as among the Ghorbats), or the ethnic (Hazara or Azeri) community, but relations outside this group are usually guided by the principles of economic interest and utility maximisation. Thirdly, while the mutual support among the drug addicts is independent of family or ethnic ties, as all of them are usually treated as outcasts by their communities, it is at the same time precarious and unreliable, even in situations of dire need.

An interesting follow-up question would be whether these alternative economic practices and relations are abandoned if there is an opportunity for the individual to leave the community for more formal employment, a more central settlement or a less marginalised community. This could indicate that the general aim of the individual remains their integration into the 'development project' (the universalisation of Western models of society, the economy and politics) and not the establishment of an alternative. Another possible outcome would be that the family and community ties are so strong that individual success and wealth would continue to be distributed among the in-group.

In the end, we can observe that on the basis of our case studies in Tehran, Esteva's (1992) hope for the economic alternatives on the margins and a 'new commons' can be empirically confirmed. However, these alternatives, in our cases, are entangled with numerous relations of power which must not be overlooked. To not mention or downplay them would indeed mean engaging in precisely the romanticisation of alternatives post-development has so often been accused of.

Acknowledgements

The authors would like to gratefully acknowledge the support of Mehrdad Tohidi and Hamid Avarzamani in conducting the empirical research.

References

Abrahamian, E. (1982). *Iran between two revolutions.* Princeton University Press.

Amanolahi, S. and Norbeck, E. (1975). 'The Luti, an Outcaste Group of Iran', *Rice University Studies*, 61(2), pp. 1–12.

Alaedini, P. and Emami, Y. (2005). 'International migration and poverty: The Iranian case', *Social Welfare Quarterly*, 5(18), pp.169–200. [In Persian].

Arakelova, V. (2015). 'On the Number of Iranian Turkophones', *Iran and the Caucasus*, 19(3), pp. 279–282.

Bajoghli, N., Nasr, V., Salehi-Isfahani, D. and Vaez, A. (2024). *How sanctions work: Iran and the impact of economic warfare.* Stanford University Press.

Bayat, A. (1997). *Street Politics: Poor People's Movements in Iran.* New York: Columbia University Press.

Corbridge, S. (1998). '"Beneath the pavement only soil": The poverty of post-development', *The Journal of Development Studies*, 34(6), pp. 138–148.

⊠juric, R., Becken, J. and Bengsch, B. (1996). *Ohne heim-ohne grab: die geschichte der Roma und Sinti.* Berlin: Aufbau-Verlag.

Esteva, G. (1992). 'Development'. In *The Development Dictionary: A Guide to Knowledge as Power*, edited by Sachs, W.London: Zed Books, pp. 6–25.

Gibson-Graham, J. K. (2006). *The End of Capitalism (as we knew it): a feminist critique of political economy.* (2nd ed.), Minneapolis: University of Minnesota Press.

Gibson-Graham, J. K. (2010). 'Forging post-development partnerships: Possibilities for local and regional development'. In *Handbook of Local and Regional Development*, edited by Pike, A., Rodriguez-Pose, A. and Tomaney, J., London: Routledge, pp. 226–236.

Haghighattalab, P., JanGhorban, M., Ghaffari, H. & Dehdar, M., (2022). *Education of immigrant children in Iran: legislative, regulatory and executive challenges and proposed solutions.* Islamic Consultative Assembly's Research Centre. [In Persian].

Harris, K. (2017). *A Social Revolution: Politics and the Welfare State in Iran*. Oakland: University of California Press.
Maljoo, M. (2017). *Moderate Politics: A Political Economic Critique*. Tehran: Lahita. [In Persian].
Momeni, F. (2015). *Iran's Economy at the Time of Structural Adjustment*. Tehran: Naghsh-o-Negar Press. [In Persian].
Nasr Esfahani, A. (2018). *In the brother's house: Afghan refugees in Iran*. Research Center For Culture, Art and Communications.
Safikhani, S., Mousavi, S. Y. and Rajablou, G. A. (2016). 'Liminal Identity of Gypsies in Tehran', *Journal of Iranian Cultural Research*, 35(3), pp. 1–29.
Salehi-Isfahani, DJ. (2020). *Iran Under Sanctions*. Washington: SAIS Johns Hopkins University.
Schöneberg, J., Haudenschild, D., Darvishi, H., Momeni, S., & Ziai, A. (2022). 'The many faces of Post-Development: alternatives to development in Tanzania, Iran and Haiti'. *Sustainability Science*, 17(4), pp.1223–1234.
Schuurman, F. J. (1993). 'Introduction: Development Theory in the 1990's'. In *Beyond the Impasse: New Directions in Development Theory*, edited by Schuurman, F. J.London: Zed Books, pp. 1–48.
Sykes, P. (2013). *A History of Persia* (Vol. 1). New York: Routledge.
The Regulation for Supporting Street Children, No. 22717T32368H (2020), Council of Ministers.
Tohidi, M., Vosoughi, M. and Baseri, A. (2018). 'A sociological analysis of the relationships and interactions of society and rough sleepers', *Journal of Organizational Behavior Research*, 3(2), pp.1–11.
Zoka, Y., 1956. *The Kowli image and its life*. Fine Arts Publication. (Persian)

10 Ontology in action

Ecocentrism as defence of place in Indigenous social movement practices, South Africa

Emile Kwa and Yves Van Leynseele

Introduction

The tarred road turns into dirt beneath the tires of the taxibus. Travelling from Thohoyandou to Tshidzivhe, a small Indigenous village in the Venda[1] region of South Africa, the landscape changes drastically. The many homesteads make way for smallholder farms, indigenous forest and the steep mountains of the Soutpansberg mountain range. Ndivhuwo, a cousin of the chief of Tshidzivhe, shows me around the village that is built on the fertile soil of a Soutpansberg hill. As we walk to the other side of the mountain, the landscape changes once again. The indigenous trees make way for a plantation of pine trees, planted in orderly straight aisles. This area, which was once part of the Tshidzivhe communal land, has been converted into a state forestry area. In addition to the hectares of indigenous forests that have been cut, the sacred natural site of the Netshidzivhe family, Thathe Vondo, has also been affected by state forestry, leaving the sacred natural site vulnerable to intrusions and disturbances by ancestral spirits.

Tshidzivhe is representative of a rural village in the former Venda 'homeland'[2] where competing imaginaries of development clash. Local development projects like mining, tourism and infrastructure, characterised by a strategic collaboration of local elites with state institutions, present new developmental opportunities for this remote area of South Africa. Opportunities eagerly awaited by many impoverished residents, officials and investors alike mirror an enduring extractivist logic that targets 'underproductive' land aimed to generate economic growth. Indigenous communities are rallying in resistance, expressing how such developmental projects are environmentally damaging and threaten to enclose their territory, denying community access to sacred sites. This combination poses an existential threat by eroding traditional livelihood options, ritualistic practices, Indigenous knowledge systems and Indigenous cosmologies at large.

New civil society alliances are emerging in defence of Indigenous rights that popularise and articulate claims in holistic and cosmological terms. This chapter unpacks these efforts through the perspective of a grassroots social movement, Dzomo la Mupo (transl. *Voice of Nature*). We will show how their ontological claims to territory open a new terrain of preservation and reparation activism, moving away from land reclamation and towards a re-affirmation of Indigenous

DOI: 10.4324/9781003477921-13

cosmologies and the advancement of the eco-centric principle of *mupo*, meaning nature, as an alternative to modernist development. The shift marks a break from earlier strategies pursued by rural NGOs which focused primarily on acknowledgement and compensation for the loss of communal land rights as a result of racially discriminatory land laws and practices. Claims were made in the context of the post-apartheid land restitution legislation and other state commitments regarding land tenure security, agrarian reform and local economic development for previously-disadvantaged communities (James 2007; Hebinck and Cousins 2013).

This chapter will describe this shifting articulation in the context of a land-based conflict between modernist development projects and Indigenous social movements, analysed through the lens of ontology. We explore how ontology is operationalised through particular social movement practices that invoke Indigenous ontology and the eco-centric principle of *mupo*. For instance, eco-mapping practices facilitated by Dzomo la Mupo are discussed as a key strategy that enables the translation of such eco-centric worldviews into formats that engage with international climate change debates, advocating for Indigenous concepts such as *mupo* as an alternative for the extractivism of development projects. We describe the hybridisation of ontological and epistemic boundaries, emphasising how the fluidity of ontological categories is employed to advance Indigenous concepts in the global bioconservation debate.

We will begin this chapter with a theoretical discussion of ontology. An outline of the methodology will follow, where we discuss the use of qualitative methods and the embedded perspective, with the Indigenous grassroots organisation Dzomo la Mupo. Next, we outline the VhaVenda Indigenous ontology in more depth, focusing specifically on the ancestral belief system and the eco-centric principle of *mupo*. Then, we discuss how Dzomo la Mupo operationalises ontology into social movement strategies. Lastly, we will discuss how, through strategic alliances and the incorporation of Western bioconservation discourse, Dzomo la Mupo articulates *mupo* as an alternative to the extractivist practices of developmental projects.

Ontological difference in political ecology

This study is informed by the 'ontological turn' in political ecology. Ontology can be defined by explaining that:

> any way of understanding the world, or some part of it, must make assumptions (which may be implicit or explicit) about what kinds of things do or can exist, and what might be their conditions of existence, relations of dependency, and so on. Such an inventory of kinds of being and their relations is an ontology.
>
> (Scott and Marshall cited in Blaser 2010: 2–3)

While not entirely immutable, up until the 1980s, the world was treated as being built from permanent and unchanging building blocks which could be understood and mastered by scientific reasoning. Following the 'ontological turn', referring to a shift in academic thought which has come to centre the issue of ontology (Escobar 2007a: 107), our current understanding of ontology has been radically reshaped by science and technology studies (STS), actor-network theory (ANT) and anthropology (De la Cadena and Blaser 2018; Pickering 2017: 138).

Ever since this re-imagining, we understand that ontology does not a priori precede practices, but that it is rather actively shaped through practices and dynamics of a network consisting of the human and the nonhuman. There is no untouched reality viewed from different perspectives, but multiple ontologies are shaped through practice (Mol 1999: 77). Mol is by no means alone in her understanding of ontologies as multiple. Recognising the plurality of ontology, Descola (2013 [2005]) differentiated four ontological categories in his book *Beyond Nature and Culture*. By analysing the differences and continuities that are established between a self and a different being throughout different cultures, Descola is able to identify four ontologies: animism, totemism, naturalism and analogism. These categories distinguish how humans construct their world based on whether they consider nonhuman entities similar or dissimilar in terms of interior and exterior qualities. The analysis of the analogism-ontology informs our understanding of the VhaVenda Indigenous ontology as will be outlined in the next section.

Descola's description of the naturalism-ontology corresponds with what in broader literature is known as modernity. The separation between nature and culture is an indicative feature of modernity that distinguishes it from other ontologies. Latour (1993), in his work *We have never been modern*, makes a distinction between moderns and nonmoderns. Modernity is characterised by the separation of nature and culture, but Latour argues that the natural world remains intertwined with our cultured world. Thus, he states that we have never been modern. While it is true that modernity has never succeeded in constituting a total reality, it still enacts the separation of nature and culture as a totalising project (Escobar 2007b: 183). That modernity produces different conceptions of nature, land and the environment from Indigenous ontologies is outlined by various other authors, including Tim Ingold (2000), who posited a 'local perspective' against a 'global perspective'. The local perspective is embedded in a practical and perceptual engagement with the world whereas the global perspective is a detached observation in which the human transcends nature and its components. From this latter perspective, the world is seen as a collection of properties and resources to be managed for public interest. The 'global perspective' is similar to the process of the decontextualisation that is present in James Scott's concept of 'high-modernism'. With a high-modernist ideology, Scott (1998: 4) refers to:

> a strong [...] version of the self-confidence about scientific and technical progress, the expansion of production, the growing satisfaction of human

> needs, the mastery of nature (including human nature), and, above all, the rational design of social order commensurate with the scientific understanding of natural laws.

Both the global perspective and high-modernism can be understood as conceptual variations on modernity.

Our analysis of the hybridisation of Indigenous ontologies places central importance on political processes of claim-making that do not fix these meanings. Rather, and in line with political ontology approaches, we need to understand ontologies as being performed and in flux, as the performance of ontology can differ depending on its specific political context (Blaser 2014). Such claims represent powerful alternatives that deconstruct essentialist renderings of a modernist ontology and present us with a more intimate, nuanced understanding of 'other-worlding' that is not the static, non-modern opposite of the totality of the developmentalist view but may be prone to situated, strategic translations.

Dzomo la Mupo: embedded research

In this section, we will first briefly introduce the grassroots organisation Dzomo la Mupo and then outline the NGO-embedded research methodology. Founded in 2007, Dzomo la Mupo is a grassroots organisation led by Indigenous traditional healer Mphatheleni Makaulule and supported by a committee of Indigenous elders, chiefs and *makhadzi.* [3] The organisation maintains a broad range of activities to which interested parties can latch on to. The main focal areas are i) protection of indigenous forests, ecosystems and sacred sites, ii) food security and food sovereignty (including plant nurseries for growing and distributing indigenous plants) and iii) intergenerational learning and the preservation of the Indigenous knowledge and cultural diversity of VhaVenda communities. Some of its recent activities will be elaborated below.

The organisation has around 250 members, which is ever increasing as Mpatheleni devotes time on movement-building, focusing especially on attracting youth. With youth members finding their way to positions in the board, the movement is showing newfound professionalisation, trying to increase coherence in their programmes and develop a more streamlined plan of action. Being reliant on donor funding, they strategically orient themselves broadly in the activist landscape in order to accommodate a wide array of academic institutes, donors, researchers and environmentalist NGOs. As a grassroots organisation, Dzomo la Mupo is not selective in their choices of partnerships, allying with as many organisations that they align with as possible. In addition, they have an accommodating attitude towards academic researchers. Mpatheleni is also a key partner and broker for Indigenous knowledge systems education at the local University of Venda.

The objectives for this research were firstly to gain an understanding of the Indigenous VhaVenda ontology, secondly to analyse the social movement practices of DLM and thirdly to describe the interface between them as expressed through storytelling 'from below'. To work towards these objectives, qualitative research methods were used, with a strong emphasis on ethnographic fieldwork and participatory observation, accompanied by semi-structured interviews. Data was collected during five months of ethnographic fieldwork research by the first author that took place from September 2022 to February 2023 with VhaVenda communities and more specifically with the social movement Dzomo la Mupo. The second author has since 2018 been involved in various ways with Dzomo la Mupo including consultation meetings and research collaboration. This established relation provided contact between the first author and Dzomo la Mupo, who facilitated further access to the field. Due to the Western European background of both researchers, results and analyses were frequently shared with Dzomo la Mupo members and an external supervisor from the local university to ensure credibility.

Gaining an understanding of the VhaVenda ontology was a key methodological challenge of this research, which was done through ethnographic fieldwork methods. Through integration into a lived reality of the VhaVenda Indigenous ontology, the first author tried to build an analysis of this ontology. Law and Lien (2012) argue how ontology can be empirically studied by focusing on practice. As practice generates ontological order, studying ontology is a matter of empirical investigation focusing on practice and performance (Law and Lien 2012: 364–365). Everyday practices thus became an object of study, with a particular focus on spirituality and interactions with the natural world.

Given that the strategies of Dzomo la Mupo are the second central component of this research, embedded research was conducted. In embedded research, the researcher works collaboratively with non-academic organisations to create a beneficial relationship, with the purpose of identifying a collaborative research agenda (McGinity and Salokangas 2014; Mosher et al. 2007; Lewis and Russell 2011). Over the course of five months, the first author took part in all organised events and activities of Dzomo la Mupo to research how the Indigenous VhaVenda cosmology is implemented and operationalised into social movement actions. The most important study sites were Vuwani, Tshidzivhe, Duthuni, Vuvha and Tshikuwi. In addition to participatory observations of everyday life, attending workshops and events of Dzomo la Mupo composed a central source of ethnographic data. During these workshops, attendees worked to unify their understanding of the VhaVenda ontology, activist strategies were aligned and the goals of the organisation were articulated.

Working closely with Dzomo la Mupo allowed us to gain insights into the strategies they employ in working towards their objectives of conservation of natural spaces and sacred sites. With this embedded research design, we wanted to capture how Dzomo la Mupo translates ontology into political and activist practices and subsequently to determine whether or how these practices gain traction within the strategic field of conservation activism. This perspective enables us to bring the social movement perspective to the field of political ecology and reconstruct how this organisation's story-telling travelled from local community settings to inter-scalar communities of practice.

VhaVenda Indigenous ontology

The Venda people are not a unified ethnic group but are composed of multiple clans and subclans, such as the VhaNgona, VhaLemba, VhaSenzi and Masingo, all with their own migrational history. The estimated arrival of the first Venda clan, the VhaNgona or *VhoNgwaniwapo* – the latter meaning 'the original people' – is dated at around 700 A.D. (Sebola 2017: 598), although multiple dates circulate (Nemaheni 2021: 116–117). The VhaNgona call themselves Indigenous and have, out of all VhaVenda clans, most strongly held on to a traditional way of living, including a strong connection to ancestral spirituality and traditional cosmology. *Mupo*, the Tshivenda word for nature, constitutes the core of the VhaVenda Indigenous cosmology. It is a spiritual principle and is as such ontologically connected to the ancestral belief system, which also constitutes an important part within the Indigenous ontology. In order for us to understand the VhaVenda ontology and the cosmological meaning of *mupo*, let us begin our exploration with the ancestral belief system. In the VhaVenda ancestral belief system, as with most other African religions, the ancestral spirits derive importance from their ability to communicate with the creator God. Since humans are unable to communicate directly with the creator, their communication with ancestral spirits is a way to connect with the divine. African spiritual religions distinguish between the material and the spiritual spheres of life. These are not separated, but interconnected (Ter Haar 2009: 19). In other words, ancestors connect the material sphere with the spiritual sphere. Through rituals, the ancestors are enabled to grant blessings to the community. But while empowered through human agency, the spirits are in full control (Sinthumule 2022b: 2). For instance, ancestors are able to bestow blessings or give guidance to community members, but have destructive capabilities as well. As ancestors reside in sacred natural sites called *zwifho*, these sites hold an important place in the VhaVenda Indigenous ontology.

Ancestral belief and sacred sites are central to the constitution of the VhaVenda ontology and their understanding of the cosmological system. Both the wellbeing and misfortune of a community are regulated through, or even determined by their relationship with their ancestors and *zwifho*. This is what Descola calls an analogy-ontology. Analogism receives its name from the analogy between heaven and earth. It

> divides up the whole collection of existing beings into a multiplicity of essences, forms and substances separated by small distinctions and sometimes arranged on a graduate scale so that it becomes possible to recompose the system of initial contrasts into a dense network of analogies that link together the intrinsic properties of the entities that are distinguished in it.
>
> (Descola 2013: 201)

This system of reference and relation extends from natural to cultural, from 'up there' to 'below here' and back; the cultural world below is an analogy of the natural order up there. Thus, everything is in relation to everything else (Kwa 2018: 266). The various chains within the analogous networks of meaning, specifically the community and the ancestors, are regulated through *zwifho* (ancestral sites): wellbeing of *zwifho* relates to the wellbeing of the ancestors, in turn relating back to the wellbeing of the community. Protecting and maintaining *zwifho* is a way of safeguarding the community. In the analogous interplay between the 'up there' and the 'below here' – the material sphere and the spiritual sphere – the opposite is also true, as destruction to *zwifho* can bring misfortune to the community.

In this analogous network, the spheres of the earth down below and the world of the ancestors 'up there' are tied together as a unified system through the principle of *mupo*. There are many translations given for *mupo*, but it is most frequently translated into 'nature'. It is described as everything which is not man-made, but everything which is created by the creator Nwali. This includes not only trees, mountains, rivers and animals, but also the sky, the moon and the stars. In this sense, *mupo* goes beyond the natural world, referring to the entire cosmos. It also goes beyond physicality as it describes processes, like the changing seasons, the tides of the sea and the cycles of the moon.

The definition of 'not man-made' does not separate humanity from *mupo*, but includes it. Processes like childbirth, menstruation and a child learning to walk, all are regulated by *mupo*. In addition, agriculture, planting seeds and keeping livestock are also *mupo*, as they entail living in accordance with *mupo*; interactions with *mupo* constitute a relation with it. A definition is not taught in classrooms, as Mphatheleni describes: '*mupo* is a word which… when growing up, we found ourselves knowing it'. Having an understanding of *mupo* and living in accordance with it is an integral part of the Indigenous VhaVenda way of life. Indigenous community members generally have extensive knowledge of their natural surroundings that, for example, aid them in agricultural practices.

Mupo is a principle of cosmic unity, an underlying totality that guides the cosmos. The ancestral spirits, as they grew up with the principle of *mupo* themselves, have become intertwined with it. Many of the questions and requests that community members ask the ancestors are related to the principles of *mupo*, of which rain is the most important. As such, the relation between *zwifho* and *mupo* becomes apparent: the state of *mupo* will reflect the relation between the custodian clan and their *zwifho*. If a clan angers or dissatisfies *zwifho* and the ancestors, *mupo* will suffer because of it. The state of the ancestral spirits is reflected in the state of *mupo*. Beings of the natural world are part of the network of relations that constitute the analogous VhaVenda ontology. These natural beings become spirits, because the wellbeing of *mupo*, the spirits of the ancestors, the community and all indigenous trees and wild animals are related, and this cements the individual elements into one unified and integrated continuum. *Mupo* and the ancestral belief systems are interwoven. Mphatheleni explains what *mupo* means to her:

> In my personal interpretation, *mupo* is beyond what we describe as God. *Mupo* is beyond what we describe in our human thinking, who is the creator. Because *mupo* is the creator. Even God is created by *mupo*. You can't see, you can't touch *mupo*, you can never see *mupo*. Here, we are in *mupo*, but *mupo* is making my voice, my mind, it's making my words. It gives me my spirit. That is *mupo*. [4]

At its core, *mupo* is a deeply spiritual principle. To Mphatheleni, it is the highest spiritual principle. *Mupo*, as a spiritual principle, finds its material expression in the natural world. Therefore, engaging with the materiality of the natural world establishes a spiritual connection. Consequently, the constitution of the Vha-Venda Indigenous ontology is intricately intertwined with interactions involving *mupo*.

Shifting grounds in Indigenous social movements

In the practices of Dzomo la Mupo lies a shift in social movement strategies that depart from the rural NGO practices that emerged after apartheid. As apartheid ended in 1994 and the South African Government of National Unity was installed, restorative land restitution programmes and the reversal of land removals were among the first transformative legislative bills passed. The Restitution of Land Rights Act (1994) marked the beginning of this envisioned transformation (Walker et al. 2010: 1). Land restitution policies made it possible for rural communities and families to claim compensation for loss of historical land rights as a result of racist land laws such as the 1936 Native Trust and Land Act. Such laws shaped the persistent system of communal land tenure in the former 'homelands', which linked land ownership to tribal identity and vested landed authority in the hands of so-called traditional leaders such as chiefs and local headmen (Weinberg 2015).

In the post-apartheid political dispensation, numerous local NGOs rallied around the land restitution programme, drawing on donor funding and state subsidies to register and support dispossessed communities reclaiming land rights. This spurred a specific type of civil society activism that directed itself at the state and formulated claims centring notions of rights to land and collective land governance.[5] James writes how these NGOs adopted a role of patronage and mediation, filling the 'gap' between people and the state, providing help to Indigenous communities with land claims, facilitating community processes and ensuring their registrations (James 2007: 217). Their orientations tended to either build on popular discourses of human rights or more political positions seeking to protect land-hungry constituents and eviction-prone farm workers (James 2007; see also Wegerif 2010).

This instrumental role of the land rights restitution programme in shaping rural land reclamation and reparation processes waned in recent years as the initial tasks of claims registration were finalised and because of other issues such as the frustrating pace of settling land claims. The inability of state and civil society to deal with overlapping community claims in the Venda region exacerbated matters, provoking intra-community tensions over beneficiation and sparking rivalry between competing claimant groups and traditional authorities (Van Leynseele 2013; Fraser 2007). As a result, Dzomo la Mupo has shifted away from reclamation practices in terms of the land restitution programme. Instead, they have shifted their articulation towards a strategy that invokes Indigenous ontology and the cosmology of *mupo*. In the following statement, Mphatheleni explains how they are not focused on land claims, but rather target the core of their Indigenous ontology:

> Our focus area is not about chieftainship or land claiming, who's the chief, who is not the chief... And Dzomo la Mupo is not about land claims, but we support land claims. But with Dzomo la Mupo, we claim the forest, the sacred forest, *zwifho*, because *zwifho* is the heart of the land. If we get back *zwifho* and use it according to the expectation of *mupo* or the creator, those who are currently holding the land will be gone: 'Ow, we will no longer be the leaders, we will no longer disturb you'. We are claiming the whole system of our Indigenous ways but the heart of everything is *zwifho*. [6]

Here, Mphatheleni explains why Dzomo la Mupo's primary concern is the protection of sacred sites, instead of disputes over chieftaincy or traditional leadership. The concern for sacred sites is in line with the Indigenous ontological understanding of the relationship between the wellbeing of *zwifho* and the wellbeing of the community and *mupo*. The formulation directs itself to the restorative powers of *zwifho* at large, since the wellbeing of the custodian clan is innately and spiritually connected to it. Centrality of the custodianship-*zwifho* relationship along these ontological lines has also justified Dzomo la Mupo's politics of representation and territorial authority. Their aim has been to restore the autonomy of VhaNgona custodian clans alongside a revival of Indigenous eco-centric ways of living and ancestral spirituality. The shifting articulation is further emphasised by the way the centrality of *zwifho* and related rights to nature also resonate with a distinctive bio-conservation framework, as will be elaborated below.

VhaVenda ontology as social movement practices

The shift towards an ontology-based social movement is operationalised through a variety of practices, including the protection of sacred sites. But what does an ontology-based social movement look like and how is ontology operationalised? In this section, we dive into eco-mapping, a community activity facilitated by Dzomo la Mupo. We will use eco-mapping to illustrate how the principle of *mupo* is centred, integrated and operationalised as a social movement practice. Eco-mapping has managed to engage multiple communities with the activist goals of Dzomo la Mupo and has therefore been a key tool in movement building. Eco-mapping, short for ecological mapping, is a communal mapping exercise which can take up to five days and usually includes groups of more than fifty community members, ranging from elders to children. The process of creating an eco-map involves visually representing a landscape and its contents through pictures and drawings. The eco-map illustrates the territory of a clan according to the cultural understanding of a local community. This territorial eco-cultural map utilises drawings and sketches to depict the evolution of land use, providing a comprehensive characterisation of the landscape. The end result is a colourful collage of pictographs and images that portrays the natural landscape, highlighting its distinctive features. A variation of the eco-map is the eco-calendar, in which traditional understanding of the seasons are displayed.

While eco-mapping has come to resonate with many local communities, it is not a traditional VhaVenda technique. Mphatheleni first learned of this technique during a visit to an Indigenous community in the Colombian Amazon, a trip that was facilitated by the Gaia Foundation. As Indigenous knowledge was lost during periods of colonisation, this Indigenous Amazon community used eco-mapping as a technique to revive and conserve Indigenous knowledge. They stressed that eco-mapping is a process, as the discussions and conversations that arise during the creation of the map are as important as the end result. Eco-mapping as a technique has proven to capture Indigenous knowledge and stories that are part of the natural surroundings and territories that communities inhabit.

The Amazonian Indigenous community taught Mphatheleni how to apply this technique in communities in Venda. Calling it a souvenir from the Amazon, Mphatheleni has applied it ever since in the local context with Indigenous VhaVenda communities. Now, Dzomo la Mupo organises eco-mapping workshops with communities, led by Mphatheleni. For such a workshop, as many community members as possible are gathered, ranging from the chief and *makhadzi,* to teens and children. Mphatheleni explains how, during these sessions, elders remember details about their childhood they thought they had forgotten.

In eco-mapping, the participants seek a collective understanding, co-creating and stabilising meaning in an ontological field. An eco-map thus goes beyond a spatial or geographical representation of a territory, as it encapsulates Indigenous understanding of cosmology and ontology/epistemology, presents Indigenous knowledge and stories, all the while conveying an ontological reality. The eco-map thus fits into the realms of both ontology and epistemology. A cosmological understanding is also illustrated in the eco-calendar, which attempts to present the temporal understanding of the cosmos, the workings of *mupo* and the place of humans within this system.

Makhadzi Tshiwela has spread the eco-map of her territory Mulambwane out on the floor: the couch had to be moved backwards for it to fit into the living room. The map, which she keeps in a black garbage bag, looks somewhat battered from all the unfolding and folding up again. Barefooted, she walks across the map as if she is back on her birth ground, from which she and her clan were removed several decades ago. Now, she lives in Tshikuwi, a hot and dry village near Mulambwane, in a house built with metallic roofing. 'I don't like this roof', she says, 'we need a grass roof. But there is no grass in this area to make that

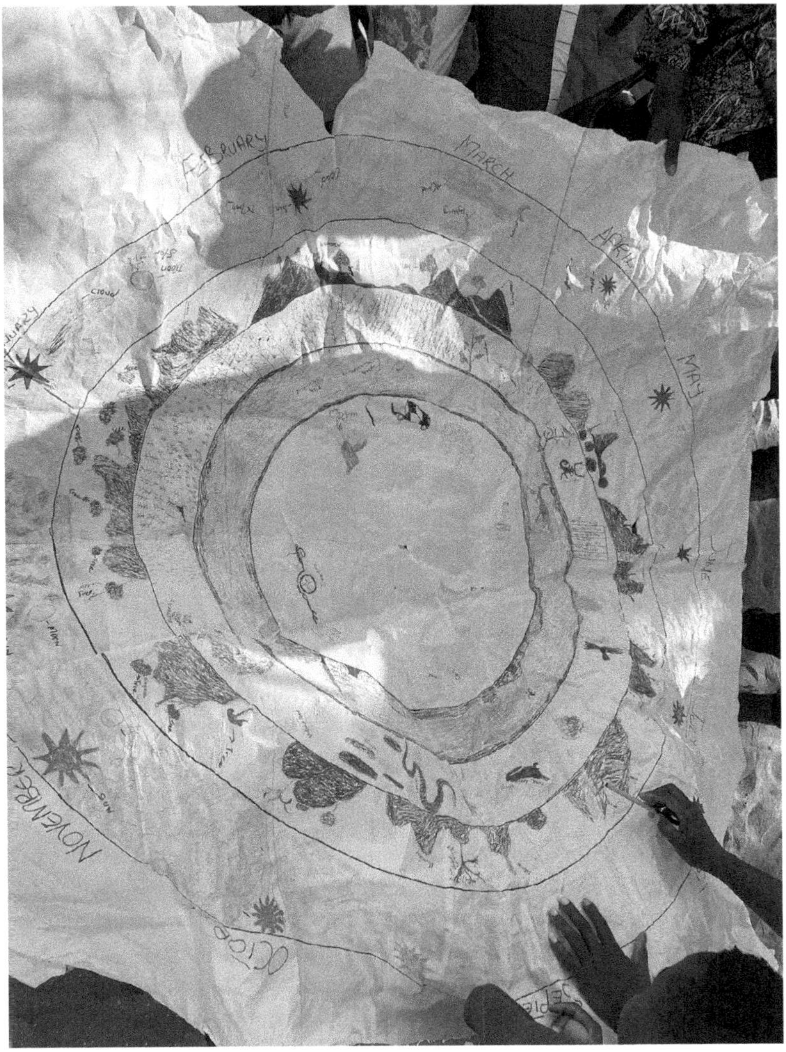

Figure 10.1 Eco-calendar (Photo by first author)

roof. Our rituals, they need grass roofs'. While walking across the map, she tells me where the grass which is suited to make roofs grows in Mulambwane.

A day earlier, we drove to Mulambwane together, but three metal fences prevented us from entering. The current owner of Mulambwane has completely fenced off the territory and Indigenous community members are not able to enter on their own accord. But through this map, Tshiwela is able to show me Mulambwane and tell me stories about her childhood on this territory; where she used to play, where the cattle grazed, which vegetables were cultivated and where the leopards lived. The youth, including her children, continue to learn about Mulambwane through this map in the same way she was teaching me about the land and its features. As a result of their removal from Mulambwane, the elders are unable to teach the youth about these natural spaces, and consequently, Indigenous knowledge gets lost. The eco-maps now function as a substitute on the basis of which youth can be educated. As intergenerational transference of knowledge is hindered, eco-mapping does work in the preservation and transfer of Indigenous knowledge. However, education through eco-mapping is removed from its original socio-cultural context and is thus unable to transfer all practices and knowledge.

Dzomo la Mupo instrumentalises eco-mapping as a tool for social movement activism. They are not the first to do so, as the Latin American Indigenous communities referred to above also used it for activist purposes. In the case of these Latin American communities, eco-maps were used to challenge Western education imposed on their communities, in spite of their Indigenous education which took place in the forest. As for Dzomo la Mupo, it has become a tool for education in and of itself, but also as an activist strategy to create a collective awareness and understanding of the importance of Indigenous knowledge and cosmology. Eco-mapping is used to co-create and mobilise ontology/epistemology in shared efforts for the defence of space, thus creating a political support base of a collective ontological understanding. Besides being a method for movement building, it also has a political application; namely it has enabled them to formulate eco-centrist alternatives that foreground their Indigenous ontology to extractive and land-grabbing industries. As such, it performs as an anti-development counter-narrative.

Eco-mapping is a vital practice for Dzomo la Mupo with regard to movement building, community building, and the transference of intergenerational knowledge and assisting communities outside of Venda in facilitating eco-mapping workshops. Mphatheleni and elders from Dzomo la Mupo have facilitated eco-mapping events in the Eastern Cape province in South Africa and in Kenya, continuing the dissemination of the technique on a global scale.

In addition to eco-mapping, Dzomo la Mupo has an array of programmes that contribute to the organisation's objectives of preservation, all the while invoking the VhaVenda eco-centrist ontology. For instance, Dzomo la Mupo has been actively involved in fencing off vulnerable wetland areas, like the Mutzinga river. They organise tours for community members to educate them on bioconservation and the importance of such wetland areas and rivers within the area. Activities like these target their core programmes: protection of ecosystems and intergenerational learning. This same principle goes for almost all their activities. For example, Dzomo la Mupo has set up a tree nursery programme for female elders. These trees are sold on commercial markets, attributing to the financial sustainability of Indigenous elders. But these trees are also planted in places where indigenous forests have been destroyed or damaged. As such, the tree nursery project targets the revitalisation of indigenous forests, seed conservation and intergenerational learning.

In the social movement practices of Dzomo la Mupo, *mupo*-spirituality is invoked through engagement with materiality of nature, which forms a central component in the majority of their practices. *Mupo* is a spiritual principle that finds its material expression in nature. Thus, planting trees, harvesting and conserving indigenous seeds and protecting a river source invoke a spiritual connection to the natural world.

Articulation and Hybridisation of Ontology

To the interest of many young people, including unemployed VhaNgona youth, development projects have been promised, to bring economic development and job opportunities to the impoverished region of Venda. However, Dzomo la Mupo worries about the environmental damage that these projects cause, making the defence of land and protection of natural spaces their central objectives. Since they have moved beyond land claims as a way of achieving these objectives, alternative routes must be found. Now, Dzomo la Mupo looks to grant indigenous forests and *zwifho* a protected status through, for example, nature conservation programmes or heritage agencies. A recent example of this is the work that Dzomo la Mupo does in defence of the Mulambwane communal land over the possible arrival of the Musina-Makhado Special Economic Zone (MMSEZ). In the appeal for a protected status, Dzomo la Mupo translates the VhaVenda Indigenous eco-centric worldview into a Western episteme and presents it as an anti-developmental counter-narrative. In the process, a hybridisation of two ontologies takes place.

The MMSEZ consists of agro-processing clusters, a metallurgical/mineral beneficiation complex and petrochemical industries. This public-private partnership programme aims to accelerate economic growth, facilitate trade, create jobs and ensure infrastructure development (MMSEZ, n.d.). It is set to be built on Mulambwane, the former communal land of Indigenous communities. On the basis of an environmental impact assessment (EIA), the MMSEZ is estimated to pose a high risk of causing environmental damage, biodiversity loss and pressure on local water supplies (Karim 2023). In defence of the Mulambwane communal land, the announcement of the MMSEZ-project was met with local resistance and the emergence of small organisations like the Mulambwane Women's Organisation.

In an allied resistance against the MMSEZ-project, Dzomo la Mupo works together with NGOs and INGOs like Earth Life Africa, Natural Justice and the Centre for Environmental Rights (CER). During joint workshops and meetings, Dzomo la Mupo plays a facilitative role in which they interlink the NGOs with Indigenous communities. Natural Justice and CER are both groups of lawyers that work on the intersection of human rights, environmental justice, conservation and activism. As the Indigenous common laws and concepts have little to no validity in relation to national and international legislature (Bavikatte et al. 2015: 5), Natural Justice assists Indigenous communities in the formulation of their cultural Indigenous identity and ontological conceptions of nature into a legislative framework. During these workshops, there is a constant interplay, or process of translation, between the VhaVenda Indigenous concepts and legislative frameworks: the local communities, under the guidance of Mphatheleni, are defining Indigenous concepts and the relation between their cultural identity with the natural environment, while Natural Justice helps to formulate this in legal language.

A similar process has been described by Escobar (1998). After demonstrating how concepts like biodiversity are constituted through the Western discourse of bioconservation, he shows how Indigenous social movements integrate this globalist discourse into their formulations of cultural autonomy and nature conservation. Through this integration, concepts like biodiversity become part of Indigenous social movement narratives of defence of culture and identity rooted in place, articulating an alternative political ecology framework (Escobar 1998:

Figure 10.2 Presentation of eco-map (Photo by first author)

60–61). In other words, social movements strategically use concepts like biodiversity and Western conservation discourses as a space to formulate a cultural identity and cultural narrative rooted in eco-centrism. Burow et al. (2018) describe a similar case and include 'ontology' in their analysis. They describe how Indigenous communities of the Confederated Salish and Kootenai Tribes in the United States strategically appropriate the modernist ontology of settler colonists during a land rights reclamation process (Burow et al. 2018: 67). The authors argue that Indigenous communities navigate multiple ontological and epistemic registers, actively reworking and hybridising ontological and epistemic boundaries in the process. Dzomo la Mupo engage in a similar hybridisation: by adopting Western discourse on bioconservation and legislative language, Dzomo la Mupo hybridises their Indigenous ontological and epistemic concepts with modernist categories as a strategy to posit *mupo* as an alternative to the extractivism of development projects.

As a result of this process of articulation, Dzomo la Mupo presents a rather essentialist account of their Indigenous worldview and concepts. During the fieldwork, we frequently encountered essentialist renderings and articulations of the VhaVenda Indigenous ontology. At face value, this can be understood as a simplification of their reality. However, it should rather be understood as a form of strategic essentialism. Strategic essentialism is a political tactic employed by a minority group acting on the basis of a shared identity in the public arena in the interests of unity, during a struggle for equal rights (Eide 2016: 2). For example, during this same workshop, meanings of Indigenous concepts like *mupo* and *zwifho* were collectively defined, finding a common understanding among all participating communities and correcting outlying interpretations to fit the broader narrative. Such situated instances of essentialism transpire during the articulation of an alternative to development practices as a strategy to distinguish the Indigenous cultural identity, traditional practices and ontology from modernist and extractivist notions on (economic) development. Essentialism thus becomes a strategy of defence to the forces that threaten their cultural identity.

Through a process of ontological and epistemic hybridisation, Dzomo la Mupo and Indigenous community members are able to formulate their Indigenous concepts in language that can engage with the dominant bioconservation discourse. By including cultural identity – rooted in traditional practices and local knowledges, right to territory and use of space, political autonomy and developmental autonomy in their narrative, Escobar (1998: 65) argues that social movements articulate an alternative political ecology framework. In other words, social movements strategically engage with dominant conservation discourses as a space to formulate a cultural identity and cultural narrative rooted in ecocentrism. The process of translating the VhaVenda Indigenous ontology into the Western episteme enables the articulation of the ecocentrist principle of *mupo* as an alternative to the extractivism of developmental practices.

Our conceptualisation of ontological translation highlights the strategic approach of small social movements and knowledge brokers as they navigate the power dynamics of the civil society activist landscape. Here, translation emphasises the instability and fluidity of meaning in its interactions with the larger 'development configuration' (Mosse and Lewis 2006: 13–14). We also draw from decolonial theory, where epistemic translation has been described as a practice of plurality. In the context of social movements specifically, translation creates a space for the intelligibility of cultural diversity and facilitates intercultural dialogues. For Boaventura de Sousa Santos, translation is a condition for the articulation of struggle, enabling social movements to challenge modernity's hegemony (Vásquez 2011; Santos et al. 2007).

Ontological hybridisation does not remain limited to these specific and situated instances. The fluidity of Indigenous and modernist ontological schemas highlight strategic ontological performance. For instance, Dzomo la Mupo encourages *makhadzis* to keep indigenous tree nurseries aimed at a commercial market for monetary compensation, embracing modernity strategically as a means to ensure financial stability. But on the other hand, ontological fluidity also shows ambivalent engagement with traditional spirituality, as many *Vhanonga* community members welcome development projects, viewing economic development as a way out of poverty and unemployment. Returning to traditional agriculture as the means to sustain livelihood with *mupo* as a guiding spiritual principle seems improbable in an impoverished South African region that wants its share of economic prosperity. The practices of Dzomo la Mupo that showcase ontological fluidity highlight the strategic negotiation in an ontological borderzone of competing developmental imaginaries.

Conclusion

In this book chapter, we illustrated the operationalisation of ontology and its subsequent articulation in the context of conservation activism from the perspective of the grassroots organisation Dzomo la Mupo. Coming to an understanding of the VhaVenda Indigenous cosmology was a central objective of the research and we found how an eco-centrist ontology is constituted and maintained through ancestral rituals in sacred sites. The enclosement of community territories by state companies and displacement of Indigenous communities under racist land laws during the apartheid era has led to the deterioration of Indigenous knowledge systems, options for traditional livelihoods and Indigenous cosmologies. The damage to sacred forest areas and the decrease of ritualistic practices saw a decline in community wellbeing, due to the innate, spiritual connection between custodian clans and their *zwifho*. Combatting the overall erosion of the Indigenous way of life, defence of communal land and protection of sacred sites has thus been a priority for Dzomo la Mupo.

In the strategies for this defence, we have observed a shifting articulation in social movement strategies. The previous focus on land restitution programmes by the state have been replaced by activist practices that centre on Indigenous cosmology and spirituality. With nature- and community-based events like ecomapping, Dzomo la Mupo is stabilising and strategically stabilising meaning in an ontological field while creating a political support base. Through the formation of a coalition with civil society organisations like Earth Life Africa, Natural Justice and the Centre for Environmental Rights, rural and Indigenous communities are enabled to engage with global discourses concerning bio-conservation. Instead of focusing on state-driven reform initiatives, Dzomo la Mupo increasingly directs their efforts towards NGOs that assist in amplifying Indigenous voices and translating Indigenous ontologies/epistemologies into a Western episteme, thus allowing Indigenous social movements like Dzomo la Mupo to articulate their cultural heritage, culture and cosmology as an alternative to the extractivist development projects; ultimately seeking legitimacy for these ontologies in the broader discourse around bio-conservation and climate activism.

In the process of epistemic translation and claim-making, fluidity of ontological dispositions is demonstrated, as translations are codified with more mainstream discourses like regional bio-conservation. The appeal to Western conservation discourse through integration of concepts such as climate change and biodiversity produces ontological hybrids and highlights the fluidity and performative nature of ontology.

Notes

1 Venda is not an official province or region of South Africa, but the word is used to refer to the area in the northern Limpopo province where the VhaVenda people live. We use the word Venda to refer to the geographic region, VhaVenda to refer to the people and Tshivenda to refer to the language.
2 The former 'homelands' or Bantustans refer to the areas designated by the South African racist, White minority regime for separate development, with governing authority, land ownership and group membership defined in ethnic, tribal terms.
3 Makhadzi means woman, aunt or female priest and is attributed key cultural and religious roles in VhaVenda cultural and family settings, including communication with the spirit world (Sinthumule 2022a: 3–6). For Dzomo la Mupo, makhadzi represents a social institution that is central to preservation of Indigenous knowledge and sacred sites.
4 Interview Mphatheleni Makaulule, Vuwani, October 13th, 2022.
5 A prominent land-based NGO in the Limpopo Province, Nkuzi Development Association, duly emerged in 1997 as a 'response to the need to assist communities within the Makhado area to lodge land claims after the introduction of the Restitution of Land Rights Act No. 22 of 1994' (https://nkuzi.org.za/about.html, accessed 5th of March, 2024).
6 Interview Mphatheleni Makaulule, Vuwani, November 30th, 2022.

References

Bavikatte, K.S., Robinson, D. and Olivia, M.J. (2015). 'Biocultural community protocols: dialogues on the space within', *IK: Other ways of knowing*, pp. 1–31.

Blaser, M. (2010). *Storytelling and globalisation: from the Chaco and beyond*. Durham, NC: Duke University Press.

Blaser, M. (2014). 'Ontology and indigeneity: on the political ontology of heterogeneous assemblages', *Cultural Geographies*, 21 (1), pp. 49–58.

Burow, P.B., Brock, S. and Dove, M.R. (2018). 'Unsettling the land. Indigeneity, ontology, and hybridity in settler colonialism', *Environment and Society: Advances in Research*, 9 (1), pp. 57–74.

De la Cadena, M. and Blaser, M. (eds.). (2018). *A World of Many Worlds*. Duke University Press.
Descola, P. (2013 [2005]). *Beyond Nature and Culture*. Chicago: University of Chicago Press.
Eide, E. (2016). 'Strategic essentialism', *The Wiley Blackwell encyclopaedia of gender and sexuality studies*, pp. 2278–2280.
Escobar, A. (1998). 'Whose knowledge, whose nature? Biodiversity, conservation, and the political ecology of social movements', *Journal of Political Ecology*, 5 (1), pp. 53–82.
Escobar, A. (2007a). 'The "ontological turn" in social theory: a commentary on "Human geography without scale", by Sallie Marston, John Paul Jones II and Keith Woodward', *Transactions of the Institute of British Geographers*, 32 (1), pp. 106–111.
Escobar, A. (2007b). 'Worlds and knowledges otherwise: The Latin American modernity/ coloniality research program', *Cultural Studies*, 21(2–3), pp. 179–210.
Fraser, A. (2007). 'Land reform in South Africa and the colonial present', *Social and Cultural Geography*, 8 (6), pp. 835–851.
Hebinck, P. and Cousins, B. (eds). (2013). *In the Shadow of Policy: everyday practices in South Africa's land and agrarian reform*. Wits University Press.
Ingold, T. (2000). *The perception of the environment: essays on livelihood, dwelling and skill*. London: Routledge.
James, D. (2007). *Gaining ground? 'Rights' and 'property' in South African land reform*. New York: Routledge-Cavendish.
Karim, A. (2023). 'MMSEZ: the battle to stop Limpopo's climate bomb', *Amabhungane*, 02 February. Available at: https://amabhungane.org/stories/220203-mmsez-the-battle-to-stop-limpopos-climate-bomb/ [23/04/2023]
Kwa, C. (2018). *What is truth? A new philosophy of the sciences and the humanities*. Amsterdam: Boom.
Latour, B. (1993). *We have never been modern*. Cambridge, MA: Harvard University Press.
Law, J. and Lien, M.E. (2012). 'Slippery: Field notes in empirical ontology', *Social studies of science*, 43 (3), pp. 363–378.
Lewis, S. J. and Russell, A.J. (2011). 'Being embedded: a way forward for ethnographic research', *Ethnography*, 12 (3), pp. 398–416.
McGinity, R. and Salokangas, M. (2014). 'Introduction: 'embedded research' as an approach into academia for emerging researchers', *Management in education*, 28 (1), pp. 3–5.
Musina-Makhado Special Economic Zone [MMSEZ] (n.d.) [online]. Available at: https://mmsez.co.za/.
Mol, A. (1999). 'Ontological Politics: A word and some questions'. In *Actor-network theory and after*, edited by Law, J. and Hassard, J.Boston, Mass: Blackwell, pp. 74–89.
Mosher, R., Long, J., Le, E. and Harding, L. (2017). 'Agency and agenda's: revisiting the roles of the researcher and the researched in ethnographic fieldwork', *Anthropologica* 59 (1), pp. 145–156.
Mosse, D. and Lewis, D. (2006). 'Theoretical approaches to brokerage and translation in development.' *Development brokers and translators: the ethnography of aid and agencies*, pp. 1–26.
Nemaheni, T. (2021). 'The Vhambedzi origin and the expansion of Zimbabwe stone building tradition south of the Vhembe river', *New Contree*, 2021(86), pp. 116–133.
Pickering, A. (2017). 'The ontological turn: taking different worlds seriously,' *Social Analysis*, 61 (2), pp. 134–150.

Santos, B.S., Nunes, J., Meneses, M. (2007). *Opening up the Canon of Knowledge and Recognition of Knowledge*. In: Santos, B.S., *Another Knowledge is Possible, Beyond Northern Epistemologies*. London: Verso.

Scott, J.C. (1998). *Seeing like a state: how certain schemes to improve the human condition have failed*. New Haven, CT: Yale University Press.

Scott, J. and Marshall, G. (2005). *A dictionary of sociology*. Oxford: Oxford University Press.

Sebola, M.P. (2017). 'The Mapungubwe story and land claims: the battle for the soul of the dead, greed and deception', *Anthropos*, bd. 112, ch. 2, pp. 596–601.

Sinthumule, N.I. (2022a). 'Gender and sacred natural sites: The role of women in sacred sites protection and management in Vhembe region, Limpopo Province of South Africa', *Global Ecology and Conservation*, 35, e02099, pp. 1–10.

Sinthumule, N.I. (2022b). 'Conservation effects of governance and management of sacred natural sites: lessons from Vhutanda in the Vhembe Region, Limpopo Province of South Africa', *International journal of environmental research and public health*, 19 (3), p. 1067.

Ter Haar, G. (2009). *How God became African: African spirituality and western secular thought*. Philadelphia: University of Pennsylvania Press.

Van Leynseele, Y.B. (2013). *Landscapes of Deracialisation*. Power, Brokerage and Place-making on a South African Frontier. PhD Dissertation. Wageningen University.

Vásquez, R. (2011). 'Translation as Erasure: Thoughts on Modernity's Epistemic Violence.' *Journal of Historical Sociology*, 24(1).

Walker, C., Bohlin, A., Hall, R. and Kepe, T. (Eds.). (2010). *Land, memory, reconstruction and justice: perspectives on land claims in South Africa*. Ohio: University press.

Weinberg, T. (2015). 'The contested status of 'communal land tenure' in South Africa. Rural Status Report 3', *Institute for Poverty, Land and Agrarian Studies*. University of Western Cape. Available at: https://repository.uwc.ac.za/handle/10566/4599.

Wegerif, M. (2010). 'The Right to Land Restitution as Mobilisation'. In *Land, memory, reconstruction and justice: perspectives on land claims in South Africa*, edited by Walker, C., Bohlin, A., Hall, R. and Kepe, T.Ohio: University press, pp. 100–115.

11 Ambivalent perspectives on degrowth and alternatives to development

Exploring notions of *kalamboan* and *ginhawa* in Siquijor province, Philippines

Joseph Edward Alegado

Introduction

The global socio-ecological crisis has catalysed various pathways to rethink neoliberal approaches to development and its consequences. Scholars and activists have proposed different perspectives on how to rethink development and its compatibility with economic growth. Since the end of World War II, development has been shaped by the Bretton Woods institutions and economic development paradigms set during the immediate post-World War II era (Wallerstein 1984). This paradigm paved the way for the successful creation of international financial institutions like the World Bank and International Monetary Fund (IMF) and the World Trade Organisation (WTO). These institutions' policies have further reinforced the economic dogmas of neoliberalism, in particular privatisation, trade liberalisation, and austerity programmes (Bello 2008).

The publication *Limits to Growth* in 1972 by Meadows et al. was a key moment in which growth imperatives were questioned and discussion intensified in relation to alternatives to neoclassical economics (Hickel 2021). Over time, these alternative perspectives have proliferated, including steady state economy (Herman Daly 1980), doughnut economics (Kate Raworth 2017) and wellbeing economy, among others.

In the Global North, the word 'degrowth' has entered the vocabulary of activists and academics since the early 2000s. The concept came from the French word *décroissance* or *la descrescita* in Italian, a term used to describe a river returning to its normal flow after a major flood (Research and Degrowth 2024). Its proponents describe degrowth as follows: 'degrowth challenges the hegemony of growth and calls for a democratically led redistributive downscaling of production and consumption in industrialised countries as a means to achieve environmental sustainability, social justice and well-being' (Demaria et al. 2013: 209). Further, key to the concept of degrowth is that reducing consumption does not mean a decrease in wellbeing. Rather, the aim is to maximise wellbeing through non-consumptive activities like having more time for family, community, art, nature and culture, and to reduce the number of working days to enhance the wellbeing of workers (Alegado and Gerber 2020).

DOI: 10.4324/9781003477921-14

Degrowth and post-growth thinking represent alternative approaches to organising economic life that have gained ground in the contemporary context, where capitalism seems to lurch from one crisis to another. They are part of a global tapestry of alternatives to growth-centric development that build on approaches such as deglobalisation, ecofeminism and emancipatory Marxism, among others (Kothari et al. 2019). These perspectives collectively emphasise various dimensions of people's relationships with one another and with the planet.

The current literature on degrowth demonstrates, however, that the concept has continued to evolve and diversify. Scholars such as Parrique (2019), Hickel (2017) and Schmelzer et al. (2022) unpack degrowth and its undercurrents. Other scholars have shown the intersection of degrowth with other social movements and their key issues, such as housing (Nelson and Schneider 2019) and transition initiatives (Liegey and Nelson 2020). Studies of the varied and explicit application of degrowth principles in daily lives by communities who want to pursue their self-determination have especially centred on the Global North. Yet scholars and practitioners from or of the Global South are also exploring and interpreting these ideas from their specific contexts (see, for example, Gerber and Raina 2018; Adityanandana and Gerber 2019; Guerrero 2019; Dengler and Seebacher 2019), making degrowth a fluid and still-evolving concept.

This chapter explores the ambivalent views held by the locals on the notions of alternatives to development vis-à-vis mainstream development thinking in a Global South setting, namely the Philippines. Specifically, this chapter is based on qualitative research fieldwork in the Siquijor island province of the Philippines. As posited by Bulloch (2017: 13), ***kalamboan*** (development) is the most commonly used term of the Siquijor locals in their native Bisaya language to describe meanings of 'mobility', 'progress', and 'development'. According to Bulloch (2017: 13), in Siquijor, people use the term ***kalamboan*** to refer both to 'communal advancement or to a personal improvement in living standards'. According to Mercado and Muyco (as cited by Tafoya 2023: 22), ***ginhawa*** is 'the life force that animates one's wellbeing, comfortable life, healthy living, good breathing, relief, food, etc.'. I argue here that the long-held value of ***ginhawa*** or wellbeing could be the key to further understanding notions of ***kalamboan***.

I will begin by providing some background on the political economy of the Philippines and how it is cultivating the current mainstream growth-oriented development paradigm, followed by an overview of the literature on post-development and degrowth thinking. This will be succeeded by a detailed discussion of the way in which ***kalamboan*** (development) and ***ginhawa*** (wellbeing) are understood among Siquijodnons.

Philippines at the height of neoliberal development

The Philippines is an archipelago of 7641 islands with a land area of 300 000 square kilometres. It is divided into three major geographical regions (Luzon, the Visayas and Mindanao), 17 regions, 33 highly urbanised cities, 113 component cities or those that are still part of provinces and 1,488 municipalities (Philippines

Statistics Authority [PSA] 2023: 1). The 2020 Census of Population and Housing puts the population of the Philippines at 109,033,245 (PSA 2023: 1). The Asian Development Bank (2021) states that 23.75% of the population were living below the national poverty line in 2021.

During the Spanish 300-year colonisation period in the Philippines, land and other natural resources became concentrated in the hands of powerful institutions and individuals, namely Spanish government officials and *friars* (Spanish priests) and local Filipino elites and collaborators. This had repercussions even when the Philippines gained its independence in 1946 as Filipinos lost their formal claims of ownership and rights over the land at that time (Constantino and Constantino 1975). Consequently, today the Philippines is plagued by pervasive inequality and political and economic powers are concentrated in the hands of a few (De Dios and Hutchcroft 2003).

The country's turbulent political history creates particular challenges for development and governance. The Epifanio Delos Santos Avenue (EDSA) People Power revolution in 1986, which overthrew the Marcos Sr. dictatorship (1965–1986), ushered in a period that rebuilt democratic institutions. However, old and new political dynasties and oligarchs remain entrenched in the country's political and socio-economic affairs, especially the control of key economic sectors. According to Bello et al. (2004), the post-1986 Philippines is marked by the institutionalisation of neoliberal policies. The presidency of former president Fidel Ramos (1992–1998), who was a military general during the Marcos regime, saw the aggressive implementation of neoliberal reforms such as trade liberalisation, deregulation of the oil industry and privatisation of state-owned assets such as power and water. As Bello (2008) notes, neoliberalism was indeed the policy of the times, rolled out through the World Bank (WB) group's loan conditionalities and policy prescriptions for loan packages that insisted on austerity measures (Tadem 2020) requiring governments to rely on conditional cash transfer programmes and other aid measures. This became a period of elite capture of natural resources through policies on mining and land reform that reveal a weak state, where well-intentioned laws are good on paper but lack proper implementation (Bello et al. 2004).

According to Espaldon and Baltazar (2004), the Philippines' population exhibited an enormous increase from 27 million in the 1960s to 88.57 million in 2007. The annual population growth rate is 1.5% in 2021. The International Fund for Agricultural Development (IFAD) noted in 2023 that more than half of the Philippines' population lives in rural areas, and 36% of these are poor and dependent on agriculture as their primary source of income. Due to a lack of opportunities in rural areas, people move to urban areas to look for jobs.

The World Bank Group (2024) notes that the Philippines is touted as one of the most dynamic economies in the East and the Pacific Region. Currently, the country is classified as a middle-income country with 'increasing urbanization, a growing middle class, and a large and young population' (World Bank Group 2024: 1), which drives consumption, a vibrant labour market and industries, and remittances from Filipino migrants abroad. As such, development in the

Philippines has been framed from a dominant economic paradigm incorporating other aspects of human development (United Nations Development Programme [UNDP] 2024). Further, development plans are created at various levels: national, meso/regional and local. For example, in 2017, the country's socio-economic planning agency, the National Economic Development Authority (NEDA), in consultation with other government agencies, launched the 'Ambisyon 2040', which sought to 'represent collective vision and aspirations of Filipinos' (NEDA 2017). At the local governance front, local government units are mandated to draft plans which seek to contribute to the overall local development of their areas.

Despite these challenges in governance and socio-economic inequality, the Philippines is also known to have a vibrant civil society (Quimpo 2008). This has been attributed to its liberal and representative democratic form of government, which provides space for non-government actors to flourish (Bello et al. 2004). More recently, due to governments which have authoritarian populist tendencies like the Duterte government (2016–2022), civil society actors have encountered challenges in policy advocacy spaces (Teehankee 2016). In 2017, the Asian NGO Coalition (ANGOC) estimated the number of development-oriented non-government organisations (NGOs) both international and local and grassroots-led people's organisations (POs) at between 3,000 and 5,000 (Asian Development Bank 2008), with over 58,000 registered sectoral organisations (Laquian 2005). At present, these figures could be greater, given the relatively open space for civil society to engage the Philippine government (Laquian 2005).

Degrowth and post-growth literature

In recent years, literature on degrowth and post-growth thinking has been increasing. This literature intersects with post-development and other paradigms advancing alternatives to development. However, the literature seems to be heavily focused on Global North-based experiments and initiatives. More recently, a few scholars have problematised the resonance of degrowth in the Global South, such as in India (Gerber and Raina 2018), Indonesia (Adityanandana and Gerber 2019) and Thailand (Chiengkul 2018). More empirically grounded studies are still needed in order to understand what degrowth looks like in the Global South.

Responding to the crises of capitalism, the concept of degrowth has emerged as a means to rethink our relationships with nature in our current economic system. Among the most comprehensive definitions of degrowth is in the Degrowth Declaration of Paris in 2008. The said declaration describes the degrowth project as a 'voluntary transition toward a just, participatory, and ecologically sustainable society' (Degrowth Declaration of Paris 2008). This transition can occur in developed countries through the downward adjustment of their production and consumption followed by the maintenance of some form of 'steady state' economy (Kerschner 2010). As defined by the Center for the Advancement of the Steady State Economy (2023), a steady state economy is defined as 'an economy of stable or mildly fluctuating size'. Further, to be sustainable, a steady state economy must not exceed ecological limits.

Drawing on the work of Kallis (2018) and Latouche (2009), Hickel (2021: 106) provides a more nuanced definition of degrowth, describing it as the 'planned reduction of energy and resource throughput designed to bring the economy back into balance with the living world in a way that reduces inequality and improves human wellbeing'. He explains that degrowth is not just about reducing the Gross Domestic Product, but about transforming our current economic system which is characterised by the 'process of elite accumulation, the commodification of commons, and the appropriation of human labour and natural resources' (Hickel 2021: 1107). All of these, as Hickel (2021) emphasises, are embedded in colonial relations. For example, the proliferation of sweatshops producing 'fast fashion' in the Global South has been the Global North's response to capitalist ideals of cheaper modes of production and labour. As Dorninger et al. (2021) have pointed out, resource consumption in the Global North has an ecological impact that registers largely in the Global South.

Numerous scholars have identified various principles and values which degrowth advocates seek to live by: sustainability, circularity, cooperation, useful production, sharing, local production, work-life balance, relational goods and conviviality (Flipo and Schneider 2008: 12). These principles and values adhere to the basic degrowth streams first identified by Flipo (2007) and later on renamed as degrowth sources by Demaria et al. (2013). Further, a common element across degrowth and its allied movements, like post-development thinking, is a rejection of the green economy because it further perpetuates business-as-usual approaches in solving socio-ecological crises. For example, in the movements working on genuine zero waste as the solution to the plastic pollution crisis, there is resistance to green techno-fixes such as waste-to-energy incinerators and other false solutions (in the view of degrowth activists) that rely on market-based approaches. There is also the inherent value of democratic decision-making processes in these movements. Schmelzer et al. (2022) have posited that in order to embrace degrowth, allied movements must orient themselves towards degrowth's ideals of democratic processes of transformation, ensuring equity and participation of grassroots voices.

As with any other political project, degrowth is still evolving – subject to continuous (re)interpretation in both theory and praxis. For degrowth to move beyond activist circles, broader cultural and political changes and shifting mindsets must be ensured (Heikkurinen and Bonnedahl 2019; Vandeventer et al. 2019). These include instituting cultural and behavioural changes and initiating local experiments that will help expand and deepen the degrowth movement. Ongoing concrete cases and local experiments on how to practice degrowth have been initiated in different countries. Most, however, are from the Global North, such as the integral cooperatives in the Catalan region in Spain (Dafermos 2017), solidarity economy networks initiatives like ethical banks in Italy and Spain, and solidarity purchase food groups (Schifani and Migliore 2011) and a vegetable box bike delivery service in Hungary (Liegey and Nelson 2020).

Despite apparent convergences of values and principles between the proposed degrowth principles discussed earlier and parallel struggles of movements in the Global South (related to land grabbing, access to basic utilities, privatisation of natural resources, etc.), scholars like Guerrero (2019) highlight the fact that movements in Asia have not taken up the language of degrowth. Some studies explore why degrowth lacks resonance with social movements in the Global South (Rodriguez-Labajos et al. 2019). For example, Chiengkul (2018) argues that degrowth in developed nations will need to be part of a global effort to tackle climate change and other socio-ecological crises and to preserve the conditions for future generations' basic needs satisfaction. In particular, the 'growth lock-in' of current societies and the ways in which a transition away from this model might therefore affect the wellbeing of citizens of developing countries seem to be a puzzle in the Global South. Hence, this probably results in hesitation on degrowth.

Addressing this issue, degrowth scholar-advocates like Hickel (2021) and Schmelzer et al. (2022) have written extensive clarifications on North-South relations with regard to degrowth. They argue that degrowth in the Global North will enable Global South economies to veer away from their expected role as exporters of cheap labour and raw materials and to focus instead on domestic reforms, namely building economies focused on sovereignty, self-sufficiency and human wellbeing. Addressing the uneven development and colonial relations between Global North and Global South countries will help enable the latter to gravitate towards degrowth's principles and ideals. Doing so will spare communities in the Global South from the 'pressures of atmospheric colonisation and material extractivism' (Hickel 2021: 1109).

While the language of degrowth has not been prevalent in the Global South, the related concept of post-growth has been taken up by scholars who have looked into parallel approaches. As defined by the Post-Growth Institute (2023:1), post-growth 'is a worldview that sees society operating better without the demand of constant economic growth. It proposes that widespread economic justice, social wellbeing and ecological regeneration are only possible when money inherently circulates through our economy'. Savini (2023) has emphasised that while post-growth is an approach, degrowth is the agenda. He further explains this from an urban development perspective in order to differentiate between the two: 'post-growth strategies combine targets of material and energy reduction with goals of social justice … [while] a degrowth agenda proposes to reduce excess consumption and production, and to redistribute wealth to meet social universal needs' (Savini 2023: 113–114).

As discussed by Guerrero (2019), the analysis and critiques of the limits of the growth-oriented model of development and capitalism were already expressed in Asia from the early 1990s through networks like the People's Plan for the 21st Century or PP21, which means aspects of the degrowth and post-growth agenda have already been taken up in the region. Gerber and Raina (2018) have explored the emergence of post-growth thinking in India and have argued that degrowth ideas have existed for more than a century in India but have been adapted to local contexts. Looking into an environmental conflict in Indonesia, Adityanandana and Gerber (2019) explore how a Balinese philosophy called 'Tri Hita Karana' resembles post-growth thinking. Similarly, Bolivia and Ecuador's *buen vivir* approach can be likened to the Philippines concept of *ginhawa* or the life force that animates one's wellbeing (Tafoya 2023). Such concepts can help us to understand how alternative approaches to development take on local cultural value and what would make it more appealing for locals to advocate for such concepts.

Post-development and degrowth in the Global South

The Global South has offered vibrant debates on the development question for decades and has already demonstrated a history of experimentation with diverse forms and models of development (Guerrero 2019). Scholars such as Escobar (2001) have been engaging with place-based movements articulating alternative paths to development by experimenting and producing counter-hegemonic praxis. Dengler and Seebacher (2019) note that there are many scholars who are taking up degrowth in non-European settings and argue that these scholars reveal the potential of degrowth and post-growth in these contexts.

Similarly, other Global South-based scholars like Kothari (see Kothari et al. 2019) argue that communities and local movements can be agents in co-creating post-development thinking. These place-based movements exemplify post-development ideals as an answer to the failures of mainstream development discourse which have failed to address socio-ecological crises (Kothari and Demaria, 2017). These scholars and activists have long been non-conformists who reject mainstream views on development. In fact, Ziai (2014) argues that these South-led alternative development approaches are tapping into local culture and, to some extent, are grounded on Indigenous People's concepts and practices like *buen vivir* in Ecuador, *ubuntu* in South Africa, and *ecoswaraj* in India.

These movements' similarities to degrowth exemplify their movement-building capabilities. As Liegey and Nelson (2020) have emphasised, the degrowth movement's building opportunities are dynamic, not static, and subject to various socio-political undercurrents and local and cultural contexts. Post-development movements that have called for systemic alternative approaches supported by climate and environmental justice movements in the Global South have also shown strong gravitation towards degrowth and post-growth thinking principles such as conviviality or living together harmoniously. Further, similar to degrowth movements in the Global North, these movements in the Global South also provide critiques of the idea of growth itself, argue in favour of socio-ecological transformation to address inequality and emphasise the urgency of putting an end to rising emissions and the depletion of non-renewable resources (Guerrero 2019).

In this section, I have unpacked the degrowth discourse and post-growth thinking's roots, values and principles, complementarity and divergences with other alternative thinking, which seeks to rethink growth-based economy in order to solve the crises of capitalism and its excesses. As Chiengkul (2018) and

Guerrero (2019) make clear, the key underlying gap in the literature relates to how degrowth and post-growth thinking apply in the context of the Global South, given the fixation on the thinking that mainstream economic growth (which has long evaded the Global South) will result in progress and development.

The section has provided various examples of ideas that are related to degrowth and which emanate from the Global South, showing that Southern scholars and civil society are actively shaping degrowth and post-growth thinking. The key underlying gap here is the need to further understand and theorise the relationships between these alternative Southern-based movements to see whether other forms of alternative development in the South can be considered as forms of degrowth and post-growth.

Methodology and conceptual framework

This chapter is part of a broader PhD project in which I try to examine the connections between degrowth, post-growth and alternatives to development from the lens of zero waste systems in two case study sites in the Philippines. In this chapter, I draw on a three-month period of fieldwork (November 2023 – January 2024) in Siquijor province. I employ qualitative methods such as key informant interviews and focus group discussions. The interviews and focus groups involved multiple stakeholders from the communities, local government officials, local grassroots groups and ordinary individuals. Participant observation methods enabled me to see connections that, at first glance, are not apparent. Coming from the environmental movement space before starting my PhD, I was able to build on connections with groups and individuals as well as local government officials who are involved in the two field sites. As such, I made it clear to them that the research is part of an independent PhD work and not part of the ongoing zero waste project supported by my previous organisational affiliations.

The methodology was enriched by a political ecology framework that offered a lens to critically interrogate the frame of development from locals in Siquijor province. Utilising political ecology helped me understand power relations, state-society interactions, forces of inequality and uneven development that are situated in broader socio-political processes and which gravely affect local communities. Examining alternative development pathways like degrowth calls for a political ecology lens because, as outlined in the literature review, these issues are mired in questions of inequality, the crisis of capital and political processes. According to Karlsson (2015: 350), political ecologists ask an overarching question: 'whose use of, claims to, and/or perceptions of the environmental prevail, and why?' Robbins (2019) further explains that the discipline is useful in understanding the relationships and the processes that go with these between environmental degradation and social marginalisation, the causes of environmental conflicts over changing patterns of access to and control of resources, and the fundamental connections between place, identity, and social movements.

Community-led initiatives occur in the broader context of neoliberal governance. These more powerful national and multinational actors tend to set the tone of community engagement and limit the opportunities for expanding community roles and participation. As elucidated by Bravo and Moreano (2015), in looking at the political ecology of alternative radical development in Ecuador, critiques of Northern-led development thinking are embedded in broader socio-political processes. As an outcome of these forces and processes, the Ecuadorian state has essentially subverted the original intention and meaning of *buen vivir*. The so-called 'greening of the state' or post-neoliberalism has ended up being co-opted by presenting and advancing a traditional programme of natural resource extraction as a form of sustainable development.

Location of the study

The island province of Siquijor is an hour away from Negros Oriental by boat. This is an area that attracts tourism for its beaches and other natural wonders. This island province in the Central Visayas region had a population of 103 295 in 2020 according to the Philippines Statistics Authority (2021). It is bounded by Cebu province in the north, the Negros provinces in the west, and Bohol province in the northeast (Province of Siquijor 2024). The main sources of livelihood are tourism and agriculture, particularly the coconut industry.

Siquijor, like other peripheral provinces in the Philippines, is mired with local political dynasties, each set to advance their own political interests (McCoy 1994). According to Siquijor-born scholar-activist Joel Rocamora (cited in Tamiki 2019: 419):

> Siquijor has a small 'upper class' of politicians, senior bureaucrats, a few professionals and Chinese traders who would be 'middle class' in the larger islands. The majority of the people barely survive on rocky, hilly land and depleted fishing grounds. In between are government clerks and teachers and petty traders mouldering in frustration and boredom. It would be difficult to organise class struggle on the island because income differences are not large. But there is a large pool of educated young people waiting to be tapped for socio-economic projects.

Siquijor is an economically small-scale province (Tamiki 2019). Like other island provinces in the Philippines, the province's economy has remained underdeveloped, characterised by poverty and a lack of economic opportunities (Tamiki 2019). Siquijor's development is state-led through national programmes funded by multilateral aid agencies, channelled through the national government in which delivery is facilitated by local politicians.

As relayed to me by one of my informants, Siquijor is known as the Isla del Fuego (Island of Fire). This name originates from the account of when Spanish colonisers first set foot on the island and described it as such. Historically, Siquijor is linked to sorcery and witchcraft (Dumont 1992). According to one of the Siquijodnons (as Siquijor locals are called) I spoke to, the island province gained that reputation because the residents used to consult faith healers when they were sick. During those times, the distance to nearby provinces (Cebu, Bohol, and Negros Oriental) proved to be a barrier for Siquijodnons to access proper healthcare services.

The remote location of the island seems to have hampered its growth and progress. In addition, it was transferred from one provincial government unit to another and only became a fully-fledged province in the 1970s. This 'underdevelopment' in Siquijor has fostered the dream of achieving progress among the locals As Bulloch (2017: 13) has stated, development is a 'salient concept' in Siquijor owing to the apparent lack of progress in the island province. People's aspirations for development are expressed in myriad ways, as will be explored below.

Notions of *kalamboan* (development) and *ginhawa* (wellbeing) among Siquijodnons

In this subsection, I will explore the underpinnings of *kalamboan* and *ginhawa* in Siquijor. As Bulloch (2017) has explained, *kalamboan* in Siquijor can be further nuanced by noting that the term refers both to individual upward mobility and to the collective, wherein visions of development are facilitated by local chief executives using a top-down approach. Some residents have expressed reservations about local development projects, but have limited choice because of the 'hardware' and 'software' development these projects provide (see Castellsagué and Panthi's chapter in this volume for a discussion of the idea of 'hardware' and 'software' development in a different context). Residents express ambivalent views towards mainstream development thinking, with some gravitating towards alternative development thinking through their articulations of *kalamboan* and *ginhawa*.

Along the streets of San Juan town in Siquijor, 32-year-old Mary Ann Pabustan sells her snacks and delicacies to the delight of tourists and locals. Mary Ann is one of the few beneficiaries of the Department of Labour and Employment (DOLE) Integrated Livelihood Program, which provides initial capital funding for the construction and setting up of food stalls as part of their livelihood programmes for low-income communities. She is one of the many migrants to the province of Siquijor who, due to their search for a better life outside their home towns, moved to Siquijor from nearby provinces. Mary Ann reports that she loves Siquijor because of the better opportunities it offers and the peaceful life she has there compared to the conflict-plagued province of Davao de Oro in Mindanao, from which she originates.

During the mornings, Mary Ann tends to her backyard garden, which is planted with vegetables and fruits. Right after having lunch, she starts preparing her goods to be sold in her food stall from early afternoon to early evening. She says that this routine is ideal for her since she can have a work-life balance. Another thing she loves about Siquijor is that it has a policy that bans tree-cutting:

> Here in Siquijor, you have to ask for a permit before you can cut trees, even in your backyard. This is the opposite of what we have in Davao del Oro where illegal logging and mining are rampant.
>
> (Interview with Mary Ann Pabustan, 26 November 2022).

In 2012, Typhoon Bopha devastated parts of Mindanao, including Mary Ann's province. Environmental groups have blamed the mining and illegal logging that were rampant in Davao de Oro for the flooding that typhoon Bopha caused in the region (Rappler 2012).

Like other Filipinos from rural areas who are in search of better opportunities, Mary Ann and other informants whom I interviewed first tried their luck in Metro Manila, the capital region which has a population of 13.5 million (PSA 2020). Urban migration seems to be a trend in developing countries like the Philippines due to the search for livelihoods and better job opportunities (Philippine Institute of Development Studies [PIDS] 2020). According to one informant:

> I used to work for five years in Metro Manila. Life in the big city was not easy. We had to pay for our rent for housing and high costs of living. We prefer rural life due to less pollution, no traffic and less congestion. We want to live closer to our families and to nature despite having simple lives and less chance of getting rich by staying here.
>
> (Interview with Nelia Pantig, 26 November 2024).

My study challenges dominant narratives about rural-to-urban migration as locals of Siquijor interviewed for my study do not insist on moving to urban areas to look for more opportunities outside the province. For some locals I interviewed, choosing to remain in Siquijor is an easy choice. There are instances, such as the case of Mary Ann, where migration from the cities to Siquijor happens because of the high costs of living in their hometowns and the attraction towards a more peaceful life in Siquijor.

In small provinces like Siquijor, people operate based on trust and social cohesion is considered as an important currency. The locals live according to an agreed set of norms, which strengthen relationships and create a sense of solidarity among members of the community. People in the villages know each other well, so that crimes are not as rampant in Siquijor as in other areas. In one instance where I had to ride *habal-habal* (pillion) on a motorcycle, my motorcycle driver told me that her motorcycle had once stopped working. She parked and left it alongside the road, asked her husband to pick her up, and returned to the area the following day to have her motorcycle fixed. It was still there and nobody had stolen it. She said that this is not unusual for Siquijor, unlike in big cities where crimes like robbery are rampant.

In a Roman Catholic-dominated country like the Philippines, celebrating the feast days of patron saints is a big thing. Traditions like this provide a glimpse into the local culture of the community and the values that they uphold. While celebrating feasts is less common today in Metro Manila and urban areas, these celebrations are still prevalent in rural areas like Siquijor. As I observed the feast day in an area of Siquijor, one of my informants, Rowena Calaod, told me that celebrating feast days in Siquijor also shows the value of reciprocity among members of the community. For that fiesta celebration, Rowena shared with me that she received Php 3,000.00 (about $50) from her best friend, Yolly, living in the next town. That amount was her friend's contribution to Rowena's budget for the fiesta celebration. Contributing this amount of money assures her friend that she is invited to the fiesta. Rowena shared with me that this practice is what they call *sangga* (taken from the word *kasangga* which means 'partner'). She explained further: 'In return, I am thinking of pledging a dish to be served during the fiesta at Yolly's town fiesta. That pledge allows me to be her guest during their fiesta celebration' (Interview with Rowena Calaod, 9 January 2024). This practice of *sangga* as a gesture of reciprocity during fiestas and special occasions can vary in form from cash to a contribution of a dish and in some instances, *lechon* or roast pig which is considered as a special dish in the Philippines, usually reserved for occasions like Christmas, birthdays, weddings and feasts.

In the interviews and focus groups I conducted, respondents said that *ginhawa* (wellbeing) for them means having a stress-free life or *hayahay* with a deeper meaning. While *hayahay* means living a chilled life in the Bisaya-speaking region of which Siquijor is part, *ginhawa* means living a comfortable life that is not necessarily materially rich but involves being 'one with nature'. For Jacqueline Pante, who teaches in a public high school in Siquijor municipality, *ginhawa* means going back to their roots as Siquijodnons and having a close relationship with nature:

> Everything in nature, our forefathers have meanings ascribed to it. Siquijodnons are known to have a close relationship with nature. It is where it came from so we have to take care of the environment. Nature has a healing power.
>
> (Interview with Jacqueline Pante, 8 January 2024).

Another informant expands on this insight as he describes the meanings of *kalamboan* and *ginhawa* in his lived experience:

> *Kalamboan* and *ginhawa*, for me, mean eating three meals a day, being able to breathe fresh air. While we may not be materially rich, but living a comfortable life for us means having less things to worry about and giving back to the environment.
>
> (Interview with Tristan Reyes, 10 January 2024).

In a photovoice exercise where I had informants answer the question 'What does *kalamboan* mean to you?' I received the replies depicted below:

> *Kalamboan*, for me, means earning just right so I can raise my children well and being able to nurture harmonious relationships with my neighbours and friends in the village. After all, it is the only thing that I can pass on to my

Figure 11.1 Photovoice activity submission from a participant who is working as a waste picker

children – a good education and a respected name. It does not have to be a rich life but a simple, healthy, and comfortable life in Siquijor.

(Interview with Eva Cunanan, 14 November 2023).

For me, *ginhawa* means a life in Siquijor that is worry-free. Siquijor has given us a lot – livelihood opportunities, tourism sites like nice beaches, and a stress-free life on this island. A *maginhawang buhay* [comfortable life] for me

Figure 11.2 Photovoice activity submission from participant

means taking care of Siquijor and being able to preserve its environment – clean and green.

(Interview with Chito Befetel, 10 January 2024).

Local politics play a highly important role in charting development plans and policies at the local level. As Hutchcroft (2024) has posited, provinces like Siquijor continue to depend on patronage relationships with local politicians who are expected to deliver goods and services to constituents. Further, local politicians serve as brokers of development between the national government and its constituency. My interviews with three local chief executives highlight that executives have different views on how development should be 'felt' by their constituents.

For Mayor Richard Quezon of Siquijor town, the capital of Siquijor province has seen progress in the last couple of years by bolstering tourism. He attributes this progress to the 'development' that local politicians have introduced in Siquijor, such as the improved livelihoods that result from boosting tourism figures and infrastructure projects which he introduced, such as the bay walk, which is a concrete pavement near the shore built by the local government:

> We developed the bay walk because we want to show that the city wants to take charge of its development. The bay walk became a tourist spot and a street food hub especially during the evenings. Siquijor used to be a sleepy town but during night-time we have plenty of people coming in the bay walk to enjoy the surroundings and eat street food there. It is part of the overall drive of the Office of the Mayor for Siquijor to be clean and green, which will translate to boosting visitors. For agritourism, we worked on developing more fishponds. Siquijor also has other tourist sites aside from beaches like mountains.
>
> (Interview with Mayor Richard Quezon, 15 November 2023).

Another aspect of ***kalamboan*** and ***ginhawa*** that comes through in the interviews with executives is how local politics frame development plans and are pivotal to how locals negotiate the meaning of development in their everyday lives. As discussed by Bulloch (2017), development has been framed by NGOs and international government aid agencies in partnership with national and local agencies. Government programmes facilitated by aid and loans from the World Bank, such as the KALAHI-CIDSS or the *Kapit-Bisig Laban sa Kahirapan* (Linking Arms Against Poverty) Comprehensive and Integrated Delivery of Social Services, are seen as one-size-fits-all models of development interventions. Local politicians see these kinds of projects as a part of their development plans for their constituents:

> Through government programmes like KALAHI-CIDSS, constituents are given funds to start initiatives that they want. By facilitating access to these kinds of programmes, we are able to equip them with their immediate needs. If we have savings, we are also able to give from the budget of the local government unit.
>
> (Interview with Mayor Richard Quezon, 15 November 2023).

Incumbent Siquijor Governor Jake Villa thinks that governance means balancing nature and economic progress. He calls this sustainable growth and suggests that the province is on track to increase development while addressing the environmental aspect:

> In our province, we achieve close to zero poverty incidence by increasing the livelihoods of the people. Our products are affordable for the people. Since

> we are an island, we need to import products. We are also conscious that we [need to] balance development and still remain a pristine island of the Philippines. Further, [there are] the services that we offer to the residents of the island for free – hospitalisations, free maintenance medicines which we give to them weekly. Even dialysis sessions for kidney patients are given free for Siquijodnons. This is part of our overall social services package.
>
> (Interview with Governor Jake Villa, 10 January 2024).

For Larena Mayor Cyrus Vincent Calibo, development should be anchored on the needs of the people. He also believes that developmental processes should be consultative and inclusive. As narrated by Mayor Calibo, the municipality exerts effort in reaching out to different sectors in crafting its development plan. The Municipality of Larena further recently established a People's Development Council (PDC), which seeks to harness the voices of various sectors in Larena in order for them to be part of policymaking and crafting the local development plan. Setting up a PDC as a governance mechanism is touted by local governance scholars as a way for ordinary citizens to be part of development:

> We recently passed a resolution establishing a Development Council in Larena. Our vision is to have this people's council comprising representatives from various sectors work hand-in-hand with elected municipal councilors, which the Vice Mayor chairs. If we are able to organise the people through a People's Council, then we can harness collective decision-making processes. In doing this, we are able to come up with the best decision for the good of everyone.
>
> (Interview with Mayor Cyrus Vincent Calibo, 11 January 2024).

Furthermore, in rural areas, especially in developing countries like the Philippines, there is the tendency to see development as related to hard infrastructure (i.e. roads, bridges, etc.) rather than to 'soft' development (social protection, health-care, etc.), (see the chapter by Castellsagué and Panthi for a similar view). A community member interviewed expressed this view:

> Here in Siquijor, we are not particular [about] the politicians at the national level. We don't care whether you are Uniteam or Pink [two political coalitions in the 2022 presidential elections] but we are active [in] local politics. For local politicians, as long as you bring development – roads and bridges, free healthcare services – to the people, it does not matter whatever your affiliations are at the national level.
>
> (Interview with Epifania Umali, 29 November 2023).

While community members like Epifania see these things as part of the inherent role of local government units, others like Dominador have a more critical stance on the role of local politicians in the development of the community:

> Local politicians in Siquijor should listen to the voices of the people. They should not be dangling us with favours and other development projects, especially during election season, in exchange for support or votes. In my 50 years of living in Siquijor, I have observed that Siqujodnons know what kind of development we want and the LGU should respect and listen to that.
> (Interview with Dominador Signio, 9 January 2024).

Ambivalent views on mainstream top-down development versus alternative development seemed to be prevalent among the locals of Siquijor. For example, Siquijodnons have also expressed their concern about 'too much development' on the island and they are worried that Siquijor will reach a situation of overcapacity similar to other tourism destinations in the Philippines like Boracay in Aklan and Siargao island in Surigao del Norte province. These two tourist destinations recently reported overcapacity, so that in 2018 Boracay had to be closed to tourists for six months in order to fix the wastage system (Rappler 2018). Progress does not necessarily translate to a good life, as Siquijodnons have expressed in their concerns about the island going beyond its capacity, especially in relation to tourism and its impact on waste in the environment.

As Siquijor has become more well-known, foreigners have begun to go to Siquijor for retirement purposes. They buy parcels of land fronting the beach and open businesses like resorts and vacation houses. Because of this, the past few years have seen increasing prices of land sold in Siquijor. This has resulted in locals who are no longer being able to own land in Siquijor:

> I hope that tourism here can co-exist with the right kind of development. I hope my town will not be like San Juan [where there's a concentration of hotels and resorts], wherein most of the lands there are already foreign-owned. I am thinking of the plight of fisherfolks in Siquijor; how can they have access to their livelihoods if the resources are already owned by foreigners? How can we ensure that Siquijodnons, especially ordinary citizens, can start their own resort businesses if natural resources are already controlled by foreigners? Yes, there's no denying the fact that the tourism surge boosted local employment, but this comes at the expense of ownership of natural resources on the island.
> (Interview with Alfredo Umali, 15 November 2023).

In the above paragraphs, I have explored how some residents of the island province seemed to have implicit degrowth and post-growth ideals in the way they think about notions of development and progress in their localities. However, facilitators of development, such as local chief executives, have a greater say in the development of the community. This can be shown by the projects and programmes they continue to introduce to 'develop' the lives of their constituents. Yet, there have been reservations about a one-size-fits-all and top-down approach to crafting development plans and processes. There is also ambivalence regarding the desire to boost tourism in the island province because while this may allow the province to reach its full potential, it could mean sacrificing access and ownership of ordinary citizens to natural resources.

Further, mainstream development plans as envisioned by national government agencies and multilateral institutions are often in contradiction to what the community envisions or intends as part of their human development. Local people express hesitation and concern about the impact of 'too much' development and capitalism's encroachment on spatial boundaries. Their sustainability is hinged on social capital, cooperation, trust and the (re)production of agreed upon norms.

Expanding on the work of Tafoya (2023: 22) on *ginhawa* (wellbeing) and Bulloch (2017) on *kalamboan* (development), my discussion shows that Siquijodnons' conceptions of both *kalamboan* and *ginhawa* may not explicitly express degrowth and post-growth thinking, but that locals' critique of mainstream development perspectives resonates with degrowth and post-growth values. For Siquijodnons, living a *maginhawang buhay* (comfortable life) may not necessarily correlate to owning material things and having upward mobility but rather to maintaining social cohesion (another aspect of *kalamboan* that I have expanded on) and being one with nature (*ginhawa*) since it is through nature that one's wellbeing is animated by having a 'comfortable life, healthy living, good breathing, relief, food, etc.' (Mercado and Muyco as cited by Tafoya 2023: 22).

As a work in progress, a community's development is never static but always dynamic. Hence, development interventions must incorporate solutions that are locally relevant, culturally rooted and community-led. When a prefigurative action from 'below' is absent, development will be premeditated and determined by actors through a top-down development intervention.

Conclusion

In this chapter, I have presented one example, from the Philippines, of the myriad ways in which patches of alternatives to development exist in Global South countries. Specifically, I have explored how locals of Siquijor province navigate *kalamboan* (development) and *ginhawa* (wellbeing) in their locality in a way that prefigures 'alternatives to development' practices despite their ambiguous views and ambivalence to current paradigms like degrowth, post-growth and post-development. Alternative development paradigms in the Global South may be less pronounced, but the values and principles are already inherent and present in Global South contexts (Adityanandana and Gerber 2019). This runs in parallel with what post-development theorists have advanced – that 'development is a cultural construct … notions of development are not singular but vary between different groups of people' (Bulloch 2011: 177).

This chapter has also shown the need to decentre notions of development in order for alternatives to development to flourish. As the fieldwork has shown, further exploration of the notions of *kalamboan* can help us in unpacking other forms of alternatives to development in the Global South. This chapter has also shown that locals continue to negotiate notions of development. Their ambivalence to mainstream conceptions of development does not necessarily translate to active gravitation towards degrowth and post-growth and forms of alternative development thinking. Yet, their concern for the environment is present as espoused in the way they articulate *ginhawa*.

Dengler and Seebacher (2019) argue that degrowth could be the 'Northern supplement to existing Southern concepts (e.g. *buen vivir, ubuntu,* radical ecological democracy), transformative movements (e.g. environmental justice movements, transition movements) and lines of thought (e.g. post-development, postcolonial feminisms)'. If that is so, then in the case of Siquijor, *ginhawa* and *kalamboan* can be Siquijor residents' contribution to already existing alternatives to development thinking in the Global South.

References

Adityanandana, M. and Gerber, J. F. (2019). 'Post-growth in the Tropics? Contestations over Tri Hita Karana and a tourism megaproject in Bali', *Journal of Sustainable Tourism*, 27 (12), pp. 1839–1856. Available at: https://doi.org/10.1080/09669582.2019.1666857.

Alegado, J. and Gerber, F. (2020). 'A degrowth economy in a post-pandemic world', *Philippine Daily Inquirer*. 06 June.

Asian Development Bank. (2008). *Asian Development Bank cooperation with civil society Annual Report 2007*. Available at: https://www.adb.org/documents/adb-cooperation-civil-society-annual-report-2007.

Asian Development Bank. (2021). *Asian Development Bank – Philippines*. Available at: https://www.adb.org/where-we-work/philippines.

Bello, W. (2008). 'The global crisis of legitimacy of liberal democracy'. In *En publicación: Globalization and the Washington Consensus: its influence on democracy and development in the south*, edited by Lechini, G. Buenos Aires: CLACSO, Consejo Latinoamericano de Ciencias Sociales, ISBN 978–987-1183–1191-3.

Bello, W. F., Docena, H., De Guzman, M. and Malig, M. L. (2004). *The anti-development state: the political economy of permanent crisis in the Philippines*. University of the Philippines Diliman and Focus on the Global South: Dept. of Sociology, College of Social Sciences and Philosophy.

Bravo, E., & Moreano, M. (2015). Whose good living? Post-neoliberalism, the green state and subverted alternatives to development in Ecuador. In *The International Handbook of Political Ecology* (pp. 332–344). Edward Elgar Publishing. https://doi.org/10.4337/9780857936172.00033.

Bulloch, H. C. (2011). 'Contending developments: local notions of development on Siquijor Island, Philippines', *Journal of International Development*, 26 (2), pp. 177–186.

Bulloch, H. C. (2017). *In Pursuit of Progress: Narratives of Development on a Philippine Island*. Honolulu: University of Hawaii Press.

Center for the Advancement of the Steady State Economy. (2023). *What is a Steady State Economy?* Available at: https://steadystate.org/discover/definition-of-steady-state-economy/.

Chiengkul, P. (2018). 'The degrowth movement: alternative economic practices and relevance to developing countries', *Alternatives: Global, Local, Political*, 43 (2), pp. 1–15. Available at: https://journals.sagepub.com/doi/10.1177/0304375418811763.

Constantino, R. and Constantino, L. R. (1975). *A history of the Philippines: from the Spanish colonization to the Second World War*. Monthly Review Press.

Dafermos, G. (2017). The Catalan Integral Cooperative: an organization study of a post-capitalist cooperative. P2P Foundation. Available at: https://commonstransition.org/the-catalan-integral-cooperative-an-organizational-study-of-a-post-capitalist-cooperative/.

Daly, H. E. (1980). *Economics, ecology, ethics: essays toward a steady-state economy*. San Francisco: W H Freeman and Company.

De Dios, E. S. and Hutchcroft, P. D. (2003). 'Political Economy', in *The Philippine Economy* edited by Balisacan, A. M. and Hall. H. Oxford University Press. Available at: https://doi.org/10.1093/0195158989.003.0002.

Degrowth Declaration of the Paris 2008 conference. (2010). *Journal of Cleaner Production*, 18(6), pp. 523–524.

Demaria, F., Schneider, F., Sekulova, F. and Martınez-Alier, J. (2013). 'What is degrowth? From an activist slogan to a social movement', *Environmental Values*, 22, pp. 191–215. Available at: https://doi.org:10.3197/096327113X13581561725194.

Dengler, C. and Seebacher, L. M. (2019). 'What About the Global South? Towards a Feminist Decolonial Degrowth Approach', *Ecological Economics*, 157, pp. 246–252. Available at: https://doi.org/10.1016/j.ecolecon.2018.11.019.

Dorninger, C., Hornborg, A., Abson, D.J., Von Wehrden, H., Schaffartzik, A., Giljum, S., Engler, J.O., Feller, R.L., Hubacek, K. and Wieland, H. 'Global patterns of ecologically unequal exchange: Implications for sustainability in the 21st century', *Ecological Economics*, 179.

Dumont, J.P. (1992). *Visayan vignettes: ethnographic traces of a Philippine island*. University of Chicago Press.

Escobar, A. (2001). 'Culture sits in places: reflections on globalism and subaltern strategies of localization', *Political Geography*, 20 (2), pp. 139–174. Available at: https://doi.org/10.1016/S0962-6298(00)00064–0

Espaldon, M.V.O. and Baltazar, M.R.M. (2004). *Participatory natural resource management for sustainable agriculture*. Quezon City, Philippines: Department of Geography, College of Social Sciences and Philosophy, University of the Philippines.

Flipo, F. (2007). *Voyage dans la galaxie décroissante*. Mouvements 50(2): 143–151.

Flipo, F. and Schneider, F. (eds.). (2008). *Proceedings of the First International Conference on Economic De-Growth for Ecological Sustainability and Social Equity*. Paris, 18–19 April.

Gerber, J.F. and Raina, R.S. (2018). *Post-growth thinking in India: towards sustainable egalitarian alternatives*. Orient Blackswan.

Guerrero, D. (2019). 'Degrowth and the perspectives about it from the South', *Global Justice Now*. 19 September. Available at: https://www.globaljustice.org.uk/blog/2019/09/degrowth-and-perspectives-about-it-south/.

Heikkurinen, P. and Bonnedahl, K.J. (2019). 'Dead ends and liveable futures: a framework for sustainable change', in *Strongly Sustainable Societies*, 1, pp. 289–301. Routledge. Available at: https://doi.org/10.4324/9781351173643-16.

Hickel, J. and Haynes, N. (eds.). (2018). *Hierarchy and value: comparative perspectives on moral order*. Berghahn. Available at: https://doi.org/10.1515/9781785339981.

Hickel, J. (2017). 'Is global inequality getting better or worse? A critique of the World Bank's convergence narrative', *Third World Quarterly*, 38 (10), pp. 2208–2222. Available at: https://doi.org/10.1080/01436597.2017.1333414.

Hickel, J. (2019). 'The contradiction of the sustainable development goals: growth versus ecology on a finite planet', *Sustainable Development (Bradford, West Yorkshire, England)*, 27 (5), pp. 873–884. Available at: https://doi.org/10.1002/sd.1947.

Hickel, J. (2021). 'What does degrowth mean? A few points of clarification', *Globalizations*, 18 (7), pp. 1105–1111. Available at: https://doi.org.10.1080/14747731.2020.1812222.

Hutchcroft, P.D. and Gera, W. (2022). 'Strong-arming, weak steering: central-local relations in the Philippines in the era of the pandemic', *Philippine Political Science Journal*, 43(2), pp. 123–167. Available at: https://doi.org/10.1163/2165025x-bja10037.

Hutchcroft, P.D. (2024). *In person correspondence with Joseph Edward Alegado.* 3 April.

International Fund for Agricultural Development. [FAD]. (2023). *Country Profiles – Philippines.* Available at: https://www.ifad.org/en/web/operations/w/country/philippines.

Kallis, G., Demaria, F. and Bakker, K. (2019). 'Geographics of degrowth: Nowtopias, resurgences and the decolonization of imaginaries and places', *Environment and Planning E: Nature and Space*, 2 (3), pp. 431-450. Available at: https://journals.sagepub.com/doi/10.1177/2514848619869689.

Kallis, G. (2018). *Degrowth.* Newcastle: Agenda Publishing.

Karlsson, B. (2015). 'Political ecology: anthropological perspectives'. In *International Encyclopedia of the Social and Behavioral Sciences*, edited by Wright, J.D. pp, 350–355. Oxford: Elsevier.

Kerschner, C. (2010). 'Economic de-growth vs. steady-state economy'. *Journal of Cleaner Production*, 18(6), pp. 544–551 ISSN 0959–6526, Available at: https://doi.org/10.1016/j.jclepro.2009.10.019.

Kothari, A. and Demaria, F. (2017). 'The Post-Development Dictionary Agenda: Paths to the Pluriverse', *Third World Quarterly*, 38 (53), pp. 1-12. Available at: https://www.tandfonline.com/doi/abs/10.1080/01436597.2017.1350821?journalCode=ctwq20.

Kothari, A., Salleh, A., Escobar, A., Demaria, F. and Acosta, A. (2019). *Pluriverse: a post-development dictionary.* Tulika Books and Authorsupfront.

Laquian, A. (2005). *Beyond Metropolis.* Washington, D.C.: Woodrow Wilson Center Press.

Latouche, S. (2009). *Farewell to growth.* Cambridge: Polity.

Liegey, V. and Nelson, A. (2020) *Exploring degrowth: a critical guide.* London: Pluto Press.

McCoy, A. (1994). *An anarchy of families: state and family in the Philippines.* Madison: Center for Southeast Asian Studies, University of Wisconsin-Madison.

National Economic Development Authority. [NEDA]. (2017). *Ambisyon Natin 2040.* Available at: https://2040.neda.gov.ph/about-ambisyon-natin-2040/.

Nelson, A. and Schneider, F. (2019). *Housing for degrowth: principles, models, challenges and opportunities.* New York: Routledge.

Parrique, T. (2019). 'The political economy of degrowth', *Economics and Finance*. Université Clermont Auvergne [2017–2020] and Stockholms Universitet.

Post-Growth Institute. (2023). *What is post-growth economics?* Available at: https://postgrowth.org/post-growth-economics/.

Philippine Institute of Development Studies. (2020). *Back to the countryside.* Available at: https://www.pids.gov.ph/details/back-to-the-countryside.

Philippine Statistics Authority. [PSA]. (2021). *Population Density Siquijor Province.* Available at: https://rsso07.psa.gov.ph/content/highlights-population-density-siquijor-province-2020-census-population-and-housing-2020-cph#:~:text=The%20population%20of%20Siquijor%20hits,population%20every%20decade%20since%202000.

Philippines Statistics Authority. ([PSA]. (2021). *Census Population and Housing Philippines.* Available at: https://psa.gov.ph/content/2020-census-population-and-housing-2020-cph-population-counts-declared-official-president#:~:text=The%20Philippine%20Statistics%20Authority%20(PSA,May%202020%20is%20at%20109%2C035%2C343.

Province of Siquijor. (2024). *About Siquijor.* Available at: https://siquijorprovince.com/.

Quimpo, N.G. (2008). *Contested democracy and the left in the Philippines after Marcos.* Yale University Southeast Asia Studies.

Rappler (2012). 'Pablo destroys quarter of PH banana crop', 06 December. Available at: https://www.rappler.com/business/17451-pablo-destroys-quarter-of-ph-banana-crop/.

Rappler (2018). 'DILG's Boracay plan: 6-month state of calamity, 2-month business shutdown', 28 February. Available at: https://www.rappler.com/philippines/197124-dilg-boracay-rehabilitation-proposal-plan-state-of-calamity-business-shutdown/.

Raworth, K. (2017). *Doughnut economics: seven ways to think like a 21st-century economist.* Chelsea Green Publishing.

Research and Degrowth (2024). *What is Degrowth?* Available at: https://degrowth.info/en/degrowth.

Robbins, P. (2019). *Political ecology: a critical introduction.* (3rd ed.). Wiley.

Rodriguez-Labajos, B., Yánez, I., Bond, P., Greyl, L., Munguti, S., Ojo, G.U. and Overbeek, W. (2019). 'Not so natural an alliance? degrowth and environmental justice movements in the Global South', *Ecological Economics*, 157, pp. 175–184. Available at: https://www.sciencedirect.com/science/article/pii/S0921800918307626.

Savini, F. (2023). 'Maintaining autonomy: urban degrowth and the commoning of housing', *Urban Studies (Edinburgh, Scotland)*, 60 (7), pp. 1231–1248. Available at: https://doi.org/10.1177/00420980221121517.

Schifani, G. and Migliore, G. (2011). Solidarity purchase groups and the new critical and ethical consumer trends: first results of a direct study in Sicily. *New Medit: Mediterranean Journal of Economics, Agriculture and Environment= Revue Méditerranéenne d⊠Economie Agriculture et Environment*, 10 (3), pp. 26–33.

Schmelzer, M. Vetter, A. and Vansintjan, A. (2022). *The future is degrowth: a guide to a world beyond capitalism.* London, UK: Verso.

Tadem, T. (2020). 'A *Panacea* Gone Awry: A Review of Water Privatization Policy in the Philippines', *Asian Politics & Policy*, 12 (4), pp. 632–646. Available at: https://doi.org/10.1111/aspp.12559.

Tafoya, H.R. (2023). *Packaged food, packaged life: corporate food in metro Manila's slums.* Ateneo de Manila University Press and Kyoto University Press.

Tamiki, H. (2019). 'Defeating a political dynasty: local progressive politics through People Power volunteers for reform and bottom-up budgeting projects in Siquijor, Philippines', *Southeast Asian Studies*, 8 (3), pp. 413–439. Available at: https://doi.org/10.20495/seas.8.3_413.

Teehankee, Julio C. (2016), Duterte's Resurgent Nationalism in the Philippines: A Discursive Institutionalist Analysis, in: *Journal of Current Southeast Asian Affairs*, 35(3), 69–89.

United Nations Development Programme. [UNDP]. (2024). *About the Philippines.* Available at: https://www.undp.org/philippines.

Vandeventer, J.S., Cattaneo, C. and Zografos, C. (2019). 'A degrowth transition: pathways for the degrowth niche to replace the capitalist-growth regime', *Ecological Economics*, 156, pp. 272-286, ISSN 0921-8009. Available at: https://doi.org/10.1016/j.ecolecon.2018.10.002.

Wallerstein, I. (1984). 'The development of the concept of development', *Sociological Theory*, 2, pp. 102–116.

World Bank Group. (2024). *About the Philippines.* Available at: https://www.worldbank.org/en/country/philippines.

Ziai, A. (2014). 'Post-development Concepts? Buen vivir, ubuntu and degrowth'. In *Epistemologies of the South: South-South, South-North and North-South Global Leanings. Other Economies*, edited by De Sousa Santos, B. and Cunha, T. Coimbra: CES, pp. 143–154.

12 Conclusion

Alba Castellsagué and Sally Matthews

Early post-development texts, such as Sachs' (1992) edited *Development* Dictionary, Rist's (1997) *The History of Development* and Esteva and Prakash's (1998) *Grassroots Postmodernism*, suggested that the era of development was coming to an end and that those in the so-called 'developing' world were rejecting development and embracing alternative ways to improve their lives. There was great optimism that alternatives to development would arise and proliferate. While some post-development thinkers, including Sachs (2010: vii) and Rist (2019: 273), have acknowledged that they had underestimated the lasting appeal of development, there is still considerable optimism among post-development thinkers about the possibility of leaving development behind in favour of radical alternatives. This optimism is reflected in recent post-development writing that asserts that communities in the Global South are embracing alternative, Indigenous concepts in preference to the idea of development (Gudynas 2011; Acosta 2013; 2017; 2019; Escobar 2015; Klein and Morreo 2019; Polo Blanco and Piñeiro Aguiar 2020; Garcia-Arias and Schöneberg 2021; Schöneberg et al. 2022). According to the editors of *Pluriverse: A Post-Development Dictionary,* there are 'thousands' of 'transformative initiatives' promoting alternatives to development, premised upon Indigenous concepts like *buen vivir, ubuntu* and *swaraj* (Kothari et al. 2019: xxviii). These transformative alternatives, it is claimed, 'encompass an ethic that is radically different from the one underpinning the current system' (Kothari et al. 2019: xxvix). This optimism about the possibility of alternatives to development, rooted in practices and concepts from the Global South, has consistently been a key feature of post-development theory.

Enthusiasm about alternatives emerging from the Global South is also a feature of the increasingly influential decolonial school of thought which shares much in common with post-development theory. One of the most distinctive features of this school of thought is its emphasis on the importance of knowledge in shaping, and resisting, coloniality (Mignolo and Walsh 2018). Consequently, the decolonial school also shows interest in exploring and valorising alternative epistemologies rooted in the knowledge traditions of communities in the Global South (Santos 2014; Ndlovu-Gatsheni 2020; Mignolo 2021).

Post-development and decolonial critics of development have made valuable contributions to resisting the imposition of Eurocentric ideas and practices on

DOI: 10.4324/9781003477921-15

communities in the Global South. They have also contributed to drawing positive attention to the concepts and practices valued by people living on the margins of the global economic order. However, one of the recurrent criticisms of post-development thinking is that it tends to focus on discourse, at the risk of overlooking the material realities of people living in the Global South (see for example Moore 1999: 657–658). Similarly, recent decolonial writing has been accused of foregrounding concerns about knowledge, to the neglect of questions of political economy (Smith and Lester 2023). Furthermore, while there is much positive talk about alternatives coming from the Global South, this talk has often not been accompanied by work based on extended fieldwork that addresses the issue from an empirical point of view.

Our goal was to produce a book that is attentive to the experiences of marginalised communities and takes their stated wishes seriously, rather than spelling out a rather general and romanticised vision of what they supposedly want. Perhaps an example is helpful to explain the approach we wanted to avoid. Boaventura de Sousa Santos, an influential Portuguese decolonial scholar, begins one of his books with a 'Manifesto for Good Living/*Buen Vivir*', followed by a 'Minifesto for Intellectual-Activists'. In these two documents, Santos speaks on behalf of the Global South: 'Who are we? *We are the Global South*... We are all indigenous people ... We are animals and plants, biodiversity and water, earth and Pachamama, ancestors and future generations ...' (Santos 2014: 2–4). Speaking for this rather vast group of beings and entities, Santos asks, '*What do we want?*' and then lists all the things 'we' apparently don't want – 'transgenic foodstuffs, bibles, intellectual copyrights, certified consultants, empowerment recipes, structural adjustments, human rights, private property, nicely wrapped democracy, bottled water, and environmental concerns' – concluding that what 'we' do want is 'to live well, both regarding ourselves and mother earth' (Santos 2014: 6). Rather ironically, he also insists that 'we do not want to be spoken about. We want to speak for ourselves' (Santos 2014: 6). While Santos (2014: 7) informs us that he is 'deeply involved in the struggles of the indigenous peoples of Latin America', nowhere in this book is there any detailed description of the lives, ideas, hopes and day-to-day experiences of any specific community in the Global South. Rather, the focus is on rather general and rhetorical claims about what the Global South wants. Resisting this kind of approach, we seek to zoom in on particular contexts and to try to provide detail and nuance about people's experiences and stated preferences.

Relatedly, part of the motivation for this book was a sense of there being a disconnect between some of the very positive discourses about alternatives from the Global South we find in post-development writing and the realities we have faced when living in or visiting marginalised communities in the Global South. There seems to be a dissonance between some of the upbeat discourse about radical, transformative practices in the Global South and the realities of deprivation and marginalisation we have sometimes encountered. While very few of the people whose experiences are detailed in this book wholeheartedly and unreservedly embrace hegemonic ideas about development, many of the people we encountered during our research long for inclusion in at least some aspects of what they consider 'development'. Complete and unambiguous rejection of development is not something any of the contributors to the book found when speaking to the various people discussed in this book, although there was great variety in how communities (and individuals within them) engage with development. It is this complicated and ambivalent picture that we believe emerges when we think of development – and alternatives to it – in relation to specific communities in the Global South.

For this reason, this book has approached the question of development and its alternatives from the perspective of different empirical realities around the world. The chapters have focused on the experiences of specific marginalised communities and their particular ways of interacting with development, demonstrating the diversity of ways in which people from the Global South currently engage with development discourses and practices, and with the supposed alternatives to development being celebrated in some post-development thinking. While recognising this diversity, the chapters in the book highlight some commonalities in how marginalised communities perceive and are affected by development.

What unites these disparate cases?

Despite geographic, socio-economic and historical divergences, the chapters show that the idea of 'development' is very familiar to those in the Global South but also that the term can carry different meanings in different spaces. Alegado's chapter discusses the way in which the terms *kalamboan* (development) and *ginhawa* (wellbeing) are understood in the Philippines and whether the use of these terms aligns with mainstream ideas of development or with alternatives such as degrowth. Castellsagué and Panthi argue for the existence of two notions of development in Nepal: hardware and software *bikas*, used by different actors with sometimes divergent interests. Several other chapters show that development can be seen as both a positive and negative thing at the same time. For example, Maheve highlights how Kanyemba residents in Zimbabwe long to receive the benefits promised to them by a national development programme, while also rejecting many aspects of this programme. Mullikin's chapter relates how Rwandan farmers feel both nostalgia for the pre-development era and a longing to realise the positive outcomes that the government promised would result from agrarian modernisation programmes. While scholars have previously referred to development as an ambiguous concept (Sachs 2010; Ziai 2016), this book reminds us that such complexity and dynamism is crucial to understanding how development is negotiated by local communities from different geographies. Whether people accept or reject development depends a lot on how they define it and they rarely accept or reject development in its entirety. The chapters also highlight the ways in which marginalised communities have come to understand development in very nuanced and complex ways which recognise the ambivalence of development. Nowhere did we find either starry-eyed advocates of development or staunch traditionalists who insist upon maintaining earlier ways of life.

Despite the assertion that development in practice can have very different meanings, there are certain aspects of development that many in the Global South seem to insist upon. As has been acknowledged, including by leading post-development thinkers like Sachs (2010: viii) and Rist (2019: 273), the idea of development lives on and many people in the Global South continue to have considerable faith in development. In particular, it is the material and infrastructural aspects of development that is longed for by many of those we discuss in this book. The demands for piped water, roads, 'proper' toilets and houses echo in a similar way in several chapters in the book (Castellsagué and Panthi; Maheve; Matthews et al.; Mullikin; Prouchet et al.). The book also shows that although many organisations and NGOs have moved away from a focus on economic development and are working towards a discourse and practice of human and sustainable development, many communities still demand infrastructural and economic development (such as income opportunities) because they don't perceive this aspect of development to have been properly achieved (Castellsagué and Panthi; Matthews et al.; Prouchet et al.).

The book has also addressed the many ways in which people are critical about development and its specific programmes. While some direct their criticism towards failures in the implementation of development, while maintaining faith in the idea of development (see for example, Matthews et al.), others express scepticism about aspects of development and a desire to explore alternatives to it. For example, the chapter by Kwa and Van Leynseele relates how a VhaVenda social movement resists extractivist models of development in order to preserve sacred sites and Maheve's chapter reveals how some Kanyemba residents long for a return to earlier ways of living. Saremi et al. show how marginalised communities in Tehran find ways around the mainstream economic market to ensure economic opportunities and survival and Alegado suggests that the ways in which residents of Siquijor conceptualise *ginhawa* (wellbeing) align with values underpinning the degrowth movement.

The evidence from around the world brought together in this book thus suggests that, in practice, development is not typically embraced or rejected as a whole, but rather negotiated in ambivalent ways by those affected by it. As Prouchet et al. argue, the idea that people resist – or adhere – to development paradigms is an oversimplification, as people's experiences in the midst of development are complex and nuanced.

The importance of the political dimension of development and its potential alternatives has also been explored in various ways in this book. Some chapters have emphasised how governments and politicians are still seen as responsible for the provision of infrastructure and services related to development (Alegado, Castellsagué and Panthi, Maheve, Matthews et al.), identifying them as key actors in the implementation of development policies. Other chapters have shown how some of the concepts that post-development thinking has generally claimed as alternatives, such as *vivir bien*, have been incorporated into the state in places like Bolivia (Córdova Suxo; Ranta and Zenteno Lawrence). Consequently, in some places, the concept of *vivir bien*, which is often represented as an anti-hegemonic alternative to state-led development, is experienced by many as something coming from and associated with those in power (see also the chapter by Prouchet et al. in this regard). The chapters on *vivir bien* highlight some of the shortcomings of state policies in implementing such 'alternative frameworks', as well as some of the gaps between state discourse and the perceptions of *vivir bien* policies among different Indigenous communities. The chapters by Córdova Suxo and Ranta and Zenteno Lawrence show how the Bolivian government's turn towards *vivir bien* policies has highlighted the cultural and social aspects of it, while failing to give adequate attention to the political and economic marginalisation which continues to characterise the lives of many Indigenous and Afro-Bolivian people. In addition, Ranta and Zenteno Lawrence consider how communities, such as the Afro-Bolivian community, feel unrepresented in state portrayals of indigeneity, and develop their own alternative concepts and practices to affirm their gender and cultural identity in such a complex scenario.

The relationship with nature and the environment is central to post-development thinking, as the portrayal of alternative ways of life is very often linked to the image of communities living in ecologically sustainable ways in harmony with nature. Indigenous communities' approaches to the environment are sometimes presented as alternatives to the extractivist and econocentric models of development associated with the West. A number of chapters in this book have discussed this issue and have shown the complex relationships between development, alternatives to development and the environment. Maheve's chapter looks at the contradictions that the people of Kanyemba see in a conservation programme that prohibits traditional hunting practices, while not fulfilling the promises of development that people were promised in exchange for cooperation with the programme. Prouchet et al. discuss the way in which a state organisation in charge of forest-protected areas was pressurised by Indigenous communities in the Peruvian Amazon to support them in commercial cacao production. While some communities resent and resist conservation programmes, other chapters talk about ways in which marginalised communities connect with global discourses on degrowth and environmentalism. Alegado's chapter discusses the ways in which residents of Siquijor island in the Philippines value their environment in ways that are potentially compatible with the degrowth movements that are becoming more prominent in the Global North. Similarly, Kwa and Van Leynseele's chapter looks at the strategies and tools used by a South African social movement to defend sacred sites in a way that engages with global environmental discourses. Taken together, the chapters in the book show that while there are Indigenous and marginalised communities who mobilise to resist hegemonic forms of development in favour of environmentally friendly alternatives (as Kwa and Leynseele's and Alegado's chapters highlight), some communities feel a sense of loss when they are excluded from mainstream development projects and long to be included in some of the infrastructural and income-generation opportunities associated with such projects (as shown in the chapters by Castellsagué and Panthi, Maheve, Matthews et al., Prouchet et al.).

Why does all this matter?

As shown above, while our book explores diverse contexts and experiences, there are some key commonalities that emerge in the book. There are also some questions that are provoked by our book. The most pressing question is perhaps, 'why should we be attentive to the ambivalences and particularities that emerge when we attend to the empirical realities of marginalised communities and their engagements with development and its alternatives?' As discussed above, this book arose out of a sense of frustration that at least some of the contributors to the book have felt when confronted with grand claims about how marginalised communities in the Global South are supposedly resisting development in order to embrace alternatives rooted in Indigenous concepts and practices. Such claims are often made by scholars based in the Global North to very appreciative Global North audiences who seem fascinated by the idea of poor communities in the Global South living in harmony with each other and nature. All the while, many of us frequently connect with people in the Global South who are devastated by their exclusion from the benefits of development promised to them by various development projects. This is clearly shown by Maheve's chapter which tells the story of people who were shown films about the benefits they would obtain (such as formal housing) if they agreed to give up their traditional hunting practices in order to participate in a state-led conservation-for-development programme. The community has ended up losing their traditional forms of livelihood without gaining much in terms of benefits from the development programme. While they are understandably critical of development, they continue to want to access the benefits they were promised. Attentiveness to such experiences suggests that marginalised communities in the Global South do not necessarily want to abandon every aspect of their previous lives in order to become 'modern', 'developed' subjects, but at the same time they may insist upon access to certain aspects of the 'developed' way of life. Furthermore, our book shows people within the same community might relate very differently both to the idea of development and to any proposed alternatives to it. This is very evident in the chapter by Prouchet and her colleagues who detail the different ways in which the Awajún communities engage with entrepreneurship-for-development programmes. Some resist them, while others want to work with them to achieve new economic opportunities.

These details matter if we are to ensure that post-development theory's important critique of the ways in which development homogenises people's experiences does not give way to new sweeping generalisations about how people in the Global South prefer to live. Post-development theory, as well as the critiques of development offered by decolonial and degrowth advocates, invite us to question hegemonic visions of development which present one way of life – the Western, industrialised society – as the only ideal. Their interrogation of this ideal is founded on a concern that rather than improving people's lives, many development projects have disrupted and destroyed people's previous livelihoods while failing to bring about the prosperity they promised. In seeking alternatives, it is important to avoid replacing the idea that development will solve all ills, with the idea that a revival of Indigenous concepts and practices, assumed to promote harmonious and environmentally friendly ways of being, will be the solution. Indigenous and other marginalised communities are not homogenous and do not all want the same thing. If we are to be mindful of what Chetty (2023: 388) calls 'the problem of the wrong natives', we must accept that people may wish to embrace the kinds of lifestyles that post-development theorists have decried as Westernised, materialistic and environmentally destructive. We cannot just dismiss their stated wishes by accusing them of being brainwashed or having colonised minds (Matthews 2017) or respond like the official quoted in the chapter by Prouchet et al. who bemoans the way in which some Indigenous communities are mistaken in their focus on generating an income. Rather than declaring those who want roads, 'proper' houses and income-generation opportunities as being mentally colonised or just plain wrong, we argue in this book that scholars, officials and others in positions of power should be attentive to such communities' experiences and their stated desires. Instead of simply assuming the desirability of Indigenous and grassroots alternatives to development, contributors to this book have tried to take seriously the experiences and wishes of particular groups of marginalised people. This is why we insisted that all contributions to the book be based on close engagement with particular marginalised communities.

Does this mean, then, that we cannot make any general claims about whether and how alternatives to development are being articulated in the Global South? No – as we show above, there are some commonalities that emerge from the various chapters which suggest that it is possible to make some generalisations about how communities in the Global South are navigating development and are proposing – or sometimes resisting – alternatives. One commonality that came through is the desire for inclusion on the part of those who continue to be marginalised and displaced both by development programmes and by the projects initiated in the name of alternatives like *vivir bien*. While people may not want to embrace all aspects of such programmes, they also do not want to be ignored or pushed out of the opportunities offered by such programmes. We can see this with the Afro-Bolivians who feel marginalised within Bolivia's *vivir bien* discourse (see Ranta and Zenteno Lawrence), with the marginalised communities who have been excluded from economic opportunities in Iran (see Saremi et al.), with the Kanyemba residents in Zimbabwe who feel that they were never given the benefits they had been promised (see Maheve) and with the experiences of others discussed in this book. Attentiveness to their experiences and stated preferences can help ensure that the commitment to radical democracy evident in some post-development texts wins out over the neo-populist variants of post-development theory which risk romanticising poverty and exclusion (Ziai 2004).

Questions for further research, discussion and debate

This book might perhaps raise more questions than it provides answers. Indeed, we hope that through such questions we can provoke further discussion about alternatives to development. We seek to continue rather than end existing conversations. As we conclude this book, it is worth highlighting some of the questions raised in the book which could generate further research, discussion and debate.

One question relates to what happens when 'alternatives to development' move from the margins to spaces of power. The most prominent example of this is the way in which the concept of *vivir bien* was institutionalised in Bolivia and, to some extent, in other South American contexts. By now, this institutionalisation of *vivir bien* has received some critical attention (Viola Recasens 2014; Ranta 2016; Domínguez et al. 2017). The chapters in this book by Ranta and Zenteno Lawrence, Prouchet et al. and Córdova Suxo all further debate on this topic by showing how marginalised communities in Bolivia and Peru have come to regard *vivir bien* as something that comes down to them from powerful state actors rather than as some kind of grassroots alternative that can be mobilised against power. Córdova Suxo's chapter also discusses how the associated idea of indigeneity has come to be mobilised by the Bolivian government in ways that do not necessarily reflect the experiences of marginalised Indigenous communities. Mullikin's chapter relates how the Rwandan government has changed the meaning of the term *ubudehe* which used to refer to a common practice where neighbours would come together to work the fields, using songs and dances to coordinate their labour and ending the day's work with the sharing of food and beer. However, the government began to use the term to refer to government-directed aid programmes, shifting the way in which this term is understood. Mullikin further notes that children are still being taught the songs associated with *ubudehe* but are learning them in school rather than in the fields. What happens when the state appropriates concepts like *vivir bien* and *ubudehe* to describe its own programmes?

The state is not the only actor capable of shifting the meaning of traditional concepts and practices. Matthews et al.'s chapter discusses accusations that the idea of *ubuntu* has been appropriated by various actors for their own ends. Who may use and adapt a concept like *ubuntu*? Kwa and Leynseele's chapter describes the way in which the Dzomo la Mupo social movement is finding ways to preserve, transfer and translate VhaVenda Indigenous concepts and practices through eco-mapping and by connecting with legal and environmentalist discourses. In what ways are these concepts and practices altered through the social movement's translation of them into discourses that resonate beyond the VhaVenda? What happens to Indigenous concepts when they are transferred and translated into new contexts and given new meanings?

The chapter by Saremi and her colleagues raises another important question: they wonder whether the alternative economic practices discussed in their chapter are simply survival tactics that would be abandoned if the marginalised communities adopting these practices were able to access the formal economy. They conclude that even if such alternative practices are survival strategies, they might serve as 'seedbeds' for the building of alternatives. It is important to consider whether some practices which look like radical alternatives could simply be coping mechanisms that those excluded from development adopt, while what they really want is full inclusion in mainstream development initiatives. Marginalised communities may adopt practices that are environmentally sustainable and that rely on mutual aid and cooperation simply because these are the practices available to them. All the while, they may be quite keen, if the opportunity presented itself, to live in a less environmentally sustainable way (with a big house and a car, perhaps) and to rely on an individual paycheck rather than practices of economic solidarity with their neighbours. However, the adoption of alternative economic practices as survival strategies could also potentially open up sustainable alternatives. Taken together, our various studies suggest that different individuals within different communities will make different decisions if economic inclusion and hegemonic forms of development are available to them. It is important to ensure that we do not assume that apparently alternative economic behaviour is necessarily embraced as a choice by marginalised communities or that those in such communities all want the same thing.

Another question that this book leaves us with is: What does the desire for infrastructure and economic opportunities mean for those who would like to promote post-development and, relatedly, degrowth? If it is not environmentally sustainable to roll out a 'developed' way of life to all, how ought degrowth and post-development activists to respond to the desire on the part of people in the Global South for inclusion in the kind of development that creates environmental destruction? At various points in this book, we suggest that it is not helpful or accurate to present marginalised communities as if they all live (and desire to live) in environmentally sustainable ways. While the poorest and most marginalised people are usually not able to have lifestyles that cause significant damage to the environment, this is not necessarily because they do not desire such lifestyles – some of those discussed in this book speak of wanting roads, houses, cars and, quite bluntly, more money (see Castellsagué and Panthi, Matthews et al., Prouchet et al.). What do such desires mean and how should advocates of sustainability and degrowth respond to them? While we argue above that the expressed desires of marginalised communities should be closely attended to, is there room for activists and scholars to try to encourage such communities to consider environmentally sustainable alternatives?

Concluding thoughts

The aim of development was not very modest: development was supposed to bring prosperity to all the world. As post-development and other critics have pointed out, it failed to do this. The aim of some advocates of post-development alternatives has also not been very modest: it has been suggested that Indigenous alternatives to development are rising from the ashes of failed development programmes to bring about a powerful alternative vision of a life in harmony with each other and the earth. Our book has more modest goals: we set out to explore the ways in which some marginalised communities are engaging with development and its alternatives. We make no claim that these communities fully represent the experiences of those in the Global South or that our book reveals a common, shared vision among such communities. We set out to complicate the picture rather than simplify it by showing the ambivalent and nuanced ways in which communities try to navigate both the idea of development and supposed alternatives to development such as *vivir bien* and *ubuntu*. We hope that the complicated picture presented here can contribute to pushing debates about post-development further and can remind those engaged in the sometimes lofty debates about post-development futures not to forget the often inconvenient details that arise on the ground in the communities most affected by the ideas and practices of development.

References

Acosta, A. (2013). *El Buen vivir: sumak kawsay, una posibilidad para imaginar otros mundos.* (1a. ed.). Barcelona: Icaria editorial (Icaria Antrazyt: Análisis Contemporáneo, 387).

Acosta, A. (2017). 'Living well: ideas for reinventing the future', *Third World Quarterly*, 38 (12), pp. 2600–2616. Available at: https://doi.org/10.1080/01436597.2017.1375379.

Acosta, A. (2019). '*living well*: ideas for reinventing the future', in *The Development* Dictionary @ 25. Routledge.

Chetty, K. (2023). 'The politics of decolonial investigations', *Social Dynamics*, 49 (2), pp. 386–388. Available at: DOI:doi:10.1080/02533952.2023.2239010.

Domínguez, R., Caria, S. and León, M. (2017). 'Buen vivir: praise, instrumentalization, and reproductive pathways of good living in Ecuador', *Latin American and Caribbean Ethnic Studies*, 12(2), pp. 133–154. Available at: https://Doi.org/10.1080/17442222.2017.1325099.

Escobar, A. (2015). 'Degrowth, postdevelopment, and transitions: a preliminary conversation', *Sustainability Science*, 10 (3), pp. 451–462. Available at: https://doi.org/10.1007/s11625-015-0297-5.

Esteva, G. and Prakash, M. S. (1998). *Grassroots post-modernism: remaking the soil of cultures.* Palgrave Macmillan.

Garcia-Arias, J. and Schöneberg, J. (2021). 'Urgencies and imperatives for revolutionary (environmental) transitions: from degrowth and postdevelopment towards the pluriverse?: Review of *Pluriverse: A post-development dictionary*, edited by Kothari, A., Salleh, A., Escobar, A., Demaria, F. and Acosta, A. New Delhi, Tulika Books', *Environmental Politics*, 30 (5), pp. 865–871. Available at: https://doi.org/10.1080/09644016.2021.1911443.

Gudynas, E. (2011). 'Buen vivir: today's tomorrow', *Development*, 54 (4), pp. 441–447. Available at: https://doi.org/10.1057/dev.2011.86.

Klein, E. and Morreo, C.E. (2019). *Postdevelopment in practice: alternatives, economies, ontologies.* Abingdon, UK New York, NY: Routledge, Taylor & Francis group (Routledge critical development studies).

Kothari, A., Salleh, A., Escobar, A., Demaria, F. and Acosta, A.(eds.). (2019). *Pluriverse: a post-development dictionary.* New Delhi, India: Tulika Books.

Matthews, S. (2017). 'Colonised minds? Post-development theory and the desirability of development in Africa', *Third World Quarterly*, 38 (12), pp. 2650–2663. Available at: https://doi.org/10.1080/01436597.2017.1279540.

Mignolo, W. (2021). *The politics of decolonial investigations.* Durham (N.C.): Duke University press (On decoloniality).

Mignolo, W. and Walsh, C.E. (2018). *On decoloniality: concepts, analytics, praxis.* Durham: Duke University Press.

Moore, D.S. (1999). 'The Crucible of Cultural Politics: Reworking "Development" in Zimbabwe's Eastern Highlands', *American Ethnologist*, 26 (3), pp. 654–689.

Ndlovu-Gatsheni, S.J. (2020). *Decolonization, development and knowledge in Africa: turning over a new leaf.* Abingdon, Oxford: Routledge.

Polo Blanco, J. and Piñeiro Aguiar, E. (2020). 'El Buen vivir como discurso contrahegemónico. postdesarrollo, indigenismo y naturaleza desde la visión andina', *Mana*, 26 (1), p. e261205. Available at: https://doi.org/10.1590/1678-49442020v26n1a205.

Ranta, E.M. (2016). 'Toward a decolonial alternative to development? The emergence and shortcomings of *vivir bien* as state policy in Bolivia in the era of globalization', *Globalizations*, 13 (4), pp. 425–439. Available at: https://doi.org/10.1080/14747731.2016.1141596.

Rist, G. (1997). *The history of development: from Western origins to global faith.* Zed Books.

Rist, G. (2019). *The history of development: from Western origins to global faith.* (5th ed.). Translated by P. Camiller. London: Zed.

Sachs, W. (ed.). (1992). *The development dictionary: a guide to knowledge as power.* London: Zed Books.

Sachs, W. (2010). *The development dictionary: a guide to knowledge as power.* (2nd ed.). London: Zed Books.

Santos, B. de Sousa (2014). *Epistemologies of the South: justice against epistemicide.* London, New York: Routledge.

Schöneberg, J., Haudenschild, D., Darvishi, H., Momeni, S. and Ziai, A. (2022). 'The many faces of post-development: alternatives to development in Tanzania, Iran and Haiti', *Sustainability Science*, 17 (4), pp. 1223–1234. Available at: https://doi.org/10.1007/s11625-022-01164-5

Smith, M.N. and Lester, C.A. (2023). 'From "dependency" to "decoloniality"? The enduring relevance of materialist political economy and the problems of a "decolonial" alternative', *Social Dynamics*, 49(2), pp. 196–219. Available at: https://doi.org/10.1080/02533952.2023.2220588.

Viola Recasens, A. (2014). 'Discursos "pachamamistas" versus políticas desarrollistas: el debate sobre el sumak kawsay en los Andes', *Íconos – Revista de Ciencias Sociales*, (48), p. 55. Available at: https://DOI.ORG/10.17141/ICONOS.48.2014.1209.

Ziai, A. (2004). 'The ambivalence of post-development: between reactionary populism and radical democracy', *Third World Quarterly*, 25 (6), pp. 1045–1060. Available at: https://doi.org/10.1080/0143659042000256887.

Ziai, A. (2016). *Development discourse and global history: from colonialism to the sustainable development goals.* New York, NY: Routledge.

Index

For Product Safety Concerns and Information please contact our EU representative GPSR@taylorandfrancis.com
Taylor & Francis Verlag GmbH, Kaufingerstraße 24, 80331 München, Germany

www.ingramcontent.com/pod-product-compliance
Ingram Content Group UK Ltd.
Pitfield, Milton Keynes, MK11 3LW, UK
UKHW020147200926
475702UK00016B/2586
9781032762968